INTRODUCTION

Amanda by Gail Satt[...]
Wesley has always b[...] [...]e expects
them to get married. [...] [...]m Christian camp have reser[...] [...]ationship.
Where, they ask, are the sparks? Amanda doesn't know until her
new neighbor Ryan Robertson moves in. Then the sparks fly—
Both men are Christians, but now Amanda must decide what
other qualities God wants in a marriage made to last a lifetime.

Belinda by Colleen Coble
Soon after Belinda's husband died their only child was born, and
Belinda committed herself to raising her daughter, running the
family business, paying off bills, and staying free of any romantic entanglements. But since the day Rick Storm strode into her
life, nothing has been the same. Can her friends ever understand
how difficult it is to trust Rick with her wounded heart?

Collette by Kristin Billerbeck
Collette Ambers has no illusions. She will stay in the States just
long enough to raise money for her late father's mission in
Kenya and to enjoy a reunion with her friends from camp.
Mysteries surround her father's work, and she must find the
answers quickly or see her father's reputation ruined. She understands that tall, handsome Kyle Brighton has only taken her on
as a ministry. Will Kyle be her ally, or is he feeding her lies. . .
and breaking her heart in the process?

Danielle by Carol Cox
Dani Gallagher can't believe she gets paid for her year-round
job at the Grand Canyon. It combines her joy in nature with her
love of people. And people love her in return. Her three longtime friends have always understood Dani's determination to stay
out of the dating game and let God bring her future husband to
her. But how will they explain the feelings she has for Chase
Sheppard—feelings that won't go away no matter how hard she
prays for God to take them?

FOREVER FRIENDS

Four All-New Novellas
Celebrating Friendship

Kristin Billerbeck
Colleen Coble
Carol Cox
Gail Sattler

BARBOUR
PUBLISHING, INC.
Uhrichsville, Ohio

Acknowledgment

For our friend and mentor, Loree Lough,
who conceived this story and brought us together.
Thanks, Loree!

Amanda ©2000 by Gail Sattler.
Belinda ©2000 by Colleen Coble.
Collette ©2000 by Kristin Billerbeck.
Danielle ©2000 by Carol Cox.

Illustrations by Mari Goering

ISBN 1-57748-645-5

Published by Barbour Publishing, Inc., P.O. Box 719, Uhrichsville, Ohio 44683 http://www.barbourbooks.com

 Member of the
Evangelical Christian
Publishers Association

Printed in the United States of America.

Foreword

There are many kinds of friendship, just as there are many kinds of friends. I like to think that the friendships we have shown in this series occur often, as every one of us needs these kinds of friends—friends for whom time and distance are meaningless. People who, when we get together after not seeing them for a long period of time, seem like they've never been separated from us.

This project on the four stories of *Amanda, Belinda, Collette,* and *Danielle* has also been a unique experience of friendship. The four authors, Colleen Coble, Kristin Billerbeck, Carol Cox, and myself, live far apart in this vast continent of North America. While doing this project together, we have corresponded daily via E-mail, and the friendship that has grown and developed among us has touched us in special ways, even though the possibility strongly exists that all of us will never meet in person.

Now that the project is over, we, too, have developed that timeless friendship that distance could never end.

Here's to you, my own Forever Friends.

Love,
Gail Sattler

Amanda

by Gail Sattler

Chapter 1

W ho were you talking to? I got tired of listening to a nonstop busy signal."

At the sudden sound of Wesley's voice behind her, Amanda jumped, sending the phone, which she'd just hung up, crashing to the floor. She whirled around, one hand at her throat. "You could always knock like everyone else."

"Me? Like everyone else? I've been with you since birth. I'll still be with you till the end of time. You wound me." Wesley pressed his hands to his chest, staggered to the couch, and flopped down. When he didn't get a response, he opened his eyes. "You didn't answer my question. Who were you talking to?"

Amanda picked up the phone and returned it to its place on the coffee table. "It's the last Thursday of the month. I was talking to—"

His loud groan cut her off. "Not another one of those conference call deals with Bellhop, Cologne, and Dandelion."

"Will you stop that? That's Belinda and Danielle. And Collette isn't back yet. But Dani got a letter from her. She says Collette is really nervous about coming home. And Belinda just met some builder or something who's new in town, and Dani is still good ol' Dani, happy to be working in the middle of nowhere at the Grand Canyon."

Wesley checked his watch. "And you had to talk forever about it. I'm glad it's not my phone bill."

"They're my friends, and I miss them."

Wesley grinned. "But you've got me." He batted his eyelashes.

Amanda wasn't falling for it, but she couldn't bite back a grin at his antics. She rested her hands on her hips and tapped her foot, pretending to be annoyed.

Wesley grinned back and slid his hands down, pressing his palms to his stomach at the same time as his tummy gurgled. "I'm hungry. Let's go out."

Amanda crossed her arms and said nothing.

"I'll pay."

It was all she needed to hear. She grabbed her purse as Wesley checked to make sure the back door was locked. Amanda ran upstairs to close the patio door. They met at the front door and walked out together.

Wesley nodded at the moving van parked in front of the house next door. "The new people are moving in today."

Amanda nodded and settled herself into Wesley's car. "Look at that big comfy couch!"

"Mind your own business, Wesley. Come on; I'm hungry, too."

Wesley grumbled playfully and waited for a car to pass as Amanda peeked back over her shoulder. She couldn't see him well, but her new neighbor appeared in the back of the open truck. He closed his eyes and stretched his arms high over his head, then pressed his fists into the small of his back, arched, and twisted first to one side, then the other. Behind him, it didn't look like much had been unloaded, and it was nearly suppertime.

Amanda couldn't imagine moving. She'd lived in the same house all her life. After her parents died, other than a new couch and upgrades to her stereo and computer, not much had changed except for rearranging the furniture a few times. Everything was as she liked it. Amanda jerked her attention forward when Wesley steered the car onto the street. As curious as she was about her neighbor, she shouldn't be spying on him.

"So, Ammers, where do you want to go?"

They hadn't gone half a block when Amanda touched Wesley's arm. "Wesley, wait. The poor guy looked alone. I think we should go back and ask if he needs help."

Wesley shrugged his shoulders and turned the car around. "Looks like we're going to order something that delivers."

<hr/>

Ryan tried to work the kinks out of his aching back. An elementary teacher by trade, the only exercise he got was playing basketball with a bunch of nine-year-olds in P.E. class. It didn't take a lot of exertion to hold a basketball over his head and stand in one spot while they all jumped to try and knock it out of his hand, although he always did let them win in the end.

He stopped once more to stretch his back and admire

his new home. The dwelling was small and old but in good shape. The elderly couple he'd bought it from had treated the humble abode with TLC both inside and out. He knew he was going to like small-town living and anticipated settling in.

But he was a long way from being settled. He was now three time zones away from his friends and alone with a full moving van.

The movers back in Toronto had done an excellent job packing the largest volume of stuff into the smallest possible space, and he'd barely managed to make a dent by creating a questionable opening down the middle. Unless he could find his pillow and some blankets, he would be sleeping on the floor for four days.

Ryan piled a few more boxes at the foot of the trailer and hopped down, ready to carry them into the house, when his neighbor's car returned. A young couple exited and approached him. He swiped a lock of sweaty hair off his forehead and wiped his damp palms on his jeans as they approached.

"Hi. I'm your neighbor, Amanda, and this is Wesley. You look like you could use some help."

He glanced up at the full van. During his thirty-two years on this planet, he'd accumulated a lot of stuff, and every piece of it was packed in that moving van. Two men and a small woman weren't going to make much of a dent, and besides that, he couldn't ask strangers to do his backbreaking work.

"I'm Ryan Robertson. Pleased to meet you." He shook their hands then looked up at the loaded truck.

"Apparently everyone at the moving company came down with a monster flu, and it was all I could do to get the truck here so I could pull out some necessities. They said hopefully Tuesday they'll be able to do it."

As Ryan watched, Wesley hopped up into the back of the trailer, then poked his head down the center path. "Wow. This is packed solid. There's a lot of stuff in here."

Before he could open his mouth, Amanda spoke. "I know. Let's call a bunch of the guys from church to pitch in. We'll have a moving-in party."

Ryan stood with his mouth hanging open as Amanda turned and ran into her house.

"Hey, Ryan. I'll start passing stuff down. You ready?"

"Uh, yeah. Thanks."

They worked in silence, the process going much faster with two people. As Ryan walked back and forth, his mind raced. The most difficult thing about moving, besides missing his friends, was the process of finding a new church to fit into. He'd felt God's call to make the move when the opening came up, and to have the first people he met happen to be Christians who were involved in their church confirmed it.

They hadn't moved more than a dozen boxes when a car pulled up, followed by another one, and before they finished introductions, yet another car arrived. Before he knew it, eight more men were unloading the trailer and hauling his belongings into his new home.

Soon Amanda appeared with a tray of iced lemonade, and a little later she reappeared with a stack of large take-out pizzas. Ryan tried not to feel too overwhelmed by the gathering as one of the men paused for a word of thanks over the pizzas, and then they all dug in, laughing and sharing stories. He tried to listen to everyone, but he watched Amanda. Even though they'd barely met, he found himself fascinated by her. When the last crumb of pizza and a few quarts of lemonade were consumed, they went back to work.

In record time every box was laid to rest in the rooms he'd carefully written on each box as he had packed, and every piece of furniture was in place. Before he could thank anyone properly, they all disappeared, except for Amanda, who was collecting her glasses and pitchers.

He stood before her. "I don't know what to say, except thank you."

"You're welcome." Her hand paused over a glass; she raised her head, and smiled. His heart raced into over-drive. Until now, he hadn't had a chance to speak to her alone or up close. The fluffiness of her hair made up for her lack of stature, which was probably why he thought she was younger from a distance. Up close, he figured her to be about thirtyish.

While not especially pretty, in her own way she was cute, with a tiny nose and pouty cherub lips. Her mousy brown hair was exactly the same shade as her eyes, and he had the insane urge to lift her large glasses and get a closer look. The eyes were a window to the soul, and he wanted to see the soul of a woman who would rally a crowd like this to help a stranger.

One day, when he finally met the woman who would be his soul mate, he hoped and prayed God would send him a woman like Amanda. Wesley was a lucky man.

"I'll be needing to find a new church. Would you mind if I checked out yours?"

Her smile widened, and her eyes sparkled. "I'm sure everyone who was here today would love to see you. I'll give you directions."

They scrounged up a pen and a scrap of paper, and Ryan watched carefully as she drew a map, showing the names of the major streets he had yet to learn. Since his fridge magnets were still in a box somewhere, he folded the paper and tucked it into his pocket.

"I'll probably see you before Sunday, since we're neighbors," Amanda said. "Until then, good night, Ryan." With another smile and a nod, she turned. Ryan escorted her to the door and watched as she entered the house next door.

Rather than follow thoughts of his new neighbor that were best unpursued, Ryan began the arduous job of unpacking. After a few hours, only a portion was unpacked and put away, and he'd never been so exhausted in his life. The only thing not in the house was one box of documents and books he'd picked up from his new principal on the way here. He needed to read through the material for the first day of school the following Tuesday. Just to say the job of moving in was complete, Ryan grabbed his key ring off the kitchen counter and plodded to his car.

As he inserted the key in the lock, he paused to inhale deeply, breathing in the cool night air to revive him, however little. Even the air was different in a small town. It was fresh, except for the hint of manure. Though it was cool at night, at least for a couple more weeks, the daytime temperature would continue to be warm.

Ryan pulled the box out of the trunk and slammed it shut, but instead of returning to the house, he stood behind the car and looked both ways down the street.

The real estate agent had told him that it was a quiet neighborhood, and she appeared to be right. It was before midnight, and most of the houses were dark. Of the few that had lights on, he could see the changing and moving colors of televisions in the living rooms. A dog barked in the background, but all else was quiet. He wouldn't miss the steady drone of traffic at all hours of the day or night.

He couldn't wipe the smile off his face as he made his way back to the house. His house. It wasn't rented. It was his. And the bank's. He ran his hand over the door, then tapped it with his fingertips. A real wooden door, not the usual hollow metal of the newer, more fashionable homes. The place had a character all its own.

Ryan shifted the box in his arms and fumbled for the old brass doorknob. Brass, not sterile chrome. He liked it.

It didn't turn.

Ryan rattled it, then tried again, but still it remained solid. He didn't remember locking it, but he was so tired it could have been an automatic reaction, a habit he would work on breaking.

He thumped the box to the ground, then picked through the key ring, and as he got closer to the last key, a sick feeling built inside his stomach. The new house key was still sitting on the kitchen table.

Ryan exhaled loudly and pressed his forehead into the door. Either he would have to break a window or he could hope and pray one of the neighbors had a spare key.

The light next door was still on. Feeling like an idiot, and with his heart in his throat, he knocked on their door and waited.

Amanda answered. Ryan cleared his throat. "Sorry to bother you again. I can't believe I did this, but I've locked myself out. Would you happen to have a spare key, and if not, can I borrow your phone?"

She looked up at him and blinked. "I don't have a key, but you certainly can use my phone." She turned, and Ryan assumed he should follow her, so he stepped forward when she did.

Before he knew what had happened, she stopped dead in her tracks. His exhausted brain was too slow on the uptake, so he didn't stop soon enough and instead crashed into Amanda hard enough to make her lose her balance. Rather than let her fall, he threw his arms around her and held her upright. Together they wobbled for a few seconds until they both found their footing.

The top of her head didn't even reach his chin, but a few strands of hair stuck up high enough to tickle it.

In addition to being short, there wasn't much bulk to his new neighbor. His hands nearly spanned her whole waist. She looked up at him, and her eyes, those same eyes that had fascinated him earlier, locked with his. He stared into their depths, unable to move, when suddenly he realized he was still holding her. Immediately, Ryan jerked his hands to his sides, then rammed his fists into his pockets.

Guilt roared through him. What would have happened if Wesley had walked in and discovered their new neighbor touching his wife? For a second he considered turning and running back home. If he could get in.

"I'm sorry," he mumbled, staring down at the ground.

She mumbled something he couldn't hear, then pointed to the phone. "The phone and the phone book are right there. Help yourself."

Ryan tried to control his shaking hands as he paged through the phone book, then dialed the real estate agent's number. Instead of an answering service, all he got was a recording and voice mail. He hung up without leaving a message.

"Well, I guess I'm on my own." He raked his fingers through his hair, trying to think of what he could do. He deeply regretted the need to break a window on his first night, but he couldn't think of another solution.

"If you left an upstairs window open, you could get in that way."

Ryan narrowed one eye to think. He remembered leaning out the upstairs for a few minutes to take in the view of the sleepy little town. "You know, I just might have." He walked to the living room to check, and sure enough, he had.

"I'll get Wesley. He'll get a ladder."

Ryan cringed. He didn't know if he could face Wesley right now. He could barely face himself.

To his surprise, Amanda walked to the kitchen, opened the window above the sink, and reached into a small bowl on the counter. She then threw what appeared to be a penny against the window of the house next door, waited about twenty seconds, and threw another one. He heard the creak of the window open, then Wesley's voice calling out.

"Do you know what time it is? Is something wrong?"

"I need you to come over. And bring your ladder."

She slid the window shut, and as she turned to face Ryan, her cheeks reddened. "Don't mind us. Wesley and I have thrown pennies at each other all our lives."

Ryan's world shifted. Wesley lived next door? Suddenly things weren't so bad after all.

Chapter 2

Amanda led her new neighbor outside to wait for Wesley. She didn't know what had happened inside, but something had, and she didn't know what to do.

She had been thinking of Ryan before he arrived, and to see him at the door had thrown her for a loop. After she discovered he was a teacher, she had thought about asking him for some tips, since she didn't have any teaching experience outside of church.

That was until he bumped into her. The way their eyes had locked was like nothing she'd ever experienced before. Without knowing why, she hadn't wanted to move away, which was wrong. It didn't matter how nice he was, nor should she have noticed how attractive he was. She had plans for her future with Wesley.

Wesley appeared from his backyard, balancing an aluminum extension ladder on his shoulder. "Here you go, one ladder. Do I want to know why you need it in the middle of the night?"

Ryan shuffled his feet, looked down, and then glanced up at Wesley. "I guess I'm more tired than I thought. I locked myself out. Short of breaking a window, the only way in is through the upstairs window, which I left open."

As Wesley and Ryan balanced the ladder against the building, Amanda couldn't help but compare the two men. She had known Wesley all her life, so she tended not to think of his appearance. While he wasn't bad looking, he was shorter than average, just like herself. His small wire-framed glasses gave him a scholarly appearance, which wasn't helped by the fact that he usually had his nose buried in a textbook.

The opposite of Wesley, Ryan was tall. His dark brown hair contrasted vividly with his bright green eyes, and he had a charming and honest smile. She found him easy to talk to, and judging from his easygoing ways, he would be good with children, and he seemed to enjoy his job as a teacher.

Ryan climbed up the ladder and squeezed through the small opening. Once inside, he poked his head and shoulders out and waved. Amanda helped Wesley steady the ladder as they tipped it down, then waved back. Wesley was already carrying his ladder home, but she continued to stare up at Ryan, and him down at her.

"Good night, Amanda," he called down after about a minute of silence.

Amanda shook her head. What was she doing? One day—she didn't know when—but one day sometime in the future, she planned to marry Wesley. Yet here she and Ryan were staring at each other like some backwards form of Romeo and Juliet.

"Good night, Ryan," she mumbled and ran back home.

Amanda nearly groaned in frustration as she hung up the phone after yet another dead end. One of the tellers had gone home sick, and it was her responsibility to find someone else to come in, shuffle duties, or fill in herself.

Fridays were always busy when people started getting home from work, but today would be especially busy since Monday was a holiday. With one person short, it would make a bad day worse.

She did her best to get ahead until a man at the counter caught her eye. At first her heartbeat picked up, but then she forced herself to control it. She wasn't supposed to be so happy to see Ryan. He was only her neighbor.

Ryan beamed from ear to ear. "Amanda! It's nice to see a familiar face. I need to change the address on my account and make my first mortgage payment."

She pulled the correct forms out of the drawer and directed him into her office. While she pulled up the program in her computer, out of the corner of her eye she watched Ryan pull one of her business cards out of the holder.

"So you're the assistant manager. Like it here?"

She nodded as she waited for the program to find his account number, concentrating much more intently than she needed to for such a simple function.

"What does Wesley do? I didn't really have time to talk to him yesterday."

Amanda entered the number and pulled up Ryan's account. "He's a student at UBC. He's getting his doctorate in entomology."

"Doesn't that take a long time?"

She nodded as she continued processing the information. After many years of university, Wesley would finally graduate next year. She had waited a long time for him, and one more year wasn't going to make much difference. "Yes, but he's always been interested in stuff like that. He thrives in the investigative process. Back in elementary school, his science project on some rare type of moth won the award for the district."

"I'm impressed."

She already knew Ryan's address, and when the change was made, she pulled up his mortgage account and entered his payment. "Are you finished unpacking?"

He sighed and shook his head. "No. But I thought I could use a break, and this is something that had to be done as soon as possible. Then I have to go grocery shopping. There's so much left to do, but I think I can finally see the light at the end of the tunnel."

With the transaction complete, she sent Ryan on his way and returned to her work. Usually Wesley came home early on Fridays, and often the two of them grabbed a burger or bought takeout for supper. She had a few errands to run after work, but she absently hoped that Ryan might join them, then mentally kicked herself for thinking that way.

Ryan flattened the last box and stood back. Finally, everything was in place, all the appliances were plugged in and working, and he had some real food in the house. It called for a celebration, except he had no one to celebrate with.

He could have phoned any of his friends to talk, but it wasn't the same as sitting with someone in person.

With everything he had done today, he was tired but at the same time restless. Part of him wanted to put his feet up and relax in his new surroundings, and part of him wanted to go out. He walked to the living-room window and parted the curtains, trying to decide what to do, when Amanda's car pulled into her driveway.

It was the perfect opportunity. He'd been trying to figure out what the relationship was between Wesley and Amanda and so far had drawn a blank. Last time he had seen her, he'd made a point of checking to see if she was wearing a ring, and she wasn't. He seriously wanted to get to know the woman with the expressive eyes behind the large glasses.

He stepped outside, reminding himself three times not to lock the front door, and hurried to meet Amanda. She stood beside her car, fumbling with two plastic grocery bags, a jug of milk, a briefcase, her purse, a pile of books, and her keys.

"Allow me," he said as he removed the bags, briefcase, and milk from her hands. "Let me help you."

She looked up at him, and for a second it startled him that she appeared taller than yesterday. As they walked side by side up the walkway to her door, he discovered the reason. He was in such a rush to talk to her, he'd forgotten to put on his shoes. He was only wearing his socks, while she was wearing the high-heeled shoes she'd worn to work. Even still, he towered above her by a head.

She picked through her key ring and opened the door. Ryan followed her inside, through the house, and into the kitchen, where she put the few things she'd brought with her into the fridge.

"I'm glad you're here. There was something I wanted to talk to you about."

He couldn't help but smile. "Name it."

"As a teacher, I was wondering if you could give me some insight into the way an eight-year-old thinks, especially a boy."

His smile dropped. He had been hoping for something centering around more personal topics, but it would do.

They retired to the living room and shared stories of their experiences with children; Ryan from his grade 4 class, and Amanda from the Sunday school, trading funny instances as well as the tearjerkers. She loved children and it appeared that not only could she relate to them, but they could relate to her.

A knock on the door interrupted them. It was Wesley, who walked past them into the kitchen, carrying a large pizza. Amanda followed Wesley, so Ryan followed Amanda.

Wesley dropped the pizza on the counter. "Hey, Ryan. You want to stay for pizza? Ammers can pull out another plate."

He didn't want to intrude, nor did he want to leave. Since he was invited, he decided to stay, and he was glad he did. Without being in a crowd, he was able to observe the interaction between Amanda and Wesley in the informal atmosphere of her home.

One would start a sentence; the other would finish it. They didn't necessarily always agree with each other, but they always seemed to know what the other was thinking. In addition, one would often preguess the other's actions. It was fascinating to watch.

All Amanda did was touch the last mushroom in the box; Wesley opened his mouth, and Amanda threw it in, without the two even looking at each other. Neither of them appeared to be aware of how natural they made it look, as if everyone behaved that way.

But the whole time, neither of them touched each other, no playful pats, no teasing jabs with elbows. Nothing. No special words were exchanged, making Ryan conclude that they behaved this way all the time, and no one around them thought it at all unusual except him.

He liked them both. Wesley tended to be quiet, but he was a very likable sort. Amanda had a comparable gentle spirit, and even though she seemed to be a bit on the prim and proper side, she possessed a quick wit and an easy laugh. When the conversation turned serious, she also displayed a maturity he admired.

While he wasn't deliberately scouting out marriageable women, Amanda held him spellbound.

He tried to stifle a yawn. It had been a long day, and while all the unpacking was done, he still had a lot of organizing to do, in addition to going through the reports and notes concerning his class at the new school, which would be starting in a few days. And for that, he needed an alert mind.

Ryan stood. "It's been a great evening, but it's been a

long day. I'd better be going before I fall asleep on your couch."

When Amanda escorted him to the door, he hesitated. Even though they'd only just met, he had to stifle the inclination to lean down to give her a good-bye kiss, and the urge surprised him. He'd never experienced such a quick connection with a woman before, and he wasn't sure how to handle himself, or if she felt the same way.

He backed up, nodded, mumbled a polite good night, and made his way back home, trying to act like it was normal for him to be walking between the houses in only his socks. He released his breath once he stood at his front door, then patted one pocket, then the other. His heartbeat quickened as he patted his shirt pocket, with the same results. The only thing he was carrying was his wallet. No keys.

He pressed his forehead into the door, unable to figure out how he could have done the same thing two days in a row. He wanted to impress Amanda, not show her what a birdbrain he was.

"Ryan? Is everything okay?"

He turned his head, his cheek still touching the door. Amanda was standing on her porch, her arms wrapped around her middle. He shuddered to think she had been watching him search for his keys.

His hand drifted to the doorknob. "Well. . ."

Rather than shouting into the door, he straightened and turned his body to face her so he could reply, and with the movement, the door opened.

Then he remembered. He'd been in such a hurry to

meet Amanda at her car, he purposely had left the door unlocked. When they went inside her house to talk, he'd forgotten to come back and lock the door.

He smiled, hoping she couldn't see the heat he felt in his cheeks. "Just enjoying the fresh air. Good night, Amanda."

Without further delay, he walked inside.

Ryan smiled as he locked the door and began to prepare for bed. She'd been watching him. He didn't know why, but the point was that she'd been watching.

Chapter 3

Ryan sipped his iced tea and flipped to the next page. Just like any other class of eight-year-olds, he could see all ends of the spectrum in the kids that would be under his charge for the next school year.

In the yard beside him Amanda sat in the middle of a bed of flowers, pulling weeds as she hummed to a familiar Christian tune coming from a small boom box beside her. The sun was warm, but not hot, a slight breeze occasionally ruffled his hair, and every once in a while Amanda looked up at him and smiled as she lifted her glasses to wipe a lock of hair out of her face.

Ryan couldn't think of a better way to spend a Saturday afternoon.

"Hey, Ammers!" Wesley's voice drifted from two doors down. "It's noon. You want a sandwich?"

"Sure!" she called back. "Tell Mom thanks, and I'll be right there!"

Ryan nearly dropped the stack of papers, then came close to spilling the iced tea down the front of his shirt as he caught the papers. Mom?

He lifted a notebook in front of his face, pretending

he was reading so Amanda couldn't see the smile he could not control. Some of the pieces of the puzzle snapped together. He would never have guessed, but now that he thought about it, even though they didn't look alike, not all siblings had to pass for identical twins.

Most brothers and sisters he knew fought as kids but usually developed a friendship when they got older, some more than others. Wesley and Amanda had been blessed by being able to share friendship as well as blood, which they'd have to if they lived next door.

Ryan couldn't shake the grin away. Now that he knew, he was going to get to know his new neighbor much, much better.

Amanda bit into her sandwich, then took a sip of milk.

She didn't know the term "absentminded professor" could apply to an elementary schoolteacher, but it certainly did with Ryan.

She could understand someone locking himself out of his home in the disorganized process of moving in, but now that she'd seen more of him, she wondered if this behavior was typical of him. When he'd rushed over and grabbed her groceries out of her hands before she dropped everything, she'd been very grateful he showed up when he did. However, it had been all she could do not to laugh when she discovered he wasn't wearing his shoes.

Instead of going back home to get them, he'd spent the entire evening in his socks, which wasn't unusual in itself, but when he went home, she couldn't help but watch. She had thought he would walk up the driveway and around, but he cut right through the grass, which was already damp with the cool evening moisture. Something made her watch as he stood at his front door, wondering if he would take off his wet socks before he stepped inside.

And then he started searching all his pockets for his keys, which meant, judging by his defeated posture when he bumped his forehead into the door, he had forgotten them again.

Even though it gave away her position that she had been watching, she had called out to help him, and when he moved, the door opened, meaning he had forgotten to lock it in the first place. In this case, two wrongs did make a right.

His forgetful nature and disorganized habits lent him a certain charm, which further confused her feelings about him. Wesley liked him; she knew that because they'd already discussed their friendly neighbor. In so many ways, she enjoyed being with Ryan, yet in other ways, he unnerved her.

Amanda had barely returned to her backyard, when she saw Ryan standing at the property line, towering above the small row of bushes that had been chosen to mark the property line rather than a fence.

"Your yard looks nice. Did you do all this yourself?"

Having him show up like this only reminded her that again she'd been thinking of him far too much. "Yes." It had taken years to bring all her plants and bushes to maturity, but it was worth it.

"The people I bought this house from loved to garden as well, I see."

"Only Mr. Wilkins. He did it all, believe it or not."

He glanced back over his own yard. "You're kidding. I don't know how I'm going to keep this looking this good."

Amanda stood, brushing some dirt off her shorts. "I can help you if you like. I'm not a great gardener, but I love plants and flowers."

Ryan's cheeks flushed. "I was going to grass over the garden, but I did want to see which of these nice flowering things I could keep alive. Actually, since you seem to know more than I do about plants, I was wondering if you could tell me if this one plant in the corner is a weed or not. I'm afraid I can't tell."

He parted the bush so she could squeeze into his yard, and she followed him to the plant in question. They hunkered down together, and he leaned forward and touched a small clump of plants with small mauve flowers.

Amanda brushed the tiny blossoms with her fingertips. "Whether or not you call these a weed depends on your definition. It's a forget-me-not, and lots of people have them for borders and fillers, but I warn you, when they go to seed they spread everywhere, and they spread fast. If you're not going to be right on top of keeping it in line, I suggest you pull it."

They both started to rise, but Ryan managed to stand first, then held out one hand to help Amanda up. She automatically took his hand, but when they were standing, he didn't let go. Instead, he wrapped his other hand over their joined hands and gently ran his thumb over her wrist.

Amanda stood frozen, watching his movements as she felt the roughness of his fingers, amazed at how much larger his hands were than hers.

He didn't stop the gentle motion as he spoke. "I think I'm going to get rid of it. But I hate to throw out something so pretty. If you want it, you can have it."

"Sure," she mumbled, still staring at his hands covering hers. "I'll take it. I've never been able to bring myself to kill a live plant on purpose. Except weeds. They don't count. Like mosquitoes."

He smiled, and Amanda's heart skipped a beat. A man should never look so good standing among flowers. "I'd offer to dig it up for you, but I'd kill it for sure."

Amanda pulled her hand away. No one had ever touched her like that, and she wasn't sure what to do. She wasn't sure if she was supposed to like it, but she did. "I had better get a shovel. Thanks."

She didn't know why she was running to get a simple gardening tool, but she was.

As she slipped through the bush on the property line, a ringing phone sounded in the distance. Ryan's eyebrows raised in shock when he traced the sound to his house, and he ran inside, leaving her to dig up the errant flowers in peace. He hadn't returned by the time she was done, so she returned home, planted it in the bed beside her front door, and went inside.

Rather than slave over a hot stove on such a nice day, Amanda chose to make a salad for supper. She had just finished eating the last crouton when a knock on the door sounded.

She greeted Ryan, who was holding a very sick plant in his hand.

"I went to the nursery to buy some shovels and stuff and came home with this."

Amanda blinked. The plant had no pot, only a torn netting that left most of the roots exposed, and most of the leaves appeared ready to fall off. The only remaining wilted flower petal fell off and fluttered to the ground as she watched. "Why?"

Ryan shrugged his shoulders. "The girl that worked there apparently dug it up a few days ago and forgot about it. She said she was new and was afraid she was going to get in trouble, so I bought it. Where do you think I should plant it?"

"I really don't know the layout of the Wilkins. . .uh, I mean, your yard. If you give me a minute, I'll slip on my sandals."

"The girl said the flowers would be red, which is the same color as the trim around my windows."

Amanda was surprised a man would notice such things. Wesley could tell her the exact colors and patterns of a butterfly wing but didn't know what color shirt he had on. It would be too much to ask the color of his house.

Fortunately, the inexperienced girl at the nursery had also sold him the proper size shovel and all the bonemeal and fertilizer he would need, giving Amanda some hope that the plant could be saved, short of praying over the poor bedraggled thing for its survival.

"Thanks, Amanda. I really appreciate this. Can I offer you coffee or something for your help?" He waggled his eyebrows. "I bought chocolate donuts."

She glanced back to her own quiet, lonely house, then

to Wesley's house next door. Two familiar cars were parked in Wesley's driveway, friends from the university. It didn't take a lot of imagination to know they would be spending the day talking about upcoming classes and professors, as classes were due to resume in a few days. They wouldn't mean to ignore her, but the study of arachnids and winged creatures was something she couldn't relate to.

It was either be bored at home alone, be bored at Wesley's, or go to Ryan's and eat chocolate.

"I'll be right back!" She ran home to fetch her keys, lock the door, and just before she left, she paused to check herself in the mirror. Her hair was a mess, her glasses were smudged, and she hadn't a smidgen of makeup on.

Amanda shook her head. It was Saturday. She had spent the day gardening. Ryan was simply her neighbor. Why should she care what she looked like?

When she knocked on the door, he called from the kitchen for her to come in. She heard the whirring of the coffee grinder and then the running water, so she made herself comfortable on his couch while he was busy. Wesley had been right on the day Ryan moved in. It was a comfy couch.

Conversation flowed easily. They drank the entire pot of coffee and didn't realize it was past suppertime until Ryan's stomach grumbled.

Knowing Wesley and his friends would be lost in their own little world until late, Amanda didn't object when Ryan offered to make grilled cheese sandwiches for supper, and they continued talking.

Amanda didn't know how long it had been dark by the

time she finally noticed. She hadn't worn her wristwatch because she had been gardening, and Ryan didn't have a clock anywhere in the living room.

"I should be going. I have to get up early for church in the morning."

Ryan stood with her. "Yes, me too. I've got your map taped to the fridge, so I guess I'll see you there."

"Yes, I hope so. I know everyone who helped you move would love to see you, too. And since it's a long weekend, the church is having a potluck barbecue at the pastor's house on Monday. Then you can meet more of the congregation."

He smiled. "That sounds nice. I'll be looking forward to that."

Amanda nodded. "Me, too." She didn't want to think of why.

Chapter 4

Ryan walked into the doors of the quaint old church. He'd expected the small old building to be quiet inside, but it wasn't. Small groups of people stood everywhere talking, children laughed and played, and pleasant music from a piano and a guitar filled the room.

He'd come alone, but once inside, a few familiar faces caught his eye. He recognized a few of the men who had helped him move, some of whom were standing with their wives and children. Everyone he recognized he joined briefly to once again extend his thanks, but they weren't whom he was really looking for.

As soon as he was done, he joined the group containing Amanda and Wesley. Like typical brother and sister, they stood side by side but were involved in different conversations.

Wesley was the first to speak to him. "Ryan! Good to see you here. Let me introduce you to some of our friends."

He had just started to talk when a group of six children approached Amanda. One of them had a small box in her hands, and judging from the ragged appearance of it, she had wrapped it by herself. She presented it to Amanda.

"Happy Birthday, Miss Gibsons. This is from me and Ashley and Kaitlin and Bobbie and Jason and Tyler."

Ryan watched as Amanda slowly accepted the box. "Why, thank you, Melissa! What a pleasant surprise. How did you know it was my birthday?"

The little girl beamed. "Wesley told me!" Her voice lowered. "He said you're thirty. That's even way older than my mom."

Amanda turned to Wesley and opened her mouth, but before she got a word out, Wesley turned his head and concentrated at some unknown point of interest on the ceiling, then started to whistle.

Her hands shook as she opened the clumsy wrapping. Inside were six bars of natural soap, all different colors. The blend of strong, soapy fragrances made Ryan's eyes water, but he suspected Amanda's eyes were watering for a different reason.

"Thank you all. This is so sweet. I don't know what to say."

Like typical kids, the girls swarmed her for a hug, the boys hung back, and then they all disappeared in the blink of an eye.

Amanda blinked, then swiped at her eyes. "They're in my Sunday school class."

"They must like you a lot."

She shrugged her shoulders, but Ryan knew the answer. It was obvious.

During the service, Ryan sat beside Amanda, with

Wesley on the other side. When the singing portion of the service ended, she left with the children, leaving Ryan sitting beside Wesley for the sermon.

He'd never felt so right with something in his life. Without a doubt, he knew this church would be his new home. Even before the close of the service, his decision was made. This was it. He could see that he would have many friends here, first and foremost, Wesley and Amanda. However, friendship with Amanda wasn't exactly what he had in mind.

Ryan wasn't foolish enough to believe in love at first sight, but something was happening. He knew that whatever it was, only time and the Lord's blessing would tell, but he anticipated what might follow this almost instant bond. Whatever was developing between himself and Amanda was growing stronger every time they were together.

Unless he was mistaken, she felt it, too.

After the service, the adults mingled around the back table and the coffeemaker, until the children arrived in a rush, heading straight for the cookie plate. Ryan made conversation with Wesley until Amanda joined them.

"I'm going to assume things are no different here than at my old church. Would you two like to join me for lunch? My treat, to say thanks for all you've done so far."

Amanda and Wesley both nodded without looking at each other. Ryan bit back a smile.

"Got a favorite place to go?"

Their voices came out in perfect unison. "Freddie's!"

He didn't know if he would hazard a guess at what

kind of lunch a place named Freddie's would serve, but he had to trust it would be good.

And it was. The place was packed with the church crowd, and although it wasn't very private, Ryan had a marvelous time. It also gave him the opportunity to watch Amanda in a crowd. He knew he was falling in deeper and deeper, and he enjoyed it, admitting to himself that he was fast falling in love with the woman of his dreams.

Amanda laughed at yet another joke. Ryan was good company, and she couldn't help but appreciate his fine wit and his friendly disposition. When she found herself staring at the adorable crinkles that appeared at the corners of his eyes when he smiled, she turned away. She wasn't supposed to be looking at Ryan.

Lunch was over all too soon. The amount of coffee they consumed, just so they could stay, was almost embarrassing. Rather than go their separate ways, the entire group somehow ended up at her house, and before she knew what happened, she agreed to provide an informal supper for eight people before they returned for the evening service. It seemed natural already for Ryan to tag along. Of course Wesley had invited him.

She always enjoyed the informal atmosphere of the evening service. Most of all, this was the time she could sit and listen to the pastor's sermon instead of leaving when it was her turn to teach Sunday school. When the service ended, their friends returned home, and Amanda, Wesley, and Ryan once again ended up at Amanda's house. Somehow, she wasn't surprised.

Wesley walked into the kitchen for a glass of water, while Amanda and Ryan sat on the couch.

"Hey, Ammers," Wesley called out from the kitchen. "Have you ever got a mess in here."

Amanda reached for the remote control. They'd lost track of the time, and she hadn't had time to tidy up. She'd only thrown about half the dishes in the sink before they had to rush out the door so they wouldn't be late for the service. "Don't worry about it," she called back. "I'll clean up later."

Ryan stood. "That's not right. You went through a lot of trouble to feed everyone on short notice, especially since today was your birthday. The least we can do is the dishes." He rolled his sleeves up as he walked into the kitchen, meeting Wesley in the doorway. "Come on, Wesley. I'll wash."

Wesley simply shrugged his shoulders and disappeared into the kitchen with Ryan.

Amanda smiled. Part of her felt guilty for letting the men clean up her kitchen, but she had worked hard to make supper for everyone, and it was nice to have someone else clean it up. And, as Ryan mentioned, it was her birthday. She couldn't remember Wesley ever offering to do the dishes, although he did help when specifically asked. She thought he could learn a lesson here from Ryan.

Completely dismissing any feelings of guilt, Amanda leaned back into the couch, propped her feet up on the coffee table, and started flipping through channels, prepared to enjoy being spoiled, even if it was only for a short time.

Just as she found a show she thought she might enjoy, the phone rang.

"Wesley! It's for you!"

Wesley picked up the extension in the kitchen, so Amanda hung up. Seconds later, Wesley appeared in the living room.

"I've got to go. Aunt Gloria's car died on the interstate, and she needs someone to go get her. See ya."

And Wesley ran out the door.

Sounds of glass clinking and water running echoed from the kitchen. She couldn't very well let Ryan do the dishes all by himself, so she turned off the television and joined him. No sooner was her hand on the dishtowel than he stopped moving, his hands still immersed in the soapy water.

"So much for all the help we thought we were going to be. And it's your birthday, too."

She picked up a pot to dry it. "Don't worry about it. It's the thought that counts. You're my guest. You shouldn't be washing dishes, but I'm not going to tell you to stop."

He grinned at her and continued washing.

While they worked in silence, Amanda thought about how often she'd seen Ryan since he moved in. Except for Wesley, who was a class unto himself, she didn't see much of her neighbors except for a friendly wave or short neighborly conversations on the street. Yet it seemed every time she turned around, there was Ryan. And somehow she either ended up at his house or he was at her house. The trouble was, every time they ended up together, she only got more confused about what was happening.

Since he was new in the neighborhood it was all right, but she couldn't allow things to progress any further. Not that he wasn't a likable sort, because he certainly was, but she didn't think she should be seeing so much of him.

They made companionable conversation until the last dish was dry and put away and the dishwasher was running.

"I guess I'd better be going. Thank you for your hospitality all day."

"You're welcome." Except for the time spent in Sunday school with the children, she'd been with him in some form of activity from sunup to well past sundown. She should have been sick of him, but she wasn't.

She escorted him to the door, but instead of leaving, he turned toward her. "I also wanted to tell you how much I appreciate everything you've done for me. Thanks for inviting me to your church. I really like it there, and I think I'm going to be very comfortable. Everyone is so warm and friendly, and from what I've seen, they follow their faith daily, as we should."

He stepped closer, and Amanda didn't know if she was supposed to say anything, so she simply nodded.

"And if it weren't for you, I'd be sleeping on the floor. Thanks again for calling everyone to help get all my stuff unloaded."

That was days ago, and he'd already thanked her. She didn't know why he was repeating himself, but when he stepped closer, butterflies started to flutter inside her stomach.

He reached forward and grasped both her hands in

his, which brought them very close together. "You're a very special person, Amanda. I think I like you very much." He released her hands, but instead of stepping back, he stepped right up to her, his hands at the sides of her waist.

His head lowered, and his eyes drifted shut.

The butterflies went into overdrive. Amanda was so shocked she didn't have time to think. When his lips brushed hers, she froze at the warm contact. He first kissed her lightly, pulled her a little closer, and then settled in for a firmer contact.

His kiss was tender and sweet, and Amanda had never been kissed like this before in her life. She should have stopped him, but found herself raising her arms and wrapping them around his neck and kissing him back.

Her brain went into a fog, enjoying both the warmth of his embrace and the gentle contact of his kiss. But when one of his hands drifted from her side to the center of her back, Amanda returned to her senses.

What was happening was wrong. She shouldn't have allowed him to touch her, and most of all, she shouldn't have allowed him to kiss her. She still couldn't believe that she had kissed him back.

She moved her hands to his chest and pushed to break them apart.

He blinked a few times, but his eyes were quite dazed as he looked at her.

Amanda swallowed hard to clear the lump in her throat. "That shouldn't have happened."

Ryan lifted his fingers toward her cheek, but she didn't

want him to touch her. It wasn't right. She'd made a horrible mistake, and she'd been wrong to allow this to spiral out of control. Guilt pierced her soul. In order to avoid his touch, she backed up. Her heart pounded in her chest at his confused expression.

His voice came out hoarse and rumbly. "What's wrong? Why not?"

She swallowed tightly, forcing the words out. "Because I'm engaged to Wesley."

Chapter 5

Ryan couldn't sleep. He found himself sitting in the dark kitchen, staring out the window into the night. Actually, he wasn't exactly staring into the night. He was staring at Amanda's house, backlit by the dim streetlight.

He buried his face in his hands. What had he done? What was happening? How could he have been so wrong? He still could barely believe that Wesley wasn't her brother. He was her fiancé.

And he had kissed another man's fiancée. A man with whom he had developed a fast friendship. He couldn't even feel jealous of Wesley; he liked Wesley; Wesley was a good man.

But that didn't ease how he felt about Amanda; it only made it worse.

He thought it was so clear; God had led him here, to a house of his own, the right place of worship, a good job in a small town, but most of all, to Amanda. Every time he was with her further magnified how he felt about her until it was like being struck by lightning.

It didn't add up. Sure, Wesley and Amanda were very

familiar with each other to the point of knowing each other's thoughts before they happened. They seemed inseparable, but something wasn't right. He couldn't quite put his finger on it for the moment, but he would.

He poured himself a glass of water, drank it, then stared into the bottom of the empty glass. As much as he didn't like it, he had to think of Amanda and Wesley together, respect the commitment they had made to each other, and step back.

He repeated the tenth commandment over and over in his head. *Thou shalt not covet thy neighbor's wife.*

Ryan slammed his fist into the table. She wasn't Wesley's wife. Not yet. And putting two and two together, she wasn't going to be for a long time, as Wesley had at least another year of university, and neither of them had made any reference to any upcoming marriage. She didn't even have an engagement ring on her finger.

He thought of what he would feel like and how he would behave around the woman who would be his wife. He knew he wouldn't want to be separated from her for long, and he knew he couldn't wait out a long engagement. Normally he wasn't an impatient man. He was thirty-two years old and up until now had been perfectly content to wait for God to place the right woman in his path. But he knew that when he met the woman who would be his soul mate for life, he would need for them to exchange their vows before God as quickly as arrangements could be made.

Ryan rested his elbows on the table, pinched the bridge of his nose, and rubbed his bleary eyes. Something was amiss, and he had to figure it out. If he didn't, he would be making the biggest mistake of his life by letting Amanda go.

He stood in the dark, set the glass in the sink, and dragged his feet all the way back to bed. He was so exhausted he couldn't think straight. Somehow, eventually, he would fall asleep, and in the morning, he would see things more clearly.

Instead, Ryan lay in bed staring at the dark ceiling as the full force of it hit him. He had fallen in love with Amanda Gibsons. His neighbor. Another man's fiancée.

Ryan picked up a plate from the pile at the end of the table and stood in the lineup. He couldn't imagine how so many people were going to eat at one house, but like any other informal gathering, groups of people stood everywhere, some sitting at the dining room table, others sitting in picnic chairs outside, and many standing all about the house while they ate. He'd looked for her, but he hadn't seen Amanda all day, and a sick feeling stuck in his gut at the thought that she might be avoiding him. He couldn't handle that. It made him want to go find her even more. He had it bad.

Wesley wasn't with her either, because Ryan was beside Wesley now.

Wesley. The man who one day would be her husband. Ryan completely lost his appetite.

Finally, he couldn't stand it any longer. He turned toward Wesley. "Where's Amanda?"

The line moved ahead, and Wesley started to help himself to the food. "She came early because she volunteered to help get stuff set up. She's around here somewhere."

As they continued to fill their plates, Ryan glanced up and around as often as he could until he finally spotted her standing in the far corner by a window with a coffee cup in her hand. "There she is."

Wesley nodded.

"She's all alone."

"Don't worry about her. Soon she'll be talking to someone."

Ryan wanted to be the one to go talk to Amanda, but it wasn't right, to be so besotted with another man's fiancée. He let his thoughts drift, imagining her expressive eyes shining for him and not Wesley and being on the receiving end of her gorgeous smiles. He wanted to make her happy, to be the recipient of all the love she had to give. To share their joys and their sorrows. To pray together in good times and bad. To share special moments that would be theirs, and theirs alone.

Ryan shook his head to bring himself back to reality. He cleared his throat. "She sure looks nice."

Wesley turned his head only long enough to glance quickly at her, then his attention returned to the food. "I suppose. She's worn that before."

"Amanda is very pretty in pink." Ryan could barely take his eyes off of her. Amanda's appearance rivaled any of the women on television, except one glance and a simple smile from her made him weak in the knees.

"She's okay. But you should see Rosalee Rothschild in pink. Now there's a knockout."

Ryan grabbed a roll. It was either that or grab Wesley's

neck. "Don't you just love her smile?"

"I keep telling her she should go to the orthodontist; one of her front teeth is crooked."

Now he really wanted to strangle Wesley. Instead, he turned to watch Amanda across the room, but she was looking the other way. He watched as she smiled a greeting at a woman with a little girl as they walked by. "I think it's kind of cute."

Wesley grunted as he bit into an egg roll.

Finally, Ryan couldn't stand it anymore. "Wesley, she's standing alone in a crowded room. Don't you want to go be with your fiancée?"

"Fiancée?"

Ryan ground his teeth for control. "You two are getting married, aren't you?"

Wesley grinned. "Oh, yeah. I guess that does kind of make her my fiancée, doesn't it? It's kind of hard getting used to thinking of her that way."

"What do you mean, thinking of her that way?"

He shrugged his shoulders. "It's been so long, I guess getting married kinda became the next step. Sometimes I forget."

Ryan shook his head, trying to grasp what Wesley could possibly be thinking. "You forget? The next step?"

"Yeah, we were in diapers together, went to school together, the whole nine yards. I don't know if we've ever been apart, except for when she goes to be camp counselor every year at that place near Seattle. It's probably time we got married or something. But we're going to wait until I graduate, and then the university is going to give me a job. They've already made me an offer. We'll get married after that."

Ryan's mind reeled, unable to comprehend what he was hearing. The relationship between Amanda and Wesley had been coasting for years, as it would for another undetermined amount of time. He didn't know how Wesley could stand it.

He grabbed Wesley by the arm and began to pull him in the direction of a vacant spot where they could talk without being overheard. Wesley protested only long enough to spoon one more helping onto his plate and then allowed Ryan to lead him away gracefully. Ryan started to eat as they stood and talked in an effort to appear casual, when deep inside he was anything but.

"What about an engagement ring? She's not wearing a ring."

Wesley laughed. "We'll get her a ring after I start working at the university and get a few real paychecks and after I've paid off my car. There's no rush. Everyone should know we're eventually getting married. After all, we've been together since forever."

Ryan stared at Wesley, struggling to keep his mouth from gaping open. When the day came that he made the commitment of marriage with the woman who would be his soul mate, he'd have a ring on her finger immediately, even if it meant a second mortgage on his brand-new house. The world would know they were engaged—no guessing involved.

If he hadn't been told, Ryan would never have known. Aside from their obvious close friendship, he couldn't even tell they were in love, at least not what Ryan considered love.

"How do you feel about her, Wesley? Deep down inside. What about love?"

"Love? Of course I love Ammers. We've been best friends all our lives."

Best friends? Ryan loved his best friend Dave, but he wasn't going to marry the guy.

"Yeah. We go way back. I've got pictures of us together as little kids. Some of them are really funny. And there was this one time that we. . ."

Ryan laid his plate down on the corner of the table beside him. He couldn't eat another bite. The favorite recipes of the congregation had begun to taste like cardboard. "What about romance? You know, hearts and flowers and stuff? When you can't stop thinking about her? When thoughts of her keep you awake at night?"

"Keep me awake? Are we talking about Amanda? Amanda Gibsons?"

"You know. When she walks into a room and it gets warmer and the light gets brighter, and your pulse increases, and you can't stand in one spot any longer."

Wesley stared at him as if he'd grown another head. "Are you feeling all right? Do you want me to call a doctor?"

Ryan couldn't believe Wesley couldn't comprehend what he was talking about, that he didn't experience that excitement when he was finally with her after being apart for a while.

Then it hit him. The friendship between Wesley and

Amanda went deep, of that he had no doubt, but it wasn't the kind of relationship that marriages were made of.

Of course a major portion of the marriage bond had to be a good solid and lasting friendship, one that would span a lifetime, but the love for a marriage partner went beyond that. It encompassed the need to bond—body, mind, and soul—with that person. Wesley didn't feel that way.

"What about when you kiss her?"

"Kiss her?"

"When sparks fly and you've got to kiss her or you might die, and when you do, fireworks go off in your brain."

"That kinda stuff just happens in the movies, Ryan. Of course I've kissed her a few times, but it's not like that in real life."

Ryan stared at Wesley in stunned silence. That kind of stuff may happen in the movies, but it also happened to him. And not with any woman he'd kissed. Only with Amanda.

Amanda was marrying a man who thought of her as fondly as a brother would. A man who had never really kissed her the way a man should kiss a woman. A man who thought marriage was merely an extension of a life-long friendship.

Some people might feel envious of the rare friendship that Wesley and Amanda had, a friendship that would surely last a lifetime, but it wasn't what a marriage was made of.

He picked up his plate. "Excuse me. I have to go."

Wesley nodded and walked into the backyard to the barbecue to get a hamburger.

Ryan headed straight for Amanda. He had to know how she felt about marrying Wesley, and there was only one way to find out.

Chapter 6

Amanda glanced toward the buffet table, then set her coffee cup on the sill. Since the lineup had shortened and the rush was over, she would now take her turn.

Just as she walked to the table, Ryan joined her, apparently for seconds, because she'd already seen him and Wesley helping themselves. That was the other reason she'd waited.

"Hi, Amanda."

She spooned a serving of Gladys's favorite chili onto her plate. After yesterday, she didn't know what to say to him, or even if she should say anything. It was not like she had never been kissed before, but except for a few friendly pecks from Wesley, she couldn't remember when. And she'd certainly never been kissed the way Ryan had kissed her.

She moved forward, forcing her concentration onto which selection she would sample next. "Hello, Ryan."

"Everything here is so good. Which is your specialty? Mine are the store-bought buns at the end."

She couldn't help but look at him. His playful wink and

frisky little smile made her insides shake almost as bad as her hands. "I brought the barbecued meatballs over there."

"Those are great. I've already had seconds on those."

She didn't want to talk to Ryan about meatballs, but she was too afraid to change the subject. Instead of commenting, she mumbled a quick thank you and kept filling her plate.

"I love potlucks more than I love going out to restaurants. This is the only time I get to taste good home cooking. Single guy stuff, you know."

She already knew he was single, and although she wasn't married yet, she wasn't single, because she and Wesley had been unofficially engaged for five years. Amanda remained silent.

"Can we go talk, somewhere private?"

As soon as she picked up one of Ryan's specialty buns, she nodded and followed him to a vacant corner, waiting for him to speak. She didn't know if she could slow down her cascading thoughts and emotions enough to make a coherent sentence.

"I know you're feeling awkward with me, and I can certainly understand. I didn't know about you and Wesley; I really didn't, so for that, I apologize."

All she could do was nod. She took a bite of lasagna, pretending the reason she didn't speak was because she had a mouthful.

"He said you two have known each other all your lives. How did you get to live next door?"

Amanda kept staring at her plate. "It was my parents' house. Wesley's mom and my mom were best friends, and when they got married they bought houses next door to each other. My parents were killed in a car accident, and I've chosen to stay in the house."

He nodded. "Wesley told me you lost your parents. I'm sorry; that must have been rough. He said his family helped you through it."

"Yes; Wesley and I grew up together."

"So you've always been close to him?"

She smiled, thinking of all the years with Wesley. Growing up through childhood, the difficult teen years, young adulthood, all the way to the present. They had laughed together in the good times and held each other up through the bad. "I can't imagine ever being without him."

"That's so rare. You've been very blessed to have such a friendship."

She nodded. She also had developed a close bond with her friends from camp, but she'd been with Wesley almost since birth. She was two weeks older than he was.

"So, when are you getting married?"

Amanda shrugged her shoulders, instantly relaxing. His honest apology and frank questions melted away the strain of yesterday. His sincere reactions to her replies told her that now they could be simply good neighbors and perhaps even friends.

"I don't know. Sometime after he graduates, when the time is right."

His eyebrows raised. "When the time is right?"

She shrugged her shoulders again. "I've been with him thirty years. One or two more won't make any difference."

"Won't make a difference? Most of the women I know

are in a rush to get married once they meet the right guy."

She smiled. Ryan couldn't possibly understand, but this was neither the time nor the place to explain. "Yes, but it's just Wesley."

"Just Wesley?"

She bit her bottom lip, but a short giggle escaped. It seemed there was an echo in here. "Wait till you get to know him better. I think you two could come to be friends. You'll see what I mean."

Amanda tried not to laugh when Ryan started waving one hand in the air as he spoke, carefully balancing his plate with the other.

"How could you stand waiting? It's not like a marriage of convenience where you're getting married because of some necessity or that it's an arranged marriage—which I know doesn't happen often in our culture, but it still can. When you get married, you shouldn't be able to wait!"

A few heads turned, and Amanda raised one finger to her lips. "Shh. . ."

Ryan's face turned beet red. His voice lowered. "What about that need to be closer to him than with anyone else in the world? When you've got to touch him, when there's nothing you need more than to be held in his arms."

"We're talking about Wesley, right?"

He dragged his hand over his face.

Amanda drew in a deep breath, completely at a loss for what to say. Obviously she wasn't making herself understood, but she didn't know how to explain it. A while back, she'd had a similar conversation with Belinda, and she had not been able to make Belinda understand either.

"Are you sure about this? Are the two of you really, really sure you're doing the right thing? I mean, what if either of you met someone else? Would you give them a chance to get to know you?"

"Of course I would. But Wesley and I have each other."

His mouth opened, but no words came out. Fortunately, Gladys and her husband appeared and joined them to talk. Amanda introduced Ryan as a newcomer, and after a bit of small talk, Ryan excused himself; she assumed to get more food.

Amanda continued to listen to Gladys, but out of the corner of her eye, she watched Ryan. Instead of refilling his plate, he placed it in the sink with the other dirty dishes, then headed straight for Wesley. Wesley smiled in greeting, but his smile dropped quickly. The men spoke for about thirty seconds, then they both turned and stared at her at the same time. Being so obviously studied nearly made Amanda drop her coffee cup.

Wesley's eyes opened wide, and he and Ryan turned away from her at the exact same second, facing each other with expressions Amanda couldn't identify. They both stiffened and continued to stare at each other, both talking at the same time, and Ryan started waving one arm again. Wesley didn't let go of his plate. She had a feeling that what was said somehow involved her, but she wasn't sure she wanted to know the details.

Ryan and Wesley started to turn away from each other, but Pastor James joined them, obligating them to chat. Amanda took the opportunity to join the other ladies in the kitchen and begin washing dishes.

By the time they were finished, few people remained. She drove home, tired, but content. At first she hadn't wanted to talk to Ryan, but now that she had, things were going to be okay.

Amanda kicked off her shoes, threw her blazer over the back of the couch, and flopped down. It had been a hard day at the bank, and she was glad to be home. She wondered what she could make for supper that didn't involve any work and was about to phone for a pizza when the doorbell rang.

She hadn't been expecting him, but she was sure it was Wesley, who would be wanting to tell her about the happenings at the university, in addition to mooching most of the pizza, which she hadn't ordered yet. She dragged her feet all the way to the door and opened it.

Ryan stood in the doorway, smiling from ear to ear and holding a small bouquet of flowers.

"Ryan? What are you doing here?"

"Aren't you going to ask me to come in?"

She quickly glanced next door to Wesley's driveway. The car was there, but Wesley was nowhere to be seen.

She backed up, allowing Ryan to enter. As soon as the door closed, he extended his hand, forcing her to accept the flowers, yellow daisy mums, her favorite.

"What are these for?"

"Can't you tell? It was your birthday Sunday, so they're two days late, but they're for you."

"In case you've forgotten, Wesley—"

He smiled and nodded. "I know. You're going to be

marrying Wesley. Well, I had a little talk about that with Wesley. He knows I'm here, and I told him I would be bringing you flowers from time to time. I also told him that until I see an engagement ring on your finger, I don't consider this arrangement you two have final or binding."

"That's not up to you to decide."

"No, it's not. It's up to you. But you said yesterday that if someone else came along, you'd at least give him the chance to get to know you better. And that's what I'm doing. I want to get to know you better. One thing I do know about you is that you like flowers."

Amanda studied the bouquet in her hand. She had said that; it was true, but she really hadn't expected this. "But I—"

"I'll bet you haven't had dinner yet. Neither have I. May I take you out for dinner?"

"Wha—what about Wesley?"

He stepped closer, and since her hands were full, she couldn't do anything when he ran one finger down her cheek, then under her chin, tipping it up. The intense eye contact made her breath catch. She couldn't have looked away if she wanted to.

His voice lowered to a gravelly rumble. "Wesley's not invited."

For a brief second, she wondered why this was happening. Was this some bizarre plot to make Wesley jealous? She supposed it could be, if she had hinted to Ryan that he bring her flowers in plain view for Wesley to see, but this was Ryan's idea. She failed to understand the reasoning behind Ryan wanting to make Wesley jealous, so she said nothing.

The flowers aside, Amanda considered that going out and having dinner with him might be a good opportunity to set Ryan straight. As much as she liked him, he was her neighbor, and she was not available as his date. No matter what Ryan might be thinking, she would accompany him only as his friend.

He left the choice of restaurants up to her, so she picked something quiet, not because she wanted to encourage him, but because it was a nice place to talk and not be disturbed, and it was close to home.

She knew the second the hostess seated them that she'd made a mistake. Soft music filled the air, and a fountain, complete with splashing water and soft multicolored lights, created a mood of intimacy, the perfect setting for a romantic evening. Worst of all, they'd been seated side by side, and the way Ryan was looking at her worked up a flock of butterflies in her stomach.

She'd been here before with Wesley, but it had never felt like this. Not only did the atmosphere of the place send her for a loop, but Ryan was the perfect companion to complete the picture. Polite, funny, and interesting, he was easy to talk to, except for the fact that as often as she tried to steer the conversation to the reason she'd accepted his invitation in the first place, he steered the topic far away.

By the time dessert came, Amanda gave up. Rather than spoil what was turning out to be a wonderful evening, she decided to relax and really enjoy herself, and she did. If she hadn't known better, she would have thought it was a date, which of course, it wasn't.

They didn't get home until after dark. Ryan saw her to

her door, and when she stepped inside and turned to wish him a good night, he stepped closer.

He picked up her hand, bent low, and gently kissed it. "Good night, Amanda. I had a wonderful evening. Sleep well."

With that, he turned, jogged across the lawns, and went inside his own door.

At the sound of his door closing, Amanda jolted back to her senses. Sleep well? Not likely.

Chapter 7

Amanda fumbled with the kettle, hoping a nice cup of tea would calm her shattered nerves.

A clink on the window made her drop the kettle into the sink with a crash. She fumbled for it, then set it on the counter with one hand and pressed her other palm to her pounding heart.

She opened the window just as another penny came flying through.

Wesley's laughter drifted through the window. "Oops!"

"What do you want!?" she barked.

"Did you have a nice night?"

She leaned over the sink so her face would be closer to the opening. Wesley did the same, the separation between them reduced to approximately four feet as they spoke. "Yes, I did, actually." She didn't want to elaborate on where she'd been or with whom, but she didn't want to deliberately mislead him or be evasive. She was so confused she nearly blurted it out anyway, but Wesley spoke first.

"Did you like the flowers?"

"Yes, they were very—flowers? How did you know about the flowers?"

"Because Ryan asked me what were your favorites and then he told me he was going to give them to you and ask you out for dinner to celebrate your birthday. I just wanted to know if you were surprised."

Surprised wouldn't have been her first choice of words. She didn't know whether to feel relieved or angry that Wesley already knew. "Yes, I was."

"Well, it's getting late, and I've got to get up early. Maybe I'll see you tomorrow."

They said their good nights and closed their respective kitchen windows, exactly the same as every other time they talked like this. Only this time, Amanda hesitated.

She hadn't exactly been on a date with Ryan, so therefore they hadn't exchanged a good-night kiss, but he had kissed her hand, which in itself was a very romantic and old-fashioned gesture.

She was supposed to be marrying Wesley. Why did they never blow kisses at each other through the windows before they went their separate ways?

Deep in her heart, she knew Ryan would have. And the thought bothered her.

Amanda pulled into her driveway. Instead of looking at her own house before she exited her car, she cautiously examined Ryan's driveway. The absence of his car indicated he wasn't home.

She scooped up her purse, lunch bag, and her library book and dashed toward her front door. Halfway up the sidewalk, her feet skidded to a halt.

Ryan was sitting on her doorstep, grinning sheepishly

up at her as she approached him.

"Hi. Can I borrow that ladder again?"

"Ladder? What are you doing here?"

"I kind of locked myself out again."

"How did you get here? Where's your car?"

Slowly, he rose, brushed off the seat of his slacks, shuffled his feet, and rammed his hands into his pockets. He kept his face down as he spoke. "I thought I'd park the car in the garage; after all, that's what a garage is for, not just an extension of a storage closet. I organized things enough to make room for the car, pulled it in, tidied up a little more, and closed the garage door, and locked it. Imagine my surprise when I discovered I'd left my keys in the car and couldn't open the front door. So the car is locked safely in the garage. I figure it's easier to climb into a window than break down my garage door."

"It's not my ladder. It's Wesley's. And neither he nor his parents are going to be home for hours."

"Then I figure I have three options. I can sit on Wesley's doorstep, you can invite me in until he gets home, or I can take you out for dinner, as long as you drive." He patted his back pocket. "At least I've got my wallet."

She certainly wasn't going to make him wait for hours outside, and she had no intention of going out on another quasi-romantic dinner with him. "Come in. I'll make us something for supper."

The first thing Amanda did was turn the television on to create some noise to override any awkward silence, but her precaution proved completely unnecessary. Conversation flowed as they worked together to make dinner. The

only time silence prevailed was the few seconds of preparation to gather their thoughts preceding giving God
thanks for the meal and the kindness of a good neighbor.

When Wesley arrived home, Amanda mentally kicked
herself that she felt disappointed because that meant she
had no excuse to continue her evening together with Ryan.
As soon as the ladder was in place, Ryan disappeared
through the same window he'd left open last time he
locked himself out.

Amanda didn't bother studying Ryan's driveway when she
arrived home from work. She tried to tell herself that she
didn't care if he was home or not, only that he'd arrived
home safely and with his keys intact.

She had just plopped all her stuff down on the kitchen
table when the phone rang. She recognized the voice
immediately.

"Hello, Ryan. I trust you're inside your house and you
know where your keys are?"

His laughter rang through the phone line. "Yes, I'm
inside, safe and sound. Pastor James called me today. He
says he heard through the grapevine that I'm a teacher,
and he asked if I'd like to help in the Sunday school, and
if so, he invited me to the meeting tonight. If you're going,
how about if we go together?"

She nearly protested, but this time, her objections were
groundless. It was just a Sunday school teachers' meeting,
and even though the meetings were always somewhat
social, it was church business.

In a way, she had always wished Wesley would take

more interest in children, but his pursuits were more academic and his presentation far above the comprehension level of the average kid.

"Sure. What time do you want to leave?"

"How about right now? We can stop for supper first. That way you can tell me all about how the Sunday school runs so I'm not walking in cold." She could hear the smile in his voice, and she could picture his face in her mind, including the cute little crinkles at the corners of his adorable green eyes.

Amanda squeezed her eyes shut to rid herself of the thought. Even though what he said made sense, she couldn't help but wonder if this whole thing was part of some plot. She'd seen him almost every day since he moved in, and some of his excuses were better than others. "I guess so."

"Great. Wesley says George's Bistro would be a good place to go because it's quiet and the service is fast."

Amanda gritted her teeth. "What do you mean, Wesley? When did you talk to Wesley?"

"Oh, he phoned me during his lunch break from the university."

Her eyes narrowed. Wesley never phoned her from school. "And you talked to Wesley about taking me to the Sunday school meeting?"

"Well, it did sort of come up in the conversation."

Amanda squeezed her eyes shut. She should have counted to ten, but the words spilled out of her mouth before she could stop them. Even though Ryan couldn't see her, she waved one hand in the air as she talked into the phone. "Why is it every time you do something with me, you talk to Wesley first? I don't need his permission to spend an evening with anyone other than him! And I don't need him to know where I am or who I'm with every second of every day! You don't have to talk to Wesley every time you want to see me!"

She squeezed her lips shut as she worked to control her breathing.

"You're shouting."

"No, I'm not!" She lowered her voice. "Maybe just a little."

"So you don't want me to talk to Wesley first before I ask you out?"

Amanda ground her teeth together. "No."

"Then how would you like to go to a show tomorrow night? I prefer comedies, but if you want to see some weepy woman's flick and then burst into tears in my arms, that's fine with me, too."

Amanda slapped her hand over her eyes. She couldn't believe what she'd just done. She tried to justify it by thinking he'd set her up, but this time she'd initiated it. She normally didn't have a rebellious nature, but now she felt obligated to go out with him just to prove she didn't have to ask Wesley first. Secondly, if she said no, it would look like he'd won whatever contest they'd had, even though she still couldn't figure out what had just happened.

"All right. I'll go. But I pick the movie."

"Fine by me. Now, about the meeting. I'm ready to go now, so whenever you are, come on over."

Amanda grunted and hung up the phone. She changed into her jeans and a baggy sweatshirt just to look scruffy, gathered her purse and notebook, and banged on Ryan's door.

He opened the door, grinning.

She wanted to stay mad at him, but she couldn't. By the time the meeting was over, he had charmed everyone in attendance, including herself, so much so that she actually looked forward to going to the movie with him.

Ryan straightened his tie, stepped back to look at himself in the mirror, ran his hand over his cheeks again to check his recent shave, patted his hair into place again, then, realizing how stupid he was acting, yanked off the tie and threw it onto the bed.

Who was he kidding? He was as nervous as a high school kid about to embark on his first date. It was just a movie, and it was just Amanda.

He sighed. It wasn't just Amanda. It was the woman he had fallen in love with, a woman who was still in her mind committed to marrying another man.

Ever since he'd learned of their unofficial engagement, he'd watched both Amanda and Wesley carefully. Now, more than ever, he was convinced that they were wrong for each other, not as friends, but as marriage partners.

He'd spent countless hours in prayer, asking and begging God for guidance. For the last week he'd been torn between feelings of guilt, first for wanting them to cancel the engagement and then for wishing Amanda could fall in love with him. Then, going in the opposite direction, more guilt piled on his head, worrying that if he let them continue, disaster would strike if they did get married, because they wouldn't be happy with each other as marriage partners. He didn't want to see either of them make a mistake. He liked Wesley as a friend, but he loved Amanda.

Many times in the past week he'd talked to Wesley, not that he'd exactly asked Wesley permission to attempt to court his fiancée, nor had he told Wesley how much he'd fallen head over heels in love with Amanda, but he had informed Wesley that he liked Amanda very much and planned to spend a lot of time with her. Strangely, Wesley didn't seem to mind.

Ryan shook his head. If he were the one engaged to Amanda, he would do almost anything to keep another man from her doorstep. As much as he liked and respected Wesley, sometimes Ryan simply couldn't figure him out.

Once more, he checked the time. Amanda would be knocking on his door any minute.

The exact second the doorbell rang, so did the phone. He yelled for Amanda to come in as he picked up the phone.

With all his attention focused on Amanda as she smiled at him and made herself comfortable on his couch, Ryan barely heard his principal's voice on the other end of the phone. His heart pounded, he nearly broke into a sweat, and he almost didn't listen to his boss until he heard one word that made his stomach turn.

He mumbled a polite good-bye, cleared his throat, and straightened his shoulders.

Amanda's smile dropped. "Ryan? What's wrong?"

Ryan pinched the bridge of his nose and shook his head. "I need to ask you a favor. Before I go out in public, I need you to check me for head lice."

Chapter 8

I beg your pardon?"

"That was my principal. There's been an outbreak at the school, and already two of the other teachers have been infested. Letters will be sent home with all the students on Monday, but Horace is calling all the teachers tonight."

"That's disgusting."

"I know. As a teacher in elementary school, I've had them before. They spread fast, so you have to catch it quickly. I know what to look for, but it's really hard to do yourself. Would you mind? If you don't want to, I'll understand. I can just stay home all weekend and have the school nurse check me Monday morning."

She hesitated only for a second, which immediately encouraged Ryan. "Just tell me what to do. I was looking forward to this movie."

He told her what to look for and sat at a kitchen chair while she stood behind him and checked for unmentionables. He shouldn't have enjoyed it, but her fingers picking through his hair felt soothing and very personal. Most of all, it felt domestic, and while she worked through the entire surface of his head, he closed his eyes and let his mind wander to a picture of what it would be like to share a home with Amanda. Kids. A dog. The whole thing—he wanted it all—and he wanted it with Amanda.

A pat on the top of his head broke him out of his daydreams. "You're clear, teacher."

Ryan blinked, then stood. "Thanks. I really appreciate that." He stood in front of her and looked down. She was a short little thing, and her large glasses accentuated her fine features. What he really wanted to do was hug her and kiss her the way a man should kiss a woman, but he didn't have that right. Instead, holding himself back, he grasped her hands and ran his thumb over the soft skin of her wrist. "You're a very special woman. Did you know your name means 'worthy of love'? And you are, you know."

She stiffened but didn't pull away, which he also thought an encouraging sign. "I think we had better leave, or we'll be late."

The entire movie, Ryan couldn't decide if he'd committed himself to an exercise of joy or frustration. Amanda had picked a comedy, and between her presence beside him, the musical sound of her laughter, and the lighthearted drama, he couldn't remember the last time he'd enjoyed himself more. But not being able to put his arm around her was pure frustration, and not being able to kiss her in the total blackness when the screen was dark was torture.

Like a perfect gentleman, he escorted her to her door, checked inside to ensure her safety, and said good night without touching her.

As he lay awake staring at the ceiling half the night,

Ryan made up his mind. He was going to talk to Wesley once more, and regardless of what Wesley said, he was going to court Amanda openly and properly. She deserved to be treated like the treasure she was, and if Wesley wasn't going to do it, Ryan was.

He held off for as long as he respectably could, but at precisely 12:30 P.M., Ryan knocked on Amanda's door. Instead of the smiling welcome he would have preferred, she stood in the doorway with her index finger pressed to her lips. "Shh. . . ," she whispered. "Wesley's sleeping."

Ryan checked the time, just to make sure he wasn't mistaken. When he walked into her living room, sure enough, there was Wesley, flat on his back on her couch, his mouth wide open, snoring like a foghorn.

"He was out late last night."

After one last look at Wesley's sprawled-out figure, he followed Amanda into the kitchen.

"Would you like a cup of tea?" she asked.

"No, thanks. But you go ahead."

He watched as she made the tea. She was dressed in comfortably worn jeans and a baggy old sweatshirt that hung halfway to her knees, with the sleeves scrunched up past her elbows, and she looked adorable. They walked into the backyard and set up a couple of lawn chairs so they could sit and talk, but every once in a while they could hear Wesley snort.

Finally Ryan couldn't stand it anymore. "You can't marry him."

She laughed, probably thinking he was joking. "Don't

be silly. I'm sure he doesn't snore like that all the time. It's probably just his allergies."

"I don't have any allergies."

She laughed again. She opened her mouth, but before she said a word, the phone rang. "Excuse me." She ran inside, and even though he couldn't hear what she was saying, he could hear the pleasant drone of her voice.

"Hi, Ryan. I must have fallen asleep. Good to see you."

Ryan nodded. "Wesley."

Wesley sank into the lawn chair Amanda had vacated. "Man, that allergy medication really knocked me out. I should have taken the non-drowsy stuff."

All Ryan could do was stare at Wesley. He'd already told Wesley how he felt about Amanda, but he'd obviously not made himself clear enough, because nothing had changed. "Before Amanda gets back, I have to tell you something."

"Oh?"

"It's about Amanda."

"What?"

Ryan steeled his nerve, knowing that by what he was about to say, he could possibly blow his chances with Amanda, but Wesley deserved to know what he was about to do. Most of all, he wasn't going to do it behind Wesley's back. Wesley was his friend.

"Haven't you ever watched an engaged couple, how they behave toward each other? How anyone near them can tell they're hopelessly in love?"

"Yeah. So?"

Ryan leaned forward, rested his elbows on his knees,

and clasped his hands. "A man gives the woman he loves flowers. He says sweet nothings. He goes out of his way to spend time with her, tries to make her feel special, because to him, she is. He showers her with hugs and kisses. And when you can't do that, you hold hands or do other little things to show her that you care."

"And your point is?"

"Wesley, you're not doing any of those things with Amanda!"

"But our relationship isn't like that."

Ryan slammed his fist into his open palm. "Well, it should be. You should show the woman you're going to marry how much you love her."

Wesley stared blankly at him. It took every ounce of Ryan's self-control not to stand up and grab Wesley by the shoulders and shake some sense into him. He stared Wesley straight in the eyes. "And if you're not going to do that, I will, because I'm in love with your fiancée."

All Wesley did was blink and stare back.

Ryan stood, walked in a few short circles, then forced himself back down into the chair. "Aren't you going to say anything?"

"What's there to say?"

Both men stood at the same time. Ryan extended his hand. "Regardless of what happens, Wesley, I hope we'll always remain friends."

Wesley nodded. Amanda walked outside as they were joined in a handshake.

"What's going on? You two look like you've just made a bet or something."

Ryan felt his face heat up. "Just a gentleman's agreement."

"Oh. I just wanted to tell you guys I'm leaving. That was Sue. She says there's a great sale at the mall, and we're going shopping."

Ryan dropped Wesley's hand. "Looks like we're being kicked out. Do you golf?"

Something had changed. Lately, Amanda thought she'd been seeing even more of Ryan, especially since he had given her a spare key to his house. At the time he gave it to her, he had teased her about it also being the key to his heart, but she had laughed it off, and so had Wesley.

If it weren't that Ryan and Wesley seemed to be developing such a close friendship, she might have questioned Ryan. Lately, she was seeing more of him than ever. Occasionally, he brought flowers, and sometimes he simply showed up at the oddest times and for no reason. Then the times that he wasn't with her, he seemed to be with Wesley. Yet when the three of them were together, he stepped back, allowing her to be side by side with Wesley, even if Wesley got distracted constantly. She couldn't figure Ryan out.

The worst part was that she was starting to miss him when he wasn't there, whether Wesley was there or not. It didn't seem quite right to spend so much time with Ryan, but not only did Wesley not seem to mind, he didn't notice how much Ryan was affecting her.

Amanda tried to fight it, but she could no longer deny that Ryan was getting under her skin, and he wasn't going to go away. She liked him, and she liked him a lot.

Whatever friendship was developing between them was very different than her friendship with Wesley, or any friendship she'd ever had with anyone.

Amanda pulled into her driveway and turned off the ignition. Ryan's car wasn't in his driveway, and she couldn't tell if it was in the garage from this angle, so she took her chances, gathered her things, and cautiously walked to her front door.

By the time she turned the key, she still had no visitors or offers of help to carry anything, so she let out her breath and allowed herself to relax. She dumped everything onto the table, and as she was about to leave the kitchen, the flashing light of the answering machine caught her eye.

Amanda hit the button. Dani's voice came on, but rather than the usual cheeriness, Dani's voice was somber.

"I'm just calling to tell you that I just got a phone call from Collette. Her father died yesterday. She sounded just awful, Amanda. She's in shock, of course, even though she knew it was coming, but it's still hard for her. Now, on top of that, she's got to wrap up their missionary project and come home because the funding's been canceled. I thought you'd like to know so you could pray for her and for her ministry. I'm going to call Belinda now. Bye."

Amanda had never met Collette's father, but she did know what it was like to experience the loss of a father. She'd gone through terrible upheaval when her parents died, but she'd had Wesley and his parents next door to help her through it. Collette was halfway across the world—and alone.

She couldn't reach Collette by phone and a letter took

too long, but she knew what she could do, even if all she was doing would be to let Collette know she would be praying for her.

She dug one of Collette's letters out of the dresser drawer, then called the florist to order a condolence arrangement and give the woman the longest message she could get away with on a small card.

Amanda hung up the phone, and suddenly her hand began to shake. Memories of her own father flashed through her mind. She ran into the living room and stood in front of the picture of her parents that hung above the fireplace. The picture of the three of them had been taken on her nineteenth birthday, which had been only a few months before their deaths. She'd been without them for ten years, and she still missed them dearly. Her parents would never see her wedding day, nor would they know their grandchildren, at least not here on earth.

She raised her fingers to touch the pictures, first of her father, then of her mother. The sting of tears burned the backs of her eyes, and she tried to fight it.

She knew from experience that if she remained alone in the living room, she would soon be reduced to a pathetic mess of tears. Rather than let the cycle continue, she had to leave the house. Without knowing where she was going, she started for the door. Suddenly she spotted the book Ryan had accidentally left behind on her coffee table after his most recent surprise visit.

She hesitated for a split second. Wesley was her fiancé —she should have gone to him—but the person she really wanted to be with was Ryan. And now she had an excuse.

Chapter 9

Amanda raised her fist to knock on Ryan's door but froze when she heard Wesley's laughter. Guilt roared through her. She should have wanted to see Wesley, but she was standing on Ryan's doorstep.

When Ryan opened the door, he smiled. Instead of moving aside, he moved one step closer and reached out to grasp both her hands. "Amanda! What a pleasant surprise! Wesley and I were just talking about you."

She stared at her hands clasped in his, then peeked to the side at Wesley, who was half-sitting and half-sprawled across Ryan's couch. Wesley smiled but otherwise didn't move.

A tightness suddenly nearly choked her. They were supposed to be getting married someday. This should have been the most romance-filled time of their lives. Instead, it had been Ryan who spoiled her and Ryan who she wanted to be with, both in the fun times and at times like this, when she needed an understanding ear.

Wesley made no move to greet her, even though she hadn't seen him for over a day. He was just as comfortable with her as Ryan's big comfy couch, a piece of furniture.

Ryan's eyes narrowed and his head tilted slightly. "Are you okay? Is something wrong?" When she remained silent, he gave her hands a gentle squeeze and massaged her wrist with one thumb. His tender touch shot a surge of heat through her, and her knees went wobbly.

Ryan's words from Pastor James's last barbecue hit her so hard she nearly lost her balance. *When there's nothing you need more than to be held in his arms.*

That was exactly what she needed right now. She wanted to be held while she tried to gain control of her cascading emotions, and then everything would be fine once again. Despite Ryan's often expressed sentiments about the absence of a ring on her finger, it was Wesley she was engaged to, and it should have been Wesley she needed to have hold her, but it wasn't. She needed Ryan.

She stared up at him, and the deep concern in his eyes was her final undoing. It was bad enough that she caught herself daydreaming about him at the bank and lying awake thinking of him at night. But now, here she was, standing on his doorstep, nearly begging him to hug her.

Her lower lip quivered. "I miss my dad," she muttered, and the tears spilled out.

Without hesitation, Ryan slipped his arms around her, guided her inside, and shut the door behind them. She knew Wesley was watching from the couch, but for the moment, she couldn't do anything else but let Ryan hold her tight as she cried herself out.

He rubbed soothing circles gently on her back and buried his face in her hair. He spoke so quietly, she barely heard him. "Please don't cry. If it helps, I love you, Amanda."

Without thinking why his touch helped, Amanda still cried so hard she couldn't respond. She needed his gentle comfort so much, she stayed pressed against him until there were no more tears left.

Slowly, she pulled herself away and swiped at her eyes with her sleeve. "Thanks. I needed that."

Wesley rose from the couch. "Come on. I'll take you home."

She really didn't want to go, but she allowed Wesley to lead her away. Rather than invite him in, Amanda assured Wesley that she was fine and sent him away. But she wasn't fine. She had to talk to someone. She just couldn't talk to Wesley.

Amanda looked at the time, then the calendar. Collette was still in Kenya, battling her own struggles. Dani would be unreachable, gallivanting somewhere in the Grand Canyon, but Belinda would be just about to close up her shop. Most important, Belinda had been married before. Even though she was now a widow, Belinda would know the answer.

Her hands shook as she dialed the number.

"Hi, Andi, can I talk to your mommy?"

Amanda held the phone away from her ear as something crashed on the other end of the line and the little girl screamed for Belinda's attention.

"Amanda? Is that you? Not that it isn't good to hear your voice again, but it's not the last Thursday of the month. Is something wrong?"

"No, nothing's wrong. Well, maybe. I don't know." She shook her head. "I'm so confused. I had to talk to someone who's been through this before. What's it like to be in love?"

"I beg your pardon?"

"Before you got married to Andrew. What was it like?"

Her friend sighed. "I trust you'd tell me if Wesley has done something to hurt you."

"No. No, he hasn't. Everything with Wesley is just fine." Amanda gulped. It was what was happening between herself and Ryan she wasn't so sure about.

"Well, I'm not sure I've ever been truly in love myself. Sure, I thought I loved Andrew. We were together all through high school, and we got married shortly after we graduated. It seemed like such a natural progression. But it didn't take long for me to see that he wasn't the man I thought he was, and I knew it was a mistake within a year. I craved security as well as sparks and electricity, but it didn't happen that way. I realized too late something was missing. Not that we weren't happy, because we were, at least most of the time, or at least we didn't fight all the time."

Belinda paused, then cleared her throat. Rather than press for details, Amanda waited for her friend to continue. Amanda could only guess how hard life had been for Belinda since Andrew's death.

"All I'm saying is, when you're in love, and I mean really in love, you'll know it."

Amanda's throat clogged, and she couldn't think of a word to say.

A loud thump in the background, followed by an ear-shattering wail made Amanda flinch.

"Oh, Amanda, I'm so sorry. I've got to go. Andi's been

chasing the cat again, and I think she's hurt herself. Bye."

A click sounded in Amanda's ear, and she stood staring at the receiver until a dial tone sounded. Gently she replaced the unit.

Sparks? Electricity? Up until she met Ryan, she would have thought those things happened only in the movies. But now she knew they happened in real life.

Up until recently, Amanda had thought she was doing the right thing. Now she wasn't sure. She went to bed, but it took a long time to fall asleep—and only after lots and lots of prayer.

As soon as she woke up, she called Wesley and asked him to come over. She was waiting at the door before he knocked. "We have to talk."

He nodded. "I know."

"About us."

"Yeah."

Amanda gulped and stiffened from head to toe. They'd never really talked about where their relationship was going, but it was time to be honest with herself and with Wesley. The answer was that their relationship was going nowhere. All she could do was stare at her best friend, whom she'd been with since she was a baby.

Wesley nodded toward the couch. "Ammers, I think we'd better sit down."

She nodded and walked with him to the couch, where she waited for Wesley to speak first.

He adjusted his glasses on his nose. "I talked to Ryan."

She choked the words out. "Why does that not surprise me?"

"What's going on between you two?"

He touched her hands, a move that surprised her, and judging from Wesley's change in expression, he'd also surprised himself.

Amanda shook her head. "I don't know what's going on. I wish I could explain it, but I can't." Her eyes started burning, tears welled up, but she blinked them back. "He said he loves me. I don't know what to do."

Wesley cleared his throat. "I've been doing a lot of thinking lately, and I've been starting to wonder if we're doing the right thing."

His bald honesty was the final trigger. The same as yesterday, the flood of uncontrolled emotions burst, and she pulled her hands out of Wesley's grip, threw herself against his chest, and let herself sob freely. She felt his hesitation before he wrapped his arms around her, which only made her cry harder.

When she gained just barely enough control to speak, she still couldn't look at him, so instead she spoke into the center of his chest. "I can't marry you, Wesley. I'm sorry."

"I know. And you're right. It's over."

She pulled herself away, knowing the tears were still streaming down her face, but she made no attempt to stop them. "We'll always be special friends, Wesley. You know that, don't you?"

Slowly, he wiped at a tear as it ran down her cheek, and the tender gesture made the tears flow harder.

"Yeah, I know. But I've already prayed about it, and I don't think us getting married is the right thing anymore. You should be marrying the man you love."

They stood at the same time. She should have been surprised, but she wasn't. Maybe she was the last to admit it. She was in love with Ryan Robertson.

Wesley cleared his throat. "I'd better go. See you around, Ammers."

And he turned and left.

Ryan threw the pile of books, his briefcase, and his lunch onto the passenger seat of his car and backed out of the driveway. He stepped out of the car to shut the garage door when he saw Wesley approaching him. He waited until they faced each other.

"I just talked to Ammers. The engagement is off."

He should have been happy, but the stricken expression on Wesley's face completely stripped away any joy he might have felt. "And?"

"And she's pretty upset. It was mutual, actually, but still, it's not easy. She was crying really bad."

He didn't know what to say, so he said nothing.

"I thought you should know. I've got to go; I'm already late."

Wesley turned and ran to his car, then drove away.

Ryan felt sick. He wanted Amanda to be happy, but instead, he'd only succeeded in making her miserable. She hadn't left for the bank yet and he wanted to talk to her, but he wasn't sure of what he would say. Instead of making a bad situation worse, he got back in the car and drove to school.

Amanda drew her fingers out of the blinds when Ryan and Wesley separated.

From the time she was a little girl, she'd always thought she'd marry Wesley, and for the past five years she'd waited patiently, as she was willing to wait some more.

Now, her dreams were shattered. Her nice controlled future was turned upside down. Everything she'd ever hoped and planned for was gone. More than anything, she wanted someone who could love her unconditionally and someone she could love until the end of time. Until she met Ryan, she'd thought that someone was Wesley. They'd been friends since birth; they'd be friends till they died, but now, they'd never be married. It wasn't that kind of love. The one she loved was Ryan, but the only time he'd said he loved her was when he was trying to comfort her. At the time it had been what she needed to hear, but now it wasn't enough.

After Ryan drove away, Amanda gathered her things and drove to work, but her job couldn't distract her enough. When she pulled into her driveway after a long and miserable day, she couldn't help but look at the two houses on either side of her own and think of her two neighbors, the two men in her life.

She turned off the ignition and stared at Wesley's house. She still was in shock at his agreement that they shouldn't get married.

"Hi, Amanda."

The sudden sound of Ryan's deep voice made her jump. Her elbow hit the horn, and she dropped her purse. She stared out the car window at him.

"Can we talk?"

She got out of the car and waited.

"I talked to Wesley, and he told me. I'm sorry, really sorry." He stared down at the ground, back up to her face, then cupped her cheeks with both hands. "But that doesn't stop how I feel. Now that you're no longer going to be marrying Wesley, would you consider marrying me?"

She knocked his hands away. "Why are you asking me that? Is it because you feel sorry for me? Because I've got no parents, no family, and now, because of you, no fiancé? If that's why you're asking, the answer is no." Amanda gulped for control and backed up a step. "Now go away and leave me alone. Haven't you done enough damage?"

Without giving him a chance to speak, Amanda ran into her house, but before she closed the door behind her, she saw Ryan still standing beside her car, his head bowed, pinching the bridge of his nose. She closed the door but didn't move. After a couple of minutes she heard Ryan's door open and close.

Amanda buried her face in her hands, then let her forehead bump into the back of the closed door. First he said he loved her to comfort her, and now he proposed marriage out of guilt. She wanted him to love her the way she loved him, totally and completely. And since that wasn't the way he felt, she couldn't live next door to him; she couldn't watch him coming and going day after day.

All her life, she'd been waiting for Wesley. Good old, dependable, stable Wesley. Her whole life had been predictable and. . .boring. Up until now, boring hadn't been a bad thing.

It was time to change.

Amanda made a quick phone call, and within half an hour, the "For Sale" sign was in place on her front lawn.

Chapter 10

Ryan nearly tripped over his own feet at what he saw in Amanda's front yard.

This was his fault. He tried to tell himself that it would eventually work out for the best that she was no longer going to marry Wesley, but the pain of knowing she wasn't going to marry him either was more than he'd ever experienced. It would be difficult to talk to her when both his emotions and hers were so raw, but he had to. He couldn't let her sell the house she'd grown up in because of him.

At that moment, Ryan made a decision. He had come to love his house, but it was only a material possession. Amanda was a person, God's precious child, and he loved her more than his house, more than his heart could bear. Tomorrow, he would put his own house up for sale, and he would tell Amanda that she didn't have to sacrifice her home because of him. But for tonight, the pain was still too sharp. He would talk to her tomorrow.

For a minute, he watched the flickering light of her television reflecting in the dark night. He pictured her sitting on the couch, relaxing in her living room, and imagined what it would be like to share a home with her. He ached inside for what he couldn't have.

Ryan opened his door, deposited the stack of books and notes from the staff meeting on the floor, then turned to retrieve his briefcase out of his car. As he turned, a gust of wind blew, and a click sounded behind him.

He whirled around, knowing the end result of any attempts would be futile, but he tried anyway. The doorknob wouldn't budge.

He slammed his fist into the door, then leaned forward until his head bumped into the wooden door. His keys were already inside the house, and this time, he knew he hadn't left a window open. His only option was to get the spare key from Amanda.

With his heart in his throat, he dragged himself next door, knocked, and waited.

The door opened, and the change from her smile to her downcast expression tore at him.

"I've locked myself out. Can I trouble you for my key?"

Without a word, she turned, dug his key out of its hiding spot, and handed it to him.

Rather than meekly accept it, he reached further and grasped her whole hand. Her entire body tensed, but she didn't pull away.

"I can't let it end like this. I can't let you sell your house because of me." At his words he felt her tension ease slightly, and he took advantage of it. He stepped forward and wrapped his arms around her, held her tightly against him, and buried his face in her hair. "I love you, Amanda. I'm so sorry about everything. I don't know how I'm going to handle it if you move away, but since you can't stand to be near me, I'm going to put my house up for sale. As soon as it sells, I'll be out of your life forever. All I need to know is that you'll forgive me. I know you wouldn't be happy being married to Wesley. I thought you could be happy married to me, but it appears I'm wrong."

He stopped just long enough to breathe in the herbal fragrance of her shampoo, memorizing it, knowing this would be the last time he would be able to touch her. "No matter what happens, I'll always love you, Amanda."

Amanda squeezed her eyes shut and gritted her teeth. All day and all evening, all she had been able to think of was the men living on either side of her. Wesley, whom she now knew she would be making a major mistake if she married, and Ryan, whom she loved the way Belinda had said love should be. Encompassed in the full spectrum of love she felt for him were sparks, electricity, and security.

He loved her so much he had stepped between herself and Wesley, knowing she could hate him for it, and from her reaction, that was probably what he thought. She'd never allowed herself to tell Ryan she loved him because she'd been too caught up in her own spiraling emotions. Yet Ryan opened himself up to her, baring his soul, and leaving himself vulnerable to however she now responded. He loved her the way she needed to be loved, and she loved him body, mind, and soul. They both loved God, and they both loved each other.

The biggest mistake of her life would be if she let him go.

Being in love meant taking risks—the biggest being

the risk of rejection. If he threw her love back into her face, it was nothing less than she deserved.

The words of Isaiah 41:10 flashed through her mind: "Fear thou not; for I am with thee: be not dismayed; for I am thy God: I will strengthen thee; yea, I will help thee; yea, I will uphold thee with the right hand of my righteousness."

Despite the risk of her reaction, Ryan had not been afraid. In faith, he did what God wanted him to do, which was to show her that Wesley wasn't the right lifelong partner for her. Now she had to trust in God's strength and wisdom and know God would hold her up.

Amanda moved her hands to Ryan's chest and very gently pushed him away. As large as he was, he moved back without resistance. His eyes were squeezed shut, and slowly, they opened. While concentrating intently on the torment there, knowing she was the one who caused it, she picked up his right hand with both of hers, lifted it, and holding tight, pressed it to his heart.

Amanda struggled to clear her throat. "Ryan Robertson, I love you. Will you marry me?"

His heart raced beneath her hands, his eyes opened wide, misted over, and before she could take a breath, his hands slipped behind her back, her feet rose into the air, and she was whirling in a circle pressed tightly against Ryan's chest.

Ryan threw his head back. "Yes!!!!!" he shouted as they continued to twirl.

The second her feet touched the ground, he kissed her so beautifully that she felt like she was once again floating.

In the back of her mind, she heard a car go by, but Amanda didn't care that the neighborhood could watch them. She was marrying the right man, the man she loved, for all the right reasons, and soon the world would know, starting with Belinda, Collette, and Danielle.

Ryan released her and cupped her face in his large hands. "Under one condition. After we get off work tomorrow, we're going shopping for a ring."

Amanda smiled. She wouldn't have it any other way.

Gail Sattler

Gail was born and raised in Winnipeg, Manitoba, and now lives in Vancouver, B.C. (where you don't have to shovel rain) with her husband, three sons, a dog, and countless fish, many of whom have names. Gail became a Christian with her husband after he joined AA. She began writing when the company she worked for closed and she chose to stay home with her children. She writes inspirational romance because she loves happily-ever-afters and believes God has a place in that happy ending. She has written novels for Barbour Publishing's **Heartsong Presents** line including *Walking the Dog, Piano Lessons, Gone Camping,* and *At Arm's Length.* She now works part-time as office manager for a web design company. Visit Gail on the Internet at http://www.gailsattler.com.

Belinda

by Colleen Coble

Acknowledgment

For our friend and mentor, Loree Lough,
who conceived this story and brought us together.
Thanks, Loree!

Chapter 1

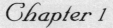

Rick Storm parked his red Jeep Cherokee in front of the huge Victorian structure and looked up at the gargoyles leering down at him from the rooftop. His foreman, Dan, who also happened to be his best friend, had told him he had to see this place to believe it, but this building was truly incredible. Once a county home for indigent residents, its crumbling brick face looked down in aging glory on the town of Wabash, Indiana. A weathered sign, Timeless Treasures Architectural Salvage, looked as though it might fall off in a stiff breeze.

He got out and tipped his Stetson to a perspiring woman whose bulk was seriously straining a pair of Lee jeans. He ignored the woman's curious stare; he'd gotten used to the disbelief at his cowboy garb a long time ago. He hailed from Arizona cowboy country and was proud of it. Eager to see the inside of this place, he headed toward the door, the peeling paint crunching under the heels of his cowboy boots. Just as he reached the top step, the rickety screen door flew open, and a little girl with curly dark hair rode her tricycle out onto the porch. She didn't look up but pedaled furiously and drove straight into his leg.

He yelped and tried to dance out of the way, then realized she was in danger of riding right off the porch. He let go of his throbbing shin and grabbed her just as the tricycle dove down the steps.

Rather than wiggling or crying out, she just looked up at him with trusting blue eyes. "I'm Andi. Are you the Lone Ranger?"

He grinned at the question. "I don't think so. I don't have a mask."

She regarded him thoughtfully, then nodded. "What's your name?"

Where are the child's parents? Don't they watch her? He frowned disapprovingly, then smiled at the little girl. "My name is Rick. Are you just learning to ride your tricycle?"

Andi nodded. "Uncle Micky got it for me for my birthday." Straightening her shoulders, she puffed out her chest importantly. "I'm three now." She waited a moment to give him time to be suitably impressed. "Mommy and me sell old stuff."

She was adorable. Rick was ready to adopt her on the spot. "You do?" He set her on the porch. "Why don't you show me?"

He took her hand, and she led the way inside. He gasped when he entered the first room. Every window had a stained-glass window hung over it, and the light through the colored glass cast dappled patterns of blue, gold, and green over the other contents of the room. More windows hung on every available wall space. Several wonderful old fireplaces lined one wall. The one in the corner looked like just what he had in mind, and he knelt to inspect it. It was in excellent shape with pillars and mantle of quartersawn oak. The price wasn't bad, either. This architectural salvage place just might be as good as he'd been told. Through the doorway he glimpsed light fixtures and beveled glass windows.

"Do you want to see Mommy?" Andi asked.

"Either her or your daddy."

"My daddy died."

Rick's heart clenched at her matter-of-fact tone. He knew what it was like to lose a beloved parent. He'd nursed his mother through a six-year battle with cancer until she'd died a year ago.

Poor little mite. He couldn't imagine where this child's mother was; such a small girl shouldn't be wandering around this huge mausoleum alone. She could get lost or worse. Andi took his hand again and led him through a labyrinth of rooms and corridors. They passed room after room of all kinds of antique plumbing fixtures, hardware, trim, windows, and doors. He wanted to stop and examine this virtual treasure trove and had to force himself to continue walking. He was beginning to think they'd taken a wrong turn when Andi stopped at a room with an ornate walnut door.

"This is where Mommy works."

He could hear music playing in the background and raised his eyebrows in surprise. He thought only cowboys and cowboy wanna-bes listened to Don Edwards croon his songs about the Old West. He grinned. No wonder Andi thought he was the Lone Ranger. Curious to see who this woman was who listened to his kind of music, he cautiously pushed open the door.

A young woman sat in an old wooden desk chair, the kind that swivelled and rocked. Her head was pillowed on her arms on top of a ledger book. She was snoring softly.

Rick put his finger to his lips and, taking Andi's hand, began to back out of the room. Andi's mother muttered and stirred. Her eyes flew open, and Rick found himself staring into the most incredible blue-green eyes he'd ever seen. Thickly lashed, they reminded him of the water in the lagoon in Hawaii where he'd gone snorkeling last summer. Almost aqua. Soft auburn hair with a face too round to be called beautiful by the world's standards, a straight nose with a tiny hump in the middle, and a lovely smile completed the picture.

That lovely smile widened in apology, and the gentleness in it went straight to his heart. She sat up groggily and put a hand to her tousled hair. She wore rumpled jeans with a wrinkled cotton shirt. Her long hair was such a riot of curls, her face was almost lost in the mass, and she wore no makeup. She evidently wasn't one to fuss with her appearance, but her eyes made it unnecessary. Her gaze flew to the pallet of blankets against the far wall.

"Andi!"

"She's right here," Rick reassured her.

Andi peeked from behind his legs at her mother. "His name is Rick, and he says he isn't the Lone Ranger."

The statement was made with a trace of doubt in her voice. "I was good, Mommy. I helped you. Rick wants to buy Mrs. Grimmley's fireplace." She looked up at Rick with a dimpled smile.

Evidently nothing much got by those blue eyes. He grinned down at her. "If Mrs. Grimmley's fireplace is the one with the quartersawn pillars, Andi is right."

The young woman scrambled to her feet and held out her hand. "I'm Belinda Mitchell, owner of this decaying heap. This little scamp was supposed to be taking a nap, and I must have drifted off myself."

"Rick Storm." He shook her hand. She had a firm handshake and gazed directly into his eyes. He liked that. She only reached his chest, and he estimated her height at about five foot two inches. Andi evidently took after her; she was quite a bit smaller than his three-year-old niece.

Her incredible eyes widened. "You're the new builder everyone is talking about. The one who uses so many antique fixtures in his houses. I read an article about your homes in the Fort Wayne *Journal Gazette*. The article said you had planned to move to Wabash, and I hoped you'd find my place."

A warm glow started in his stomach. "It's nice to know my work is appreciated. Finding your place seems to be a lucky break for me. It has a much better selection than most, but I didn't get a chance to really look since Andi was set on dragging me off to find you. Would you mind showing me around?"

She nodded eagerly. The tour lasted nearly an hour. Her selection was huge, and Rick was impressed. He knew he'd be back here often. He bought the fireplace, a spandrel, and two stained-glass windows. He noticed Belinda's eyes grow brighter with every purchase. Taking a fresh look at

Belinda and her daughter, he noticed the worn condition of Belinda's jeans and the holes in Andi's sneakers. Calling himself a sucker, he recklessly added a huge stack of woodwork to his order. He'd do anything to see her smile again.

Belinda totaled the order on a sales pad and handed him his copy. Rick was surprised at the total. He had a head for numbers and had already figured what the cost would be. "Did you forget to add something? The spandrel was fifteen hundred dollars all by itself."

"I dropped the price a little since you bought so much," she said. She rested her chin on the tips of her first two fingers in a way he thought utterly charming.

He dragged his gaze from her animated face. "You don't need to do that. Your prices are very reasonable." He fished out his checkbook and, adding in an extra five hundred dollars, wrote out a check for four thousand dollars.

Her eyes widened when he handed it to her. He saw her swallow, and tears shimmered on her lashes. She quickly turned away to begin to gather his things. Her small hands were nicked with cuts and abrasions, and he realized she must do some of the demolition needed to acquire these treasures by herself. How long had she been widowed? Andi hadn't said. It was none of his business, of course, but he longed to know what lurked behind those beautiful eyes.

"Don't worry about that stuff now," he told her. "If you'll have it ready by tomorrow morning, I'll send my foreman, Dan Johnson, after it." For some reason, he was reluctant to leave. Something about her little-girl-lost quality tugged at his heartstrings. He searched for something to say to continue the conversation. "Uh, do you have any ideas about churches around here? I just moved to town three days ago and haven't found one yet."

Belinda's face grew even more animated. "My church is wonderful! Actually, Sunday is Friend Day, and I'd be pleased to have you come as a friend for me and Andi. It's New Life out on County Road 300 North. I teach Sunday school for three- and four-year-olds, but you could sit with us during the worship service."

"I'd love to come. What time shall I pick you up?"

She gave a self-conscious laugh and twirled a curl around a finger. "You don't want to drive clear out here. I can meet you there."

He shook his head firmly. "I want to pick you up. Unless there's some other man who would object?" He cocked an eyebrow questioningly.

Her cheeks grew pink, and she shook her head. "If you are sure you don't mind, Andi and I will be ready at nine."

"And to say thank you for taking pity on a lonely bachelor, we'll eat lunch afterward. Pizza okay?"

She nodded uncertainly. "Andi loves pizza. We don't get it very often, though."

Probably because they can't afford it, Rick surmised. "It's a date!"

Immediately Belinda looked alarmed. "A—a date?" she stammered. "Andi will like that. You've made quite a hit with her."

Rick was smiling as he drove away. The move to Wabash just might prove very interesting.

Belinda and Andi watched Rick drive away in his flashy red Jeep Cherokee.

Andi looked up at her mother and squeezed her hand. "I like him, Mommy. He's nice."

Belinda ruffled her daughter's hair. "Yes, very nice," she said. "And isn't God good!" She'd fallen asleep crying over the bills when that cowboy-type showed up and bought all that merchandise. The wonder of it made her want to clap her hands for joy. And as an added bonus, he was coming to church with her! They'd been having a special outreach summer, and she hadn't found a visitor to bring with her since her brother came for a visit. She wondered if Rick would wear his western getup to church. It seemed odd to see someone decked out in western clothes when he wasn't going to a country-western concert or something like that. He looked good in those clothes, though. Stocky and broad-shouldered with gray eyes that tilted up at the corners and looked right through a person. She assumed his hair was as black as his eyebrows.

She took Andi's hand, and they walked back to the office. The phone was ringing when she opened the door. Tripping over Andi's doll in her hurry, she was breathless when she picked up the phone.

"Belinda, it's me." Dani's familiar voice was a welcome surprise. "Are you busy?"

"Where have you been?" Belinda asked. "I've been trying to call you for three days, and I was beginning to worry."

Dani gave a chuckle. "You worry too much. Have you

heard anything from Collette or Amanda?"

"I got a letter from Collette yesterday. She's heading for the States, you know. Poor thing, California is so different from Africa. I wish I had the money to fly out to California to meet her when she comes and help her get settled." The four of them had been friends since they were at summer camp ten years before. They came from such different walks of life, but no friends could be closer.

"The little mother." Dani's voice was indulgent. "What would we do without you? What's up? Any interesting men in your life yet?"

Belinda sighed. "You know there will never be another man in my life. I'm still in love with Andrew."

"You mean, you're still filled with guilt over his death," Dani corrected. "It wasn't your fault, Belinda, and it's been almost four years!"

Belinda sighed again, a heavy sound of exasperation. Dani had been getting more and more insistent every time they talked. She didn't seem to understand how she still heard the sound of screaming tires and Andrew's shout of alarm. "If we just hadn't been arguing."

"He needed to grow up and get a regular job," Dani said firmly. "He was way too set on that business. It was time to move on."

Belinda was silent in the face of the familiar argument. They'd gone over this time after time. If only they hadn't argued; if only she'd had a chance to tell him they were going to be parents. But all the what-ifs hadn't changed anything. Andrew had lost control of the car on a patch of ice. She'd awakened to icy rain falling on her face and the surreal sound of the blaring horn. She'd had her seat belt on, but her macho husband had never worn one. He'd gone through the windshield and died instantly. She decided to change the subject.

"A new builder is in town. He bought four thousand dollars worth of stuff today."

Dani whistled softly. "That will keep the wolves from the door a little longer, although I'm not sure that's a good thing in the long run. That place holds too many memories. I think the only reason you're determined to make a go of it is because Andrew loved it. Is this builder married?"

Belinda grinned wryly. Dani never gave up, but she loved her in spite of her meddling. "No, and he's coming to church with me, and we're having pizza after." She held the phone away from her ear at the excited buzz on the other end. When the noise died down, she cautiously put it back to her ear. "But don't get any ideas. He's much too good-looking to be interested in someone like me, and I'm not in the market either. He's just looking for a friend."

Dani gave an exasperated sigh. "You'd be lovely if you'd just take a little care. Play up those eyes and that wild mass of hair. You'd have men tripping over one another to get to know you."

"I don't want a man. Andi and I are perfectly happy."

"Where is my darling goddaughter, anyway?"

"I'll let you talk to her." While Andi talked with Dani, Belinda picked up the ledger book and looked at her accounts. That four thousand dollars was really going to help. She silently sent another prayer of thanks heavenward.

The next day she paid bills and was thrilled to discover

there was five hundred dollars left. She could stock up on a few more groceries and maybe buy Andi a pair of sneakers if she could find a good sale. Business was brisk on Saturday, and she went to bed feeling incredibly blessed.

Sunday morning she dressed in a denim skirt and a bright yellow T-shirt. She ran a brush through her thick hair, then slipped on a headband. There was nothing much to do with hair as curly as hers anyway. Sliding on a pair of sandals, she hurried to get Andi ready, but she was too late. Her daughter had tried to dress herself and had put on a green-and-blue plaid skirt with a red blouse. Belinda hid a smile; her daughter had inherited her mother's sense of style, poor thing.

"I think another blouse might be better with that skirt, sweetie," she said, going to the closet. "How about this navy one?"

Andi was amenable to the change, and they both ate a bowl of cereal and were ready for Rick by 8:30. Belinda picked up the few rooms they called home while she waited. Sometimes she wished they had a neat little apartment with sleek kitchen cabinets, tons of closets, and wall-to-wall carpet instead of this apartment of four rooms carved from one wing of the building. These rooms with their wavy plaster walls, wide plank floors, and old painted wooden cabinets were home, though, and the old place had its charms. The wide woodwork was lovely, and the ceilings were high and airy. The place could be nice if she ever got far enough ahead to fix a few things and hang some new wallpaper. She gave a tiny sigh. A girl could dream.

At the sound of tires crunching on the gravel, she took

Andi's hand and hurried to the door. Rick was just getting out of his Jeep when she shut the screen door behind them and came down the porch steps. Rick's smile was wide and welcoming. He looked different all dressed up; it was a far cry from the cowboy costume yesterday. She'd looked at the article in the paper again and noticed that it mentioned he had been born and raised in Tucson, Arizona. He obviously made no effort to leave his roots behind. His black hair matched his straight, winged brows, and he had a dimple in his right cheek. She hadn't noticed that yesterday.

"Um, do you mind getting Andi's car seat from the front porch?"

"Sure." He bounded up the steps and carried it back to the Jeep.

Belinda was relieved that he didn't mind messing with things like that. Some men would grumble about every little delay. Andrew always had. She started to put Andi in the car seat, but Rick took her daughter and buckled her in himself. He kept up a running chatter with her the whole time, and Andi giggled. Belinda slid into the front seat and fastened her seat belt. The Jeep was obviously new with that lovely scent of new leather. It would be nice to go to church in something besides her rusty ten-year-old Ford Escort.

"You'll have to direct me," he said. "I still haven't found my way around Wabash yet. It's quite a different place from Fort Wayne."

"What made you decide to move down here?" she asked.

He shrugged and began to back out of the driveway. "I got tired of the traffic and crowded stores. I still build a lot of houses up there, but I wanted to settle in a place with small-town values and a little slower pace."

Settle. It had been Belinda's experience that only married men were looking to settle down, and that made her wonder if he had a girlfriend.

The streets were quiet on this early Sunday morning. As they drove though town, they saw a couple of boys playing baseball in one yard and two toddlers splashing in a small pool in a side yard. She told him where to turn, and they pulled into the church parking lot at 9:15. She introduced him to a few people, then hurried toward her classroom. On the way, Mary Bickel stopped her and asked if she would take care of her cat while she was on vacation. She agreed with a bright smile, not really sure how she had come to be considered the pet sitter. Mary was the third person to ask her to pet-sit so far this year, but she didn't mind. It felt good to be needed.

After Sunday school, she looked around for Rick, but she'd worried about him needlessly. She found him chatting with several of her friends, and he seemed relaxed and at ease. People here always lived up to the church's reputation of being one of the friendliest around. She slid into the seat beside him at the opening chords of "Amazing Grace." All through church she found it hard to concentrate on the sermon. She hadn't been this close to any man except her brother since Andrew died. She glanced at Rick occasionally from under her lashes. He listened with a thoughtful expression on his face that Belinda found refreshing. Andrew had come to church with her but generally fidgeted through the sermon and was always eager to leave as soon as it was over.

"Some of us are meeting at the Great Wall for dinner. You want to come?" Dawn Porter, one of her good friends, asked.

Dawn was obviously curious about this guy Belinda had brought to church. She glanced from Rick to Belinda, and Belinda could tell Dawn thought there was something going on between them. She felt a hot tide creep up her neck to her cheeks. Was that what everyone thought —that she was seeing a man now? This had obviously been a mistake, but she wasn't sure how to get out of it gracefully. She'd already promised to have lunch with him. Maybe it would be easier to go with a group. She opened her mouth to agree, but Rick spoke first.

"Thanks, but we're headed for pizza." He smiled nicely as he declined their offer.

So that idea was out. She'd just have to try to think of things to talk about and get back to the safety of her apartment. She waved good-bye to her friends and followed Rick to the Jeep.

"I liked your church a lot," he said once they got under way. "Pastor Parks is a good teacher, and I think I could learn a lot under his ministry. I don't think I need to look any further for a church home. Thanks for inviting me."

Belinda wasn't sure what to say. She loved her church, and their pastor was terrific, but now she'd be seeing Rick at least every Sunday. She wasn't sure that was such a good idea.

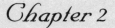

Chapter 2

C hattering happily, Andi clung to Rick's hand as they walked into Pizza Hut. The place was packed, but they only had to wait a few minutes for a table. Rick could tell Belinda was uncomfortable for some reason. She kept glancing around anxiously, as though she were afraid someone would see them together. And while he didn't consider himself God's gift to women, he still wasn't used to a woman acting as though she was half ashamed to be seen with him. He decided whatever it was, it wasn't as important as enjoying their company.

Andi immediately got out the crayon she'd been given and began to color her picture. When the waitress came to take their order, Andi looked up at her mother with pleading eyes. "Could I have a breadstick, too, Mommy?"

Belinda hesitated, and Rick plunged in. "Sure you can, sweetheart." He ordered a Supreme Pizza with only cheese on one side. When Belinda lifted her eyebrows in astonishment, he grinned. "My nephews refuse to eat pizza with anything but cheese. My brother says all kids are like that."

Belinda smiled. "You're an observant man."

"Observant enough to know something is bothering

you. Anything I can do to help?"

A delicate wash of color rose on her cheeks. "I'm fine."

"Then why do you keep looking around with an expression of dread on your face?"

She bit her lip, looked over at Andi's bent head, then stared down at the table. "Not now," she said.

He had to be content with that for the time being, but he intended to bring the subject up again later. Andi's eyes grew bright when the waitress brought the breadsticks. Rick put one on her plate and was touched to see she wouldn't eat it until she made sure her mother got to have one too. Then she picked it up and started to put it in her mouth but put it down and bowed her head.

"Thank You, Jesus, for this food. You know it's my favorite. Thank You for my new friend, and help Mommy not to be sad. Amen." She picked up her breadstick again and bit off a piece with a blissful expression on her face.

Rick smiled at her tenderly. Belinda had done a good job of raising her by herself. He turned to tell her so and found her fighting tears.

"What's wrong?" he demanded in a whisper.

She shook her head and picked up her breadstick. Avoiding his gaze, she bit into it, but he could tell she wouldn't have known if it was a piece of wood instead of food. Andi chattered happily throughout the meal, but Rick was conscious of Belinda's tense posture for the whole hour they were in the restaurant. He got up to pay the bill, and when he came back he found an older woman standing at the table talking to Andi and Belinda. Belinda was practically cowering. The woman gave him a brief glance, then swept past him and out the door.

"Who was that?"

Andi bounced in her seat. "That was Grandma. Daddy was her little boy. She's coming to take me for an ice cream tomorrow."

"I see." What he saw was Belinda in an frantic hurry to get out to the Jeep. She was obviously afraid of her mother-in-law for some reason. Belinda must have seen her as soon as they had come into the restaurant. He'd only had a glimpse of the woman, but the steely look in her eyes didn't seem like enough to send Belinda running for safety. With a wrinkled brow, he puzzled over the situation all the way to the Jeep.

Belinda's face was white with strain, and she fumbled with the catch on Andi's car seat. He gently pushed Belinda out of the way and snapped it into place himself. He shut the back door and took her elbow. "Tell me what's wrong. Let me help you."

"You can't help," she whispered. "Please, let's just go home."

He gave an exasperated sigh, but there was nothing he could do. He shrugged and got in the car. Belinda kept her hands tightly clasped in her lap, her gaze staring straight ahead through the short trip home. She practically jumped out of the car and hurried to get Andi out. The little girl was asleep in the backseat.

"I'll carry her in," he said. He gently lifted Andi out and followed Belinda into their apartment. He was pleasantly surprised by the hominess of the apartment. Warm wood contrasted with the deep, rich jewel tones she'd chosen for fabrics. The oriental rug and furniture were obviously cheap, but care had been taken to make it warm and inviting. It looked like a place where he'd like to spend a lot of time. He followed Belinda through the parlor and into Andi's bedroom.

She'd taken even more care in decorating her daughter's room. Winnie the Pooh prints hung on the walls, and a Pooh border brightened the color-washed walls. A rocking chair sat beside the bed, and a small bookcase filled with children's books showed she'd spent a lot of time reading to Andi. He loved Winnie the Pooh himself. He still remembered his mother reading him stories about Pooh and his friends when he was a child. He put Andi on the bed and pressed a kiss to her forehead, then backed out of the room.

"Thanks for everything," Belinda said.

She shut the bedroom door and went toward the front door, but Rick didn't follow her. He was determined to find out just what had happened in the restaurant. He sank onto the sofa and, leaning back against the plump cushions, patted the spot beside him.

"I'm not leaving until you tell me what happened today. Was it your mother-in-law?"

She perched nervously on the edge of the chair across from him and twisted a curl around her finger. "Yes," she admitted. "But there's nothing anyone can do. Alice, Andrew's mother, owns the title to this place. She's been threatening to sell it out from under me."

"Would she do that to her own granddaughter?"

"She says that if I don't have a job, she would be able

to get custody of Andi."

"Anyone with half an eye can see you're a terrific mother," Rick said.

Belinda sighed. "There's no way I could take care of Andi if I had to get a regular job. I don't have any skills, and minimum wage would be the best I could hope for. By the time I paid for day care, there would be nothing left. I'd have to let Alice take Andi." Tears pooled in her eyes. "When she saw me there with you, she assumed I was dating you. She said she was going to put the business up for sale tomorrow."

"Would it help if I called her and explained?"

Belinda shook her head. "I tried to tell her I'd just met you and invited you to church, but that set her off even worse. She hates religion and thinks I'm warping Andi by taking her to church."

"I'm sorry. I feel like this is all my fault." Rick pulled on his earlobe, a habit he'd had since childhood.

Belinda attempted a weak smile. "Don't blame yourself. This has been coming a long time." She swallowed hard and bit her trembling lip. "I'm sorry for being such a crybaby, but I just don't know what to do." She stood to her feet. "Can I get you some iced tea or coffee?"

Rick shook his head and stood. "No, thanks. I'm going to shove off now." She walked him to the door, and he put a hand on her shoulder. She laid her hand over his, and the brief contact speeded up his heart. He looked down into her remarkable eyes and wondered why he'd ever thought she was plain. She really was quite lovely. He wanted to kiss her, but he knew she didn't feel the same way about him—yet. As he got into his Jeep and drove away, he vowed to figure out a way to help her. Someday he wanted to see those eyes light up with joy when she looked at him.

Belinda sank onto the couch and clutched a pillow to her chest. The tears she'd been holding at bay spilled over onto her cheeks. What was she going to do? Alice was a formidable opponent. She'd never thought Belinda was good enough for Andrew, and now she didn't think she was fit to raise Andi. It had been a constant struggle since he'd died, and she'd reached the end of her rope.

"What do I do, Lord? Is my life always going to be one struggle after another?" The tears fell faster.

The answer came to her heart. *Trust Me.* She remembered the words to one of her favorite songs. *When you can't trace His hand, trust His heart.* Gradually, her tears stopped, and she felt a sense of peace. One day at a time. That's all she had to do. Get through one day at a time. She knew God was building her character, but the pressure was so hard sometimes.

She glanced at her watch. Nearly two o'clock. She had time to bake some brownies before Andi got up from her nap. She always gravitated to the kitchen in a crisis. There had been plenty of those these last three years, which was probably why those fifteen pounds remained stubbornly attached to her hips.

She'd just finished sliding the pan of brownies into the oven when the phone rang. Still licking the spoon, she ran to grab it before it woke Andi. For some reason she thought it might be Amanda.

"Hi there!"

There was silence on the other end of the line. "Belinda?"

She gave a tiny gasp. It was Alice, not Amanda. "I'm sorry; I thought it was someone else." As soon as the words were out of her mouth, she realized how her mother-in-law would take it.

"You were expecting a call from that man." Her frigid tone dared Belinda to contradict her.

She tried anyway. "No, of course not. You remember Amanda, Collette, and Dani, don't you? I thought it might be one of them."

"Harump," Alice said. "Do you really expect me to believe that after what I saw today?"

"He was just a new customer, Alice. Truly. I don't really know him at all." Belinda clutched the phone so tightly her knuckles turned white.

"If that is actually the case, it won't be a problem for you not to see him again." Alice's husky voice brooked no argument.

Belinda gripped the phone even tighter. Some spark of defiance raised its head unexpectedly. "I'll probably see him again occasionally. He liked the church, and he's a customer." Her voice trailed off at the gasp of outrage on the other end.

"If I see you with him again, I'll have no choice but to sell the business. I can't have Andi growing up under the influence of another man. I don't want her to forget who her father is."

"I talk to her about Andrew all the time," Belinda said

wearily. "And I'm not interested in marrying anyone else. Rick is just a new friend and a customer."

Alice gave a snort. "It's unlikely he'd be interested in you, anyway. You dress like a frump; you don't watch your weight; you never do anything with your hair. I don't know what my son ever saw in you."

Personally Belinda had never been sure of that herself. She silently acknowledged the truth of Alice's hurtful words. Sick from the tension and strife, she took a deep breath. "You're right, of course. What time did you want Andi tomorrow?"

Mollified, Alice softened her tone. "About eleven-thirty, I think. We'll go out to lunch and then to get an ice cream. I have a bridge game at three, so I'll have her home for her nap by two."

"That will be fine." Belinda just wanted the call to be over. "We'll look forward to seeing you then." She hung up the phone with profound relief. It sounded as though Alice wasn't going to put Timeless Treasures up for sale tomorrow. But with each threat, the reality loomed closer. She just didn't know what to do.

The phone rang again just after Andi awakened, and this time it was Amanda. They were only able to talk for a few minutes before Andi had a run-in with the cat, and Belinda had to go play referee. Something was up with her friend, and she wasn't quite sure what it was. She'd asked about love. Belinda hoped she'd been able to help her. She'd hate to see Amanda make the same mistake she'd made. She'd settled for spark and no security, but from what she'd heard about Wesley, she was afraid

Amanda was about to settle for security and no spark. You needed both, she'd told her.

❧

The next few days flew by. She tried not to think about what Alice might be planning. She had quite a few people stop by and was beginning to hope her reputation was finally getting around. Another reason for her good mood was that on the last Thursday of the month, Amanda was going to connect with Belinda and Dani through a conference call. And next month they would actually get to hear Collette's voice as well. She would be in the States next week.

Thursday morning Belinda was on the ladder hanging light fixtures when the buzzer on the door rang. She was stretched as high as she could reach and could only call out to whomever it was. "I'm in here!" With a grunt, she managed to slip the metal ring over the hook she'd screwed in the ceiling.

"Can I help?" Rick's deep voice startled her so much, she wobbled and lost her balance. Her arms flailed out, but she couldn't regain her equilibrium. She seemed to fall in slow motion and waited for the floor to rise up and smash her. Instead, she felt Rick's strong arms catch her and hold her tight against his chest. The breath whooshed out of her lungs, and she stared up into his concerned face.

"I'm so sorry. I didn't mean to startle you."

He made no move to release her, and she was in no hurry to free herself. He had his cowboy hat on again, and he looked incredibly handsome in his black Stetson and turquoise shirt. Her mouth went dry, and suddenly alarmed, she struggled out of his arms. He let go instantly.

He cleared his throat. "Where's my girl?"

"She's in her room, playing with her doll."

"Can you get her? I have a surprise for her." He looked like an eager little boy.

"What is it?"

"It's a surprise for you, too."

She laughed out loud. "You look just a little guilty. Am I going to like it or shoot you?"

"I'm not sure myself," he admitted.

They both turned at the sound of Andi's high piping voice as she skipped down the hall. She was singing the countdown song and shouted, "Blast off," just as she reached the doorway. She squealed when she saw Rick. "Mr. Ranger!" She ran to him, and he scooped her up.

"I brought you and your mommy a surprise, but you have to close your eyes."

"Mommy, too?"

"Mommy, too." He waited until they closed their eyes obediently, then took them each by the hand and led them out the screen door to the porch.

Belinda liked the warmth of his hand way too much for her own peace of mind. She knew she should draw back, but she didn't want to. They reached the porch, and he let go.

"No peeking," he warned.

They heard rustling, then a funny squeak. Belinda's eyes flew open when she heard Andi squeal.

"Mommy, it's a puppy!"

She opened her eyes and saw Andi holding a wriggling

golden retriever puppy with his little fat belly exposed. "Oh, what a darling!" Cooing as though she was talking to a baby, she knelt and scratched the puppy's head. He yipped and nuzzled her hand, trying to suckle her finger.

"His mother died, and Dan had to find homes for all the puppies. He isn't fully weaned yet, so he's going to take some extra care." With a silly grin on his face, he stroked the silky ears. "I love dogs. I had one almost like him when I was a boy. Oscar and I had a lot of good times together."

"What's his name?" Belinda put her face against the puppy's head, and he nibbled on her chin.

"That's Andi's job. I take it you want him? I don't have to take him to the pound?"

"You wouldn't dare," she said indignantly.

Andi was still wiggling with excitement. "Can he sleep with me, Mommy? Please?"

"We'll see," she said. She turned to Rick with a big grin. She could just hug him. She'd wanted a dog for Andi for ages, but she'd never had the money for one.

"Can we call him Ranger?" Andi asked. "Ranger is a good name." She flashed her dimples at Rick.

"Ranger it is," Belinda agreed. She glanced at her watch and took off for her apartment. "Oh my!"

"What's wrong?" Rick followed her with Andi and her new pet trailing behind him.

"I'm expecting a call," she said over her shoulder. She hoped she hadn't missed the call from her friends. She threw open the door to the apartment and heard the answering machine kick on. She snatched it up eagerly. "Hello."

"Where were you?" Amanda's voice demanded. "We were about to hang up."

"With a customer."

"The bachelor builder?" Dani put in.

She looked back over her shoulder at Rick playing with Andi and the puppy. "Yep."

They talked for nearly an hour. When she hung up the phone, she found Rick and Andi asleep on the floor with the puppy lying on Rick's chest. Rick was snoring loudly, a rhythmic sound Belinda found oddly soothing. Andi was curled against Rick's back, and she looked cold. Belinda fetched a quilt and spread it over all three of them. Ranger lifted his head and whined, then went back to sleep.

She decided the best way to show her gratitude for the puppy would be to make Rick some fudge. Her brother was crazy about her peanut butter fudge, and she hoped Rick would like it.

She got out her favorite pan and the ingredients. She had just turned the burner on when she heard a frantic yelp from the parlor followed by a yowl. She dropped the spoon and dashed toward the sound. Their cat, Toto, named after the famous dog in *The Wizard of Oz*, had cornered the cowering puppy under the couch. Toto's back was arched, and every orange hair bristled with outrage. She hissed and spat and tried to swat the intruder. Ranger yelped when she batted his ears. He ducked farther under the couch until all that could be seen were his pleading brown eyes.

Belinda tried to grab the enraged cat but only managed to get scratched in the process. Rick and Andi jumped up and entered the melee, too. Andi was screaming for the cat not to hurt the dog; Rick grabbed the blanket and threw it over Toto, while Andi snatched up the puppy and carried him off to her bedroom.

Rick's hair stood up on end, and he looked like a little boy who had just awakened. "Where do you want me to put this tiger?" The quilt squirmed, and Toto yowled with outrage. Before Belinda could answer him, the cat gave a final flip and managed to get a paw loose. He promptly proceeded to rake Rick across the forearm.

"Ouch!" He dropped the bundled cat, and Toto streaked off with one last outraged yowl.

Rick burst out laughing. "Things are never dull at your place," he grinned. "Where did you find that man-eater?"

Belinda grinned feebly. "He was a stray. I've never known him to act so vicious." She frowned worriedly. "Are we going to be able to keep the puppy? Do you think Toto will hurt him?"

"You'll probably have to keep an eye on them for a while, but the cat will probably get used to him eventually."

Belinda noticed the blood streaming down his arm. "Oh, my, I'd better take care of that scratch. She nailed you good." She hurried to the bathroom and rooted around in the medicine cabinet until she found one last bandage. She grabbed some antiseptic and a washcloth and went back to the living room.

"Sit down," she ordered, pointing at the kitchen chair.

He saluted. "Yes, mother." He sat in the chair and held out his arm.

She washed it with the antiseptic, dried it, and put the

bandage on. Only then did she realize it was a pink Barbie Doll bandage. It looked incongruous against the dark hair of his arm. She suppressed a grin.

He saw the mirth in her eyes. "You won't think it's so funny when I sue you for owning a menace to society," he threatened with narrowed eyes. He glanced down at his arm and saw the real reason for her mirth. He uttered a strangled sound.

Belinda couldn't hold it back anymore. She burst into giggles, and Rick's scowl turned into a grin.

"I'll never live this down on the construction site."

Belinda laughed harder then finally got herself under control. "Let me see if I can find another one."

"What? Rip this one off my arm before it's ready to come off? Not on your life, lady. I wear my battle scars proudly." He grinned again then got to his feet. "I'd better get going before that orange menace you call a cat gets loose again."

Her lips twitched with mirth. "Thank you for the puppy. Don't forget to say good-bye to Andi. She'll be mad if she comes out and finds you're gone."

He snorted. "She won't notice me anymore with her new puppy around." But he went down the hall.

Belinda wished she'd gotten the fudge done, but she could make it and give it to him later. She stopped in consternation. She was actually expecting to see him again. That wasn't good. She didn't intend to allow herself to get close to any man. She vowed to continue to keep him at arm's length and treat him like a brother.

Chapter 3

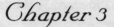

"S wing it this way!" Rick shouted over the roar of the boom lift. His foreman, Dan, nodded and swung the pile of drywall in the direction Rick had indicated. Rick made a cutting motion with his hand, and Dan stopped the forward movement and began to lower the pile. Rick grabbed hold of the rope and manually swung the drywall through the window opening and into the upstairs. Dan lowered the drywall until it rested on the floor, then cut the motor of the boom and scrambled down to help.

When he looked at Rick, he had a peculiar look on his face. Rick saw his expression and frowned. "What's wrong?" He saw where Dan was looking and glanced down. The pink Barbie Doll bandage was peeking out from under his rolled-up shirt. He flushed, then grinned.

Dan quirked an eyebrow. "Aren't you a little old to be playing with dolls, boss?"

Rick grinned feebly. "Cat scratched me."

"Yeah, and whose dainty little hands put that bandage on? Does she by chance have a little girl?" Dan punched him in the arm. "You gettin' soft on me? Playing with dollies and courting fast women?"

Rick chuckled. "This lady is the farthest thing from a fast woman you've ever seen. So far she's only interested in mothering me. But I aim to change that!"

Dan smacked him on the shoulder. "Go get 'em, Ricky boy."

Rick grimaced. He hated that nickname. No grown man of thirty-five wanted to be called Ricky. It made him think of toy fire engines and Hot Wheels.

Dan saw his expression and grinned. "I have a feeling this little gal is going to change your whole outlook on things, my friend."

The next few days flew by. Rick didn't have a chance to stop by Timeless Treasures. He thought about "his girls" endlessly, thoughts of them taking possession of his mind. He wondered what Belinda would say to such familiarity. He also thought about her problem with the business. Had her mother-in-law put the place up for sale? He hated that there was something like that hanging over Belinda's head all the time, but it wasn't his place to tell her to buck up and stand her ground. He wasn't the one with a three-year-old daughter to raise.

Sunday morning he got dressed and drove to New Life again. He'd been impressed with the preaching and the friendliness of the people. He had to admit the draw of seeing Andi and Belinda again increased his eagerness. Several people were lined up at the door, greeting those who came in. Rick got the impression it wasn't an organized thing; it was just that the people were friendly and were eager to see each other and their visitors.

Dawn Porter was one of those who grabbed his hand when he arrived. "Rick! I'm so glad we didn't scare you off last week. Are Belinda and Andi with you?" She looked past him out the double glass doors.

"Nope. I'm hoping to see them today, though." He stared at her thoughtfully. Would she help him get to Belinda?

"Did you meet my husband last week?" She introduced him to Sam, a tall man with curly blond hair who kept hitching his pants up over his slight paunch.

"So, how long have you known our Belinda?" Sam asked after the introductions were over.

"Just about a week and a half," Rick admitted. They chatted a bit longer, then Sam invited him to attend the Lifebuilders Sunday school class. Rick enjoyed the class tremendously. It was a discussion in a relaxed atmosphere with friendly people near his own age, ranging from college students to young marrieds with small children. By the time the class was over, Rick felt a welcome part of the little group. They invited him to go on a horseback riding trip on Saturday.

"Is Belinda going?" he asked.

Sam grinned. "Yeah, she's in charge of reserving the horses. You've got it bad already, buddy." His smile faded. "Just make sure you don't hurt her. She's suffered enough."

"She doesn't talk much about her husband. Did she love him very much?"

Sam shrugged. "He treated her like dirt. Gone all hours, married more to Timeless Treasures than to Belinda. It wouldn't have surprised me to hear they were heading for the divorce court, but Belinda is a faithful little thing. She kept praying for him and encouraging him. It's been hard for her since his death. She won't accept help from the church, but it's hard to watch her struggle. She's the little mother of the church. Always ready and willing to step in and help someone out."

Rick thought about Sam's words as he stared thoughtfully at the back of Belinda's head during the singing. She had hurried into worship late and hadn't seen him sitting two rows back. Why was he so interested in her? Was it only because he was so taken with Andi, or was it something more? He shrugged the questions aside and focused on the preaching.

Andi was in junior church, but as soon as worship was over, she spotted him and came running up. "Mr. Ranger! The puppy cried all night. Mommy got him a hot-water bottle and a clock that went *ticktock, ticktock,* but he still cried. Finally Mommy let him sleep with me."

He picked her up and hugged her. "Did he keep you awake?"

Andi shook her head. "He bited my ear sometimes, but he just wants to play."

"Does Toto like him yet?"

Andi gave another shake of her curly head. "She hates him. Mommy has to keep them apart."

Belinda saw them. She hesitated, then came up to them. "I didn't know you were here."

"I went to the Lifebuilders class."

He could see she felt awkward and hurried to fill the silence. "Andi says the cat still hates Ranger."

She smiled and nodded. "Yesterday I found Toto eating Ranger's food while the puppy cowered in the corner in abject worship. For some reason, that silly dog loves that mean cat."

"We love what we can't have, I guess."

"Oh, how's your arm?" she asked.

"Just fine. I got a little ribbing at work about the Barbie bandage, but it was a nice reminder of our day."

Dawn came up. "Are you still going to Great Wall with us, Belinda?"

"Sure," she said.

"You want to come, Rick?" Dawn asked.

"You bet," he put in eagerly. He saw Belinda hesitate, but he didn't give her a chance to back out. "Can Andi ride with me?"

He saw her relax and realized immediately the reason for it. She thought he just cared about Andi. He suppressed a grin.

"That's okay. We'll just meet you there," Belinda answered. Over Andi's protest she waved and hurried out the door.

Dawn was smiling when he turned back to her. "You like her a lot, don't you?"

"Guess it shows, huh?" He felt like a schoolboy with his first crush.

"Just a little." She eyed him appraisingly. "I think you'll be good for her. Want some help?"

His grin widened. "I could use all the help I can get. Got any ideas?"

She laughed. "I've got tons of them. Why don't you

ride to the restaurant with me and Sam, and we'll talk about it?"

Monday morning's cold spell broke the unseasonably hot and humid temperatures. Belinda frowned at the weather forecast. Rain was predicted all week. There probably wouldn't be many customers. She had Andrew's school loan coming up next week. Just two more payments, and it would be paid off. Dawn had been appalled when she realized Belinda was still paying it. By all rights, Andrew's mother should have paid it off, she'd declared. But Belinda hadn't asked. When she married Andrew, she'd taken on his responsibilities, as he'd taken hers. Besides, she wasn't about to ask her mother-in-law for anything. Alice already had too much control over her life.

She sat at the kitchen table with a cup of tea and her Bible for her devotions. Andi was still asleep, and Belinda cherished this quiet time in the morning. She looked up when the buzzer on the door went off. Probably an early customer. She was glad she was already dressed. She hurried out into the front display room. A huge bouquet of flowers sat on top of the fireplace. She saw the Love Bug Greenhouse van pulling out of the parking lot.

She began to sneeze and backed away from the flowers. Her eyes watered, and her skin itched. She had to get them out of here! She ran back to her apartment and grabbed a long-sleeved jacket and a pair of gloves. Pulling them on, she went back down the hall. The door buzzer sounded again, and she saw Rick standing by the door.

"I'm so glad you're here," she said. "Could you take

those flowers outside? The hives are already popping out on my arms."

He looked at her doubtfully. "You don't want them?"

"I'm allergic! Please, get them out of here!"

He shrugged and picked up the vase of flowers. "Do you want the card?"

"I know who sent them," she said crossly. Why was he arguing with her? She was in no mood for it. She'd had about all she could stand from Alice. "I'm not an idiot."

His eyes sparked dangerously, but he carried the flowers outside. She saw him dump them on the trash heap and breathed a sigh of relief. She still felt itchy, so she went around and opened all the windows.

He came back in with the crystal vase. "Do you at least want the vase?" His mouth was pinched in a straight line of disapproval.

"Don't look like that! You have no idea what that woman is always pulling. I've half a mind to call her and tell her she can't have Andi this afternoon." She marched toward the phone.

"Wait," he called down the hall. "Who do you think sent them?"

"I know who sent them," she snapped. "My loving mother-in-law, that's who! She's done this before. She knows I'm allergic, but she sends flowers anyway on our anniversary. Then she claims she forgot how allergic I am. Today is my birthday, so she's evidently expanding her little game."

He was silent for a moment. "Uh, she didn't send them."

She stared at him. "Did you see the card?"

"I didn't need to. I sent them."

"You? Why would you send me flowers? Or were they for Andi?"

"They were for both of you. Yesterday Dawn told me your birthday was today. When I saw how gloomy it was today, I decided to send them to cheer up your day."

He was scowling, and Belinda felt terrible. She'd acted badly, and she had to make it up to him. "Have you had breakfast?"

His scowl disappeared, and he grinned. "I'm famished."

"How about some pancakes? Andi should be up any minute, and you can have breakfast with us."

His smile widened. "I haven't had pancakes since my mother died."

"Well, you haven't eaten pancakes until you've eaten mine."

❧

Andi was awake and watching *Sesame Street* when they walked back into the apartment. She had Ranger on her lap while Toto glared at both of them from her perch atop the couch. Toto saw Rick and streaked toward the bedroom in a flash of orange fur.

Rick nodded toward the departing cat. "Think she'd like me any better if I started bringing some cat treats?" He sat down on the couch and pulled Andi onto his lap. She was still in her pink pajamas with fuzzy bunny slippers on her feet, and she snuggled sleepily against his chest, her eyes glued to the television set where Big Bird was singing about the letter M. He inhaled the little girl scent of her baby shampoo and powder. He glanced at Belinda where she bustled around in the kitchen clanging pots. He didn't know when he'd felt so content and at peace.

Is this what has been missing in my life, Lord?

He rested his chin on the top of Andi's head and relaxed. This was his family. He knew it deep in his heart. But convincing Belinda was going to take some effort. All she seemed to want to do was to mother him the way she did everyone else. He was going to have to get with Dawn and plan a strategy.

"Pancakes are ready," Belinda called from the kitchen.

They smelled wonderful. He stood up with Andi still in his arms and took her to the kitchen with him. She protested a bit over missing *Sesame Street* but quickly quieted when she saw the pancakes. Rick watched Belinda stand at the counter and cut Andi's food into small bites until she started on his plate.

"I think I'm big enough to have an intact pancake," he objected.

Belinda flushed, and her hand fluttered to her face self-consciously. "I don't know what I was thinking. Sorry." She put both plates on the table and turned to flip the next batch.

"Aren't you going to eat with us?"

"I'll eat when you're through. Tell me when you've had enough." She took the pancakes off the griddle and poured more batter on it.

"Uh-uh; no way am I going to sit here and eat a stack of pancakes when you haven't even had one yet. Andi and I will wait on you, right, Andi?" He looked at the little girl with a coaxing smile.

"Mommy always does that," she confided.

"Well, not today." He folded his arms across his chest and waited.

"But your pancakes will get cold if you wait until they're all done," Belinda protested.

"You've got a microwave."

She bit her lip, but didn't argue the point. Once the plate was piled high with pancakes, she sat at the table with them. Rick said grace, and they all dug into breakfast together.

It felt so right to Rick to be sitting at the breakfast table across from Belinda. He watched the sunlight catch the copper lights in her hair. She ate almost absently with delicate movements. Catching his intent stare, she flushed and looked down at her plate. Rick forked another bite into his mouth. He'd been too busy watching her to really pay attention to the food. The nutty flavor of the pancakes was different than any he'd had before.

"What's the nutty flavor?" he asked.

"Wheat germ." He raised his eyebrows, and she hastily added, "It's very nutritious. Andi and I like it on ice cream, too."

Wheat germ. He'd never even heard of the stuff. Did he dare take another bite? He looked in Belinda's beautiful eyes and decided he'd dare anything for her. He took another bite. It was good. Maybe this healthy stuff wasn't so bad. They finished their breakfast, and Rick leaned back in his chair. "Now wasn't this more fun than eating by yourself?"

Her face pink, Belinda nodded. Her eyes really were

most amazing, Rick decided. He could gaze into them for hours. The color was unusual, but even more than that, he'd never seen anyone with such love and concern in their eyes. If eyes were the window to the soul, then Belinda's soul was extraordinarily beautiful.

He stacked the dishes and carried them to the sink.

"I could have done that," Belinda protested.

"It didn't hurt me to help. After all, you did the cooking." He grabbed his hat and bent down to kiss Andi on the cheek. "I have to go to work. Be good, Kemosabe."

Andi smiled and clapped her hands. "I knew you were the Lone Ranger! Can I be Tonto?"

Rick grinned and put on his hat. "We'll talk about it," he promised.

Belinda followed him to the door. "Thanks so much for the flowers," she said. "I'm sorry I acted so badly."

"That's okay. I wish I'd known about your allergy. You're a guy's dream, you know that, don't you?"

"What?" She looked confused.

"What a cheap date you'd be! You're allergic to flowers, and I'll bet you hate chocolate, right?"

"You'd lose that bet, mister." Her cheeks bloomed with a delicate wash of color, and she looked up at him with a shy grin. "I happen to love chocolate. I'm not a complete embarrassment to my gender."

His smile died, and he took an involuntary step toward her. He touched her hair and wound a coppery curl around his finger. It felt just as he'd imagined, silky and soft as a kitten. Her eyes widened, and he gazed deep into their depths. His hand brushed the firm line of her jaw, and he ran his thumb over her lower lip. He bent his head, but before he could kiss her, the doorbell buzzed behind them. She sprang away from him like a startled doe.

She swallowed hard and opened the door with relief written on her face.

Mary Bickel stood on the threshold with a huge tiger cat in her arms. "I hope I'm not too early," she said with an apologetic smile. "If you'll take Duke, I'll run back to the car and get his things." She passed the cat over to Belinda and hurried back outside.

Rick patted the cat, which promptly hissed and raked his arm with his claws.

"You do have a way with cats." Avoiding his gaze, Belinda laughed nervously.

I moved a bit too fast, he thought, but he'd never felt this way before. He'd had casual relationships, but he'd been too busy early in his career to develop any serious romance. Later, when he'd had time, he'd been occupied with caring for his mother. But he didn't want to blow this. It was too important.

"I'd really like to take you and Andi out for supper to celebrate your birthday," he said, moving toward the door.

She hesitated, and he could see the regret on her face. "I've already promised to watch a friend's little boy," she said.

"On your birthday?" What kind of friend would take advantage of her like that?

"She had to work and she couldn't find anyone else." She smiled that warm, loving smile that did such funny things to his insides. "I don't mind. Little Cody is a darling.

He's six months old, and Andi adores him."

"How about if I bring a pizza over after work then?"

"Andi would like that." She finally met his gaze, and Rick saw the pity in her eyes. She still thought of him as someone to mother, but he was determined to change that. He didn't know how he would get past her defenses, but he wouldn't give up until he did.

Chapter 4

Toto jumped on Duke's head, and the tiger cat yowled and shot under the couch. Belinda sighed. Toto was good at terrorizing other animals. First Ranger and now Duke. The last time she'd watched Duke, Toto had accepted him within a few hours, but she had a feeling it wasn't going to be so easy this time. Toto was still adjusting to the puppy. She debated whether she should ask Rick to take Ranger home with him for a few days but decided against it. She'd already thrown his flowers in the trash; she didn't want him to think she didn't appreciate anything he did.

Her heart sped up a bit at the thought of Rick. She had thought he was about to kiss her this morning, but he was just lonely. Once he got settled into town and met some available women, he wouldn't give her a second look. She knew she was no beauty. Her frizzy hair was a fright; she really ought to get it styled. Her skin was good, but she still carried those stubborn extra fifteen pounds around her hips. She gave an exasperated sigh. She was being ridiculous even thinking about her looks. Rick wasn't really interested in her. The only reasons he was hanging around were that he liked Andi and he didn't have any other friends in town. She should try to think of some nice young women to introduce him to. She thought of several she knew, but the thought of them with Rick didn't appeal to her. She'd just have to let him handle his love life by himself.

Andi got up from her nap at about three and asked to take the puppy outside to play. Belinda told her to stay in the backyard where she could see her through the kitchen window while she baked some cookies. She wanted to thank Rick somehow for the flowers. It really had been very thoughtful.

The rest of the afternoon dragged by. Surely she wasn't pining to see Rick, was she? She was scandalized at the thought that he might have become so important to her. *He's just a lonely friend, that's all,* she told herself fiercely. The cookies were cooling on the rack under the window when she heard the distinctive sound of the engine in Rick's Jeep. Her mouth went dry, and she glanced in the mirror and nearly moaned with despair. Her hair stood on end, and she had flour on her nose. She quickly swiped at the flour and brushed at her faded jeans.

"Are those cookies I smell?" Rick looked tired, but his smile was wide. He took his Stetson off and hung it on the coat tree by the door. He carried a pizza and a plastic bag from Wal-Mart.

"You have a good nose. I hope you like chocolate chip. They're a thank you for the flowers."

"Oh, yes, the infamous flowers," Rick said. He thrust his hand into the bag and handed her a box of Russell

Stover chocolates. "Happy birthday."

Before she could thank him, Andi squealed and ran to clutch his leg. "Lone Ranger! I was very good today. Do I get to be Tonto?"

He knelt beside her and stared into her face. "Were you very, very good?" When she nodded, he smiled and reached into his bag again. "In that case, you'd better put this on." He drew out a braided leather strap for around her forehead. "No self-respecting Indian would go around without his headband." He put his hand into the bag again. This time he pulled out a small tom-tom.

Andi's eyes grew wide, and her mouth opened in a perfect O. She looked at her mother. "Can I keep it?" When Belinda smiled and nodded, Andi danced around with joy. She grabbed the headband in her small fist and waved it in the air. "Put it on me, Mommy, put it on!"

She was dancing around so much, Belinda had trouble tying it in back. "I have to see!" She dashed to her bedroom, and they heard her shriek of joy. "I'm Tonto, Mommy!" She came back to the living room, whooping and beating on the tom-tom.

"It's a good thing you don't have any neighbors," Rick said. "I hope you'll be able to stand the noise."

He sounded apologetic, but Belinda felt such a wave of thankfulness and joy that her eyes welled with tears. "Thank you so much," she whispered. "Andi's never had someone treat her so special."

He touched her cheek. "You're welcome. She's a precious little girl, and so is her mommy."

Belinda swallowed hard. He was making it very difficult

for her. She had to remember that he would find someone worthy of him one of these days. She wasn't that someone. She hadn't been the kind of wife she should have been to Andrew, and Rick was too special to get tied up with a widow and her daughter. She bit her lip and turned away.

"I thought you promised me a pizza," she said, changing the subject. "I'm starved."

The tender expression was gone from his face in an instant to be replaced with a neutral nod. "We'd better eat it before it gets cold."

They had just finished their pizza when the doorbell buzzed. "That must be Stacey with little Cody." Belinda jumped to her feet and hurried toward the door.

"I hope we're not interrupting dinner," Stacey said when Belinda opened the door.

Cody's dimples flashed when he saw Belinda. He held out chubby hands for her and gurgled. "Aa–obay," he chortled.

"Don't ask me what he said," Stacey said when Belinda looked to her for clarification. "Here, he wants you." She thrust him into Belinda's arms.

Belinda cuddled him and buried her nose in his neck. Inhaling the sweet scent of baby powder, she kissed his chubby cheek, and he grabbed a fistful of her hair.

"Oh, ow," she muttered. Disentangling his grip, she introduced Stacey to Rick.

"You're the new bachelor in church," Stacey said, fluttering her eyelashes at him.

Rick grinned. "News must travel fast," he said, shaking her hand.

Belinda noticed the way Stacey clung to Rick's hand. She supposed they would make a good match. Stacey was an out-of-wedlock mom who was struggling to make ends meet and had often lamented to Belinda that there were no good men left, especially not at their church. No wonder she was flirting with Rick.

But Rick didn't seem interested. He withdrew his hand and moved back a step. He folded his arms across his chest and, ignoring Stacey's smile, watched Belinda with the baby in her arms. Belinda felt flustered with his gaze on her. She bounced Cody up and down gently while she chatted with Stacey for a few more moments.

"Nice meeting you, Rick," Stacey said, her hand on the door to leave.

"You, too," Rick murmured.

Stacey gave a little shrug and shot a rueful grin at Belinda. "I'll pick him up around ten," she said. "Thanks again, Belinda."

"Didn't you like Stacey?" Belinda asked, shutting the door behind her friend.

"I didn't want to encourage her," Rick said with a shrug. "I figured if I dealt with it now, she wouldn't think I was interested."

"She's a very sweet girl," Belinda said. "She had a rough childhood and got into trouble, but she was saved three months ago, and God has really turned her life around." She realized she was more interested in his response than she should have been.

"That's great," Rick said. "But I didn't want her to think I was interested in anything more than friendship.

How about a game of Monopoly?"

And that was that. Belinda wasn't sure if she was relieved or disappointed. He was going to make a wonderful husband and father, and if he couldn't be hers, it would be nice if he could take care of someone as sweet as Stacey. But she had to admit she really wasn't eager to see him turn his attention to someone else.

Belinda didn't see Rick the rest of the week. She assumed he was busy with his new subdivision, but her heart still jumped every time the phone rang. On Friday she packed a small case for Andi. Andi was going to stay with her grandma Alice for the night, and Belinda was going horseback riding with her Sunday school class.

Her heart sank at the disapproving look on Alice's face when she came to pick up Andi and Belinda told her what plans she had for Saturday.

"I believe I've made my views known on the ridiculous amount of time you spend with that cult of yours, Belinda. I really must insist you begin to back off from being so involved. I refuse to let Andi grow up with such a narrow-minded view of life." She fixed her imposing stare on Belinda as if daring her to try to defy her.

Belinda took a deep breath. "My church is not a cult, Alice. And I must ask you not to voice such opinions in Andi's presence." Andi was playing with the puppy, but there was no telling how much she had heard.

Alice drew her shoulders up and glared at her. "I'll voice whatever opinion I want, you little upstart! How dare you tell me what I can and cannot say to my own granddaughter! How can you be so gullible as to believe in some unseen God who is looking out for you? Where was He when my son died in that accident? You were the one who should have died." She thrust her face into Belinda's until she was almost nose to nose. "Need I remind you that I can have you begging on the street like that?" She snapped her bony fingers in Belinda's face.

Belinda quailed, but then an odd peace swept over her. Why had she gotten into the habit of thinking her future depended on Alice's goodwill? God was the One who held her future in His hands. If Alice shut down her business, the Lord would provide another source of income. He had seen her through this far; He wasn't about to stop now. She pulled herself up to her full five foot two inches and calmly pushed down the finger that Alice was pointing in her face.

"You can say whatever you want about me, Alice, but I won't take any more remarks about my Lord or my church. If you can't agree to my rules, Andi will not go home with you tonight." She knew every line of her body told of her determination. She wasn't one who could hide her feelings.

Alice stared into her eyes and slowly began to get her anger under control. She sniffed. "Very well. But don't think you've heard the last of this. I'm calling my lawyer tomorrow."

Belinda seldom lost her temper, but this was the limit. "Go ahead. Call him!" She grabbed her purse and fished around for her keys. "I'm sick of hearing about it. I'm not going to let you hold this over my head forever. We'll just go to court and let a judge decide who is fit to raise Andi. Do you really think he'll choose a bitter, crabby old woman instead of Andi's mother who loves her?"

Angry red color swept over the older woman's face, then receded, leaving her white with rage. She sputtered, too enraged to get the words out. Taking several deep breaths, obviously to compose herself, she took a step forward. "Very well, Belinda. You've won this round. I'll hold my peace for now. But don't think you've heard the last of this." She picked up Andi's suitcase and called to her granddaughter. "Time to go, sweetheart." Her spine was stiff with outrage, but the words were sugary.

Andi gave the puppy one last pat and jumped to her feet. "I gotta kiss Mommy good-bye." She ran to her mother, and Belinda knelt to hug her. "Don't fall off the horse, Mommy," she said seriously.

Belinda kissed her soft cheek. "You be good for your grandma."

"Is Mr. Ranger going with you?"

The words were innocent enough, but Belinda could tell by the look on Alice's face that she knew exactly who Andi meant. "I'm sure he's too busy working to go with us," she said. "You'd better run along with Grandma."

Alice shot her a venomous glance before taking Andi's hand and heading toward the door. "Don't think you can pull the wool over my eyes as easily as you do this child's," she muttered under her breath. "I know what you're up to, and you'd better watch your step."

Belinda felt limp and weak from the stress of the confrontation. She really shouldn't have spoken to Alice like that. She sent a quick prayer for forgiveness heavenward then went to the bedroom to change. Horseback riding was the last thing she wanted to do right now. She'd have to put a smile on her face and pretend to be happy and joyous when her whole world was falling apart. That final parting shot of Alice's meant real trouble. She just might call the lawyer tomorrow. Then what would she do? Near tears, she found her jacket and picked up her car keys. She was in charge of this little get-together, so she had no choice but to go. She prayed for strength, then got in her rusty Escort and headed toward church.

The parking lot was full of cars when she pulled in. Dawn waved at her when she stopped and got out. She was talking to a man wearing a Stetson hat, and Belinda's heart gave a jump. It had to be Rick. She hadn't known he was coming. Dawn must have invited him. She pinned a smile in place and walked toward them.

Rick looked good. Too good for her peace of mind. His jeans were dark and almost looked starched with a center press like the country western stars wore. His snakeskin boots gleamed, and the black shirt stretching across his wide shoulders darkened his gray eyes. Dawn waved at Belinda and darted over to talk to another group. She was the greeter in the class.

Belinda stopped beside Rick. "Hi," she said.

"Hi yourself," he said softly. "Where's Andi?"

She relaxed. He really was just interested in Andi. It would keep things a lot simpler if it stayed that way.

"She's with my mother-in-law," she told him.

His eyes raked her face. "What's wrong?"

How had he known she was upset? She'd been care-ful to keep the smile pinned on. She forced her smile wider. "Nothing's wrong." She tried to change the subject. "I didn't know you were coming. I suppose you can ride?"

He gave a snort of laughter. "Do I look like a green-horn to you?"

She smiled. "You look like you could rope a calf with one hand and wrestle bulls with the other."

He took her elbow and guided her a bit farther away from the group. "Don't think you can sidetrack me. I'm like a lamb clinging to its mother. I know something's wrong. You can tell me about it."

Tears welled up in Belinda's eyes, and a lump grew in her throat. It had been such a long time since she'd had anyone to share her burdens with. It somehow seemed unspiritual to even admit everything wasn't always won-derful and joyful, so she usually kept her worries to herself and tried to concentrate on helping others with their problems. She blinked back the tears and told him about her argument with Alice.

"That woman sounds like a menace." His expression was grim. "Do you think she'll really close down Timeless Treasures?"

"I have a feeling this is it," Belinda admitted. "I think I pushed her over the edge."

"It's not your fault," he said. "You've been way too patient with her meddling." His warm fingers touched her chin, and he tilted her face up so he could gaze into her eyes. "You put a smile on that pretty face today and re-member God is in charge of this situation. Let's have a fun time, and we'll worry about this later."

Belinda swallowed the lump in her throat and nodded, then followed him to the church van. He'd called her pretty! She suddenly felt pretty. Even Andrew had never called her pretty. He said she looked interesting, whatever that meant. She glanced at Rick through her lashes. Did he really see her that way? She gave a rueful grin. There was no accounting for tastes.

Sam drove the church van, and Rick rode in the other front seat as navigator. The trip to Logansport went quickly, and Belinda was surprised to find she was enjoying herself.

She was given a black mare with a white blaze on her forehead. Rick pulled his gray mule beside her and smiled down at her. "First time I ever rode a mule," he said. "This fellow is huge. He must be eighteen hands. Richard said his mother was a Belgian."

Their guide, Richard, led them out of the stable and down the track to the meadow. They went single file, and some of the trees hung so low Rick had to duck to avoid being brushed off. When they came to the creek, Richard stopped and warned them to be careful and go across single file. This was the part of the trip Belinda hated. In her mind, she could see herself pitching over the horse's head and landing in the water. The water ran swift, but it wasn't deep, so she wasn't quite sure why the thought bothered her so much. She was the last one across. Her horse dipped down for a drink, and she jerked on the reins after a minute to get the mare moving again. She felt relieved to be safely on the other side with no mishap.

They reached the meadow, and Richard told them how to press down with their feet in the stirrups to avoid being jarred when cantering. Belinda caught Rick's grin and knew he could probably do a better job of instructing than their guide. He was a good sport to go along with everything, though. She forced her attention back to the instructor. Dawn was eager to try and took off across the meadow, with Rick shouting encouragement as he galloped beside her. It was a beautiful sight with the gelding's mane and tail flowing in the wind. Belinda wished she could be more adventurous like her friend. By the time everyone else was cantering and galloping around the meadow, she had finally gathered enough courage to try it herself. She didn't want Rick to know what a complete coward she was.

She dug her heels into the mare's flank and leaned slightly forward like she'd been told. The mare took off like she'd been shot out of a cannon. The force of the forward leap caused Belinda to lose her balance, and her right foot came out of the stirrup. Her foot shot into the air, and she flipped off the saddle backwards and landed on the ground. The force of the fall pushed the air out of her lungs, and she lay there a moment gasping for breath. Finally rolling over to her stomach to get to her feet, she found herself face-to-face with a snake.

Its tongue forked out of its mouth, and it raised its head and stared at her. Her tongue dried up in her mouth, and she froze in place. She wanted to scream, but the muscles in her throat wouldn't work; the only sound she could make was a faint rattling sound. The snake's head came down, and its tongue flicked her hand, then it slithered across her arm. That broke her paralysis. She leaped to her feet and shrieked at the top of her lungs. Dancing around in a circle, she shrieked again and again. Her horse bolted for quieter parts, Dawn's horse reared and threw her to the ground, and the guide stopped in midsentence with his mouth hanging open. Rick had been at the opposite end of the meadow instructing Sam, but he turned his mule and galloped to her side at the commotion she was making.

He slid out of the saddle and took her arm to calm her. At the touch of his fingers, she practically climbed into his arms. Realization dawned on his face, and he picked her up and carried her toward the woods.

"A snake, a snake," she sobbed. She buried her face in his neck and felt his arms tighten around her. She shuddered again at the memory of the feel of the snake's scales against her skin.

Rick patted her back and murmured to her. "It's okay; I've got you. The snake is gone."

Moments later the rest of the class members had clustered around her. When Dawn heard about the snake, she shuddered. "I don't know about you, but I'm ready to get out of Dodge and back to civilization."

"Me, too," Sally Montel said. "I don't want to see a snake."

At the sound of the disquieted murmurs around her, Belinda gathered herself together and slid out of Rick's arms. She was reluctant to leave the safety of his embrace, but she couldn't let her terror ruin the day for the rest of the class. With a final shudder, she squared her shoulders and raised her hand to quiet the group.

"Sorry I was such a ninny," she said, wiping the tears from her cheeks. "I'm not leaving until I learn how to gallop. The snake is gone, so let's mount up and have some fun!"

Rick's mouth dropped open, but he quickly closed it and gave her an approving smile. She felt warmed by his approval. It gave impetus to her resolve, and she gingerly stepped across the meadow to catch hold of her mare's reins.

Rick was right behind her. "You're something, you know that?" He twisted a curl around his finger and gazed down into her eyes. "Scared to death, but brave all at the same time." He grinned. "Has anyone ever told you what your name means?"

When she shook her head, he leaned forward. "Beautiful serpent," he whispered in her ear. "Funny how your namesake just opened my eyes a bit. You're beautiful, Belinda, inside and out." He helped her into the saddle and adjusted her stirrups before going off to find his own mount.

Bemused, she stared after him. From pretty to beautiful. The man was blind, but she couldn't help the warm feelings the words gave her. Unfortunately, she knew he'd open his eyes soon and see her as she really was. Belinda realized she hated to think of that day.

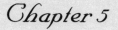

The next few weeks flew by. Timeless Treasures was busy as people tried to get some last-minute projects done before the temperatures plummeted and snow fell. Belinda had a run on porch posts and gingerbread as well as the usual bathtubs and stained-glass windows. She felt very thankful for the income, especially since she didn't know just what Alice was planning. She felt as though she were walking on a minefield every time the phone rang or she went to the mailbox.

She was washing windows when Andi came barreling into the west display room that housed the lighting fixtures. "Mommy, Mommy!" Skidding in her haste, she nearly knocked her mother off the ladder.

"Be careful, Andi," Belinda scolded.

"Mommy, the mailer man has a letter for you. He says you have to sign it."

Belinda's heart dropped. It must be a registered letter. There was only one person who would send her a registered letter. She laid her squeegee on the top of the ladder and climbed slowly down. Her heart pounded so hard, she felt as though she might suffocate. She followed Andi to the front display room and signed the card for the mail-man. Mallory & Mallory, Attorneys at Law was in the upper left-hand corner. Tears came to her eyes, and she just held the letter in her hand for a moment and stared at it. Her life was about to change, and she didn't know how she could handle the confrontation barreling toward her. She prayed quickly for strength, then opened the letter with numb fingers.

The cream sheet of linen stationery informed her that she must vacate the premises within thirty days, and that, furthermore, Mrs. Alice Mitchell was suing for custody of the minor child Andi Mitchell. The words blurred in front of her eyes, and she felt faint. With one swoop, her mother-in-law was taking away her livelihood and attempting to take her child. Did she hate her so much? Biting her lip, Belinda fought the tears welling in her eyes. She'd tried to get close to Alice over the years, but Andrew's mother had always felt her son had married beneath him. Her daughter-in-law was too plain, too poor, and too pious, all things Belinda couldn't change.

"Mommy, why are you crying?" Andi tugged at her hand, her blue eyes anxious.

"I'm all right, pum'kin." She scooped her into her arms. "Are you ready for some lunch?"

"Can I have Spaghetti-Os?" She smacked her lips and peeked at Belinda.

"You had Spaghetti-Os yesterday. Wouldn't you like something different? How about a peanut butter and jelly sandwich?"

"No!" She wiggled to get down.

Belinda set her on the floor, and her daughter raced toward the kitchen. "Okay, you can have Spaghetti-Os." She went numbly about the task of preparing lunch, but inside she felt like a quivering child afraid of the dark. She longed for someone with whom she could share her burden. After lunch, she could call one of her three camp friends. They were far enough away from the situation that they could give some perspective. She hated to bother Collette. She'd talked to her last week, and she'd been tearful and frightened of California. Maybe she'd call Dani or Amanda.

She put Andi down for a nap after lunch, then sank weakly onto the sofa. She knew she had to contact a lawyer, but she couldn't seem to get past the paralyzing fear. She wanted to throw herself across the bed and let out the tears she'd been choking back. The business doorbell buzzed, and she forced herself to her feet. How could she go out there and smile when her heart was breaking? She wiped at her face and opened the door.

Rick's engaging grin faded when he saw her face. He pushed his Stetson back and simply held out his arms, and she fell into them. She released all the tears she'd been holding back since she got the mail. His chest was broad and firm, and she could smell the freshness of the fabric softener he used mingled with the musky scent of his skin. It was a comforting smell that made her feel safe and protected. Rick patted her back and let her cry. After a few minutes, he guided her toward the sofa and sat down, pulling her onto his lap. Still she sobbed, and he stroked her hair and held her close.

After a while she lifted her head and hiccupped. "I'm

sorry," she whispered.

He thumbed away a tear from her wet face. "Don't apologize," he said. "I was glad I was here. You needed to get that out. What's wrong? Did you hear from your mother-in-law?"

Her jaw dropped. "How did you know?"

"Only something catastrophic would make you cry like that. Want to tell me about it?"

When she explained what the letter said, he frowned. "I have a friend in Fort Wayne who's a crackerjack lawyer. Want me to call him?"

"I don't know if I can afford him," she said haltingly.

"He's a friend. It won't be expensive. Get me the phone, and I'll call right now."

Sliding off his lap, she wished she could stay in the warm haven of his arms. She'd made a complete fool of herself, but he didn't seem to mind. She handed him the phone, and he punched in the numbers. While he was talking, she washed the few lunch dishes and tried not to fret. The Bible said not to worry, and though it was hard to leave it in the Lord's hands, that's exactly what she had to do. She thanked God for sending Rick to help her. She'd felt so alone, but now she felt strong enough to tackle the problem.

He came into the kitchen with a smile on his face. "Charles says the first thing we have to do is find you another job or another location for your business. Which do you prefer?"

Neither solution held much promise. She didn't have the money to rent another location big enough to house the stock, and she had no skills for another job. She opened her mouth to tell him so, when he smiled as though a light had dawned.

"Let me see if I can get her to reconsider. You try not to worry about it." He sprawled on the sofa and grinned up at her. "I don't suppose you would like to sit on my lap again, would you?"

She felt the hot color sweep up her cheeks, and she shook her head. She wanted to nod and go right back to his arms, but she knew it wasn't wise. She had to guard her heart. He would soon find some beautiful girl who deserved him. In the meantime, she could at least take care of him as best she could. "How about some lunch?"

Jacob Mallory made a teepee with his fingers, pursed his lips, and stared at Rick speculatively. "Where did you hear about this property being for sale, Mr. Storm?"

"I stopped by to buy some lighting fixtures, and the owner mentioned she wouldn't be open much longer." Rick was not impressed with Mr. Mallory. He oozed self-confidence with his three-piece suit, slicked-back hair, and round yuppie glasses. But Rick didn't have to like the man; he just had to do business with him. He didn't trust him, though, not even as far as the next room.

Mr. Mallory named the asking price; Rick dickered with him a bit, and they settled on a price. Rick whipped a purchase agreement out of his briefcase, filled out the amount, and wrote him out a check as earnest money.

Mr. Mallory smiled thinly. "I see you came prepared."

"I'm a builder, Mr. Mallory. I buy a lot of property. I

didn't become successful by lack of preparation." Rick normally didn't brag, but the smarmy man got his goat. He didn't want him to think he was dealing with an amateur. "I want you to call Belinda Mitchell and tell her the property has been sold, but that the new owner is not in any hurry, and that she may stay there rent free until further notice. It will be at least a year."

He felt about ten feet tall when he left the office building on Canal Street. Now he had to figure out how to give it to Belinda without her getting all prickly about it. He'd been thrilled when she came right into his arms today. Maybe she was beginning to care about him. Holding her had felt so right. She was the only woman he could imagine as his wife. He wanted to build her a beautiful neo-Victorian home and fill it with their children. The house could ring with the sounds of love and laughter. He just had to convince Belinda.

He could hear Andi's *Sesame Street* tape playing the theme song when he got out of his Jeep. It was nearly six o'clock, but he hoped they hadn't had supper yet. He felt like celebrating. Wait until Mrs. Mitchell found out just who owned Timeless Treasures! He suppressed a grin. He had to wait for the right time to let Belinda know, too. She wouldn't take kindly to charity. If he ever broke through her defenses, this building would make a great wedding gift.

When she opened the door, he caught her in a bear hug. After a moment's hesitation, she hugged him back, then pulled away with an embarrassed look on her face.

"I can't believe it!" Her eyes were shining.

"What?" He figured the only thing it could be was that the Mallory fellow had already called.

"This place has been sold already, but I don't have to move. They aren't in any hurry and won't need it for at least a year. I can stay here rent free. It gives me some time to figure out what to do. That's so much better than I'd even hoped for. At least I don't have to deal with Alice anymore."

"Well, that's great news! Let's celebrate. I'll take you both to Bob Evans." He stepped farther into the living room and called to Andi. "Hey, Kemosabe, you want to go out to eat?"

She jumped up and ran to hang onto his leg. "Ranger pottied on the rug, and Mommy spanked him with the newspaper." She stuck out her lower lip. "He cried."

"Looks like he got over it." He nodded down at the puppy growling at the metal toe of his boot.

Belinda patted the puppy. "He just needs to learn how to behave. You've gotten spankings, too, Andi."

Rick staggered back in mock dismay. "You've disobeyed your mommy and had to be spanked? I'm shocked, Andi."

She giggled, and he picked her up and kissed her. The feel of her small body brought out all kinds of fatherly feelings he hadn't realized he had. She and her mommy belonged to him.

He put Andi down and smacked her small bottom lightly. "Go get your coat so we can go. I'm starved." He turned to Belinda when Andi had run off to find her coat. "You don't have to worry about who sees us anymore.

Mrs. Mitchell can't touch you now."

Her face brightened, and she smiled. "That's right! I hadn't thought of that." She grabbed her coat and slipped it on. "Now I feel like celebrating!"

Over supper Rick kept glancing at Belinda. What was it about her that made her so different from every other woman he'd met? It was hard to put his finger on just what made her so appealing. She was a good mother, gentle but firm; she was strong and independent but womanly all at the same time; but most of all, her love for God and other people shone out of her extraordinary eyes. Who wouldn't fall in love with a package like that? He knew he wanted her at his side for the rest of his life, but he didn't know what it would take to make her fall for him. What if she never did? What if she never loved him the way he loved her? He didn't want to face the thought.

Traffic was light on Highway 24 as Belinda drove to Fort Wayne to see the lawyer. The sun was shining, although there was the typical brisk November chill to the air. She needed to think seriously about doing some Christmas shopping. She would have Rick to buy a gift for this year. She smiled at the thought. Her parents were both dead, and her brother, Mickey, lived in Washington State. They exchanged occasional letters and phone calls, but they lived too far apart to exchange presents. When he came for Andi's birthday last summer, it had been the first time she'd seen him in two years.

She only had a wait of five minutes before the receptionist showed her back to the office. When she walked in, she was surprised to see Rick sitting in a chair across the desk from the attorney.

"Hope you don't mind," he said. "I was up here on business anyway and thought you could use the moral support."

She'd never been so glad to see anyone. How had he known she needed some bolstering? She gave him a wide smile. "Thank you," she told him.

"I'm Charles Barker," the man sitting at the desk said. He stood and shook her hand. "I won't hold it against you that you're a friend of Rick's. Have a seat." He pointed to the chair beside Rick.

Belinda liked him immediately. His brown eyes displayed a keen intelligence, and his ready smile put her at ease. He was about Rick's age, short with thinning brown hair and bushy eyebrows. She sank down into the chair he'd indicated.

He rifled through some papers. "So the grandmother is suing for custody. Does she have visitation now?"

"Oh, yes. Anytime she asks for her, I let her take her."

"Hmm, that's good." He leaned back in his chair. "I don't think she'll be able to get custody, but you never know with judges. Tell me a little bit about your circumstances."

Belinda told him about her widowhood, what she did for a living, and how they lived. Rick sat quietly beside her and didn't interrupt.

"It doesn't sound like she has much ammunition," Charles said. "Of course, if you were remarried, it would make your case even stronger. Any chance of that happening in the next six months?" He looked at Rick when he asked.

Rick grinned. "You never know."

Belinda laughed nervously at the joke. "I have no plans for marriage." She wanted to cry. It was sweet of Rick to try to make Charles think some man would be interested, but she knew better. It was unlikely any man would want her with her plain appearance and the added baggage of a small daughter. She'd resigned herself to the cold hard facts long ago.

Charles told her not to worry, then Rick walked her to her car. "I have to go out of town on business for a few days," he said. "I should be back by Sunday, though. Do you have plans?"

She shook her head. "The only plans I have are to talk to my camp friends this Thursday. We always talk the last Thursday of the month."

"I'm going to have to meet them someday," he said. He pressed her hand. "I'll come over when I get back. Tell Andi I'll bring her a surprise."

"Not another puppy, please," Belinda said with a smile. "Ranger has already destroyed my slippers and my favorite socks. I can't afford to lose any more stuff."

"I won't bring anything live," he promised. "Try to miss me a little." He waved and ran across the street to his Jeep.

A little? She would miss him a lot. She knew she should stop seeing so much of him. But it was already too late to guard her heart. It would be devastating to her and Andi when he stopped coming around. She watched him drive away, then sighed and went to her car. The old Escort balked at the first attempt to start it, and she was afraid she was going to have to go back inside and ask for help, but it finally turned over. She had better get a new battery at the mall when she went.

The mall had just opened when she went inside. She found a couple of outfits for Andi on sale at Penney's then wandered over to L. S. Ayres. It was too expensive for her budget usually, but sometimes when they had a sale, she found some good buys. It was fun to look anyway. The store wasn't busy, and when she went by the makeup counter, a smiling young woman offered her a free makeover. She started to say no, then decided why not. She'd never had a makeover before. She could sure use some help.

She sat on the stool, and the young woman who said her name was Darcy pulled her hair back and started in.

"You have lovely skin," Darcy told her. "I'd kill for skin like that."

Belinda didn't say anything. She knew these sales-women had to say things like that, although she had to admit Darcy's skin was blotchy and spotted with pimples on her chin. Darcy used a nice-smelling cleanser on her face and neck, then applied toner and moisturizer. Belinda was surprised at how wonderful her skin felt.

Darcy explained each step as she applied foundation, blush, eye shadow, and mascara. The whole process took nearly half an hour. Belinda was glad she didn't have to go through this every morning. But when Darcy was finished and Belinda looked in the mirror, she was astonished at her reflection. She looked so different—almost, well, pretty. Fascinated, she turned her head from side to side and just stared. Was that really her? She wished she could afford these products, but Darcy told her that everything she had used today would cost over a hundred dollars. She thanked her and got up to leave.

"Wait a minute," Darcy said. "I almost forgot we're drawing a name in fifteen minutes for a free kit of smaller bottles of this same makeup. Here, sign up." She slid the form across the counter to Belinda.

Belinda filled it out, but she'd never won anything in her life, and she knew she wouldn't win now. But it didn't cost anything to try. She gave the completed form to Darcy and wandered around the store. She found a pair of shoes for Andi on sale, then stared longingly at a red dress for herself. Even on sale, it was fifty dollars, so she put it back. She wouldn't be able to buy Andi's shoes if she bought the dress.

A voice over the loudspeaker announced that there was a winner of a makeup kit. When her name was announced, she thought it must have been in her head. But the announcer said it again, and she realized she really had won. She hurried back to the counter.

Darcy was watching for her. "I'd hoped you'd win," she said. She handed Belinda the makeup kit.

"Now if I can just remember everything you did," Belinda said.

"Just a little practice, and you'll be fine," Darcy told her. "Now go home and wow that man of yours."

What man? She wished there was a man. She couldn't even get Rick's reaction. He was going to be gone until late Saturday night. She put the makeup in her bag and headed for the car. She had to fight lunch-hour traffic and felt wrung out and exhausted by the time she stopped to pick up Andi at Dawn's.

Dawn squealed when she saw Belinda. "You look fabulous. I've never seen you with makeup on before. What's the occasion?" She patted a spot on the couch beside her. "Sit down."

Belinda sat obediently. "I won a makeup kit," she told her. "Does it look okay?"

"It looks more than okay." She looked at her critically. "Now if you'd just let me do something about your hair."

Belinda suddenly felt reckless. Dawn had been bugging her to let her fix her hair ever since she'd graduated from beauty school. "Why not? I've come this far."

Dawn whooped, then put her finger to her lips. "Shh; the kids are asleep." She took Belinda's hand and dragged her to the kitchen. "Sit." She pushed her down onto a chair and began to run her fingers through Belinda's thick mass of curls. "Don't chicken out on me—I just have to go get my scissors."

"Scissors?" Belinda wasn't so sure about this. She had worn her hair long for so many years; she didn't know if she could face something totally new.

"Don't panic," Dawn laughed. "Just a little snip."

The little snip turned out to be a layered cut that released the curl in her hair. Dawn cut a few wispy bangs, then pulled the top back from Belinda's face and let the curls cascade down her back. After pulling a few strands free to curl around her cheeks, she was satisfied. She took Belinda to the full-length mirror in her bedroom. "What do you think?"

What did she think? Belinda wasn't sure she recognized herself at all. Her round face was contoured with blush, and the few wisps of curl around her cheeks and the bangs emphasized her eyes. Would Rick like it? She was mortified to discover that question was her first thought. This had gone way too far. She looked again at the stranger staring back at her from the mirror.

"I think I like it," she said.

"I love it!" Dawn fluffed the curls at Belinda's cheeks a bit. "Now I have the perfect dress for you to wear to church." She went to her closet and pulled out a tangerine dress with a cream collar and sleeves.

"Orange?" Belinda protested.

"It's not orange. It's more red than orange," Dawn said. "Trust me; it will look wonderful."

And it did, Belinda decided. The color brought out the reddish highlights in her hair and brightened her eyes. "Are you sure you don't mind if I borrow it?"

"It's yours," Dawn said. "It doesn't fit me anymore since I lost weight."

"You're a doll." Belinda hugged her. "Now I'd better wake Andi up and get home."

Andi was too sleepy to notice her mother's changed appearance, but Belinda kept looking in the rearview mirror and wondering who that woman was.

Chapter 6

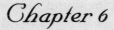

Over the next few days, Belinda practiced the art of applying her makeup until she could do it in fifteen minutes. The days dragged by, and she missed Rick with a sharp ache. She hated to admit, even to herself, that she had fallen in love with him. She was sure he just thought of her as a friend, though. He'd never even kissed her. He'd hugged her when she was upset, but that didn't count. She didn't know what to do about it. She had to get over this feeling somehow.

Sunday morning she dressed carefully, arranging her hair in an artful cascade of curls, putting her makeup on, and slipping a pair of extra nice pantyhose on before putting on her dress. *I look pretty good.*

Andi stared at her mother, then smiled. "You look pretty, Mommy."

"Thanks, sweetie, so do you. We'll be the beautiful Mitchell girls today."

When they got to church, she looked all around for Rick but didn't see him. Disappointed, she sat next to Mike Meredith, but she kept checking behind her to see if Rick had come in. Mike looked at her a bit strangely

168

then sidled over closer and began to talk to her. Before she knew it, he had asked to take her and Andi to lunch. Peeved because Rick wasn't there, she said yes. She used to wish Mike would notice her, but he never had before today except when he wanted her to care for his pet gerbil once when he was out of town.

She didn't much enjoy lunch with him. He ignored Andi and talked about himself the whole time. When he walked her back to her car at church after the meal, he tried to kiss her, and she was forced to push him away. He was moving way too fast.

Rick's Jeep pulled up when Mike's arms were still around her. Her heart leaped when she saw his tall figure get out and come toward her. She jumped guiltily away from Mike and said a hasty good-bye. Had Rick noticed that Mike's arms had been around her?

Andi squealed. "Mr. Ranger!" She kicked her feet in the car seat and waved at him.

He blew her a kiss and opened her door. "Hey, Kemosabe, did you miss me?"

His answer was a stranglehold around the neck when he got her out of the car seat. He was grinning broadly when he turned to Belinda. His smile faded. "What did you do to your hair?"

"Don't you like it?" She asked while touching her hair self-consciously.

"I didn't say that, but it's different. You look different." He didn't sound too happy about it either.

"We eated a pizza with Mike," Andi announced.

"Mike?"

"Mike Meredith from church," Belinda explained. "You've met him. He just left." She hadn't wanted him to know. It had been a silly impulse to even accept; she'd regretted it as soon as she'd done it.

Rick frowned. He put Andi back in the car seat and turned to go. "I'd better shove off," he said.

"You want to come to my house?" He had to have seen her. He would hardly look at her.

He just shook his head and strode toward his car with an angry stride. Belinda watched him go with a breaking heart. Her brief moment of pique at his late appearance had ruined it all.

❧

The last three days had been murder. Rick was hurt and angry. He hadn't expected her to try to find another man while he was gone. Maybe he should have let her know earlier in their relationship just how he felt, but he'd been afraid of scaring her. Now he'd blown it; she was obviously on the prowl for a man with that new hairstyle and makeup. She'd looked beautiful, though. But he'd liked the old Belinda, the one who made cookies and got flour on her nose. The one whose smile lit up the room. She didn't need makeup or a new hairstyle for him to see her beauty. Too bad the other guy didn't think she was good enough just like she was.

He decided to go to the custody hearing, in spite of his hurt. Maybe the other guy wouldn't be able to show up. He sat at the back of the courtroom and listened. The smarmy Mallory person didn't fare very well. Every time he tried to bring up a point, Charles countered it. When the hearing was over, the judge threw out the petition, slapped a fine on Mrs. Mitchell for filing a frivolous lawsuit, and also ruled in favor of Charles's request for supervised visitation when he pointed out she'd threatened to take Andi out of state. Mrs. Mitchell stalked out with angry tears streaming down her face. He didn't think it was because of love for Andi, but because she hated to lose. She would no longer be able to hold anything over Belinda's head. He slipped out before Belinda could see him.

He hadn't been to church in weeks, and he missed it, but he just couldn't face the thought of seeing Belinda with her new beau. He knew he needed to find another church, but he had liked New Life so much that he hated the thought of switching. It was wrong to stay away from church, though. He was going to have to do something this Sunday.

The last day of the year he ran into Dawn at Daywalt's Drugstore.

"Where have you been?" she demanded.

He smiled. Good old Dawn didn't pull any punches. "Around. I've been busy."

She regarded him with a skeptical gaze. "Too busy to come to church, but not too busy to break Belinda's heart, not to mention Andi's."

He sighed. "Belinda and I were just friends."

"Oh? Is that why she looks like she's been crying every time I see her?"

He stared at her. "What about her new boyfriend?"

Dawn looked puzzled. "What new boyfriend? She hasn't been out with anyone but you."

"Mike Meredith. She won't even have to change her initials when she marries him."

Dawn burst out laughing. "She's not interested in Mike! Whatever gave you that idea?"

A pulse of hope began to beat in Rick's chest. Had he really messed things up? "When I got back from my trip, she'd gone out with him for the first time. I saw him with his arms around her."

"Oh? It must have been something very casual because she never mentioned it to me. He's been bringing some bleached blond to church for the past two weeks."

Rick began to smile. He took off toward his Jeep at a dead run.

"Hey, where are you going?" Dawn called after him.

"To propose," he yelled back.

"All right!" Dawn danced a little jig in the parking lot.

❧❧

Belinda took down the last of the Christmas decorations and put the box in the corner to be taken to the attic. She usually left the decorations up until after New Year's, but her heart just wasn't in it. The one brightly wrapped package on the table was for Rick, but he hadn't been over since that first day she'd gone to church with her new look. Had he disliked her appearance that much, or had seeing her with Mike made him mad? She would probably never know the reason. He had never come back. If he'd even given her a sign that he was jealous, she could have explained or apologized, but there was only silence.

She peeked in on Andi and smiled when she saw her sucking her thumb in sleep. She only did that once in a while now. Her baby girl wouldn't be a baby much longer. She closed the door softly behind her and went back to the kitchen. She heard a car door and looked out the window. Her heart pounded when she saw the red Jeep parked in front of the sign. Was it Rick? Hope made her tremble. She put a hand to her throat when the doorbell chimed. She took a deep breath and went to the door.

Rick stood there gazing down at her. "I love you, but I have to know one thing," he said. "Can you ever possibly learn to love me back?"

"No," she said after a slight pause.

The hopeful smile faded from his face, and his shoulders slumped. "That's all I wanted to know." He turned to go, but she laid her hand on his arm.

"I already love you, Rick. I couldn't love you more than I already do."

He stopped in his tracks and turned slowly. She let all the love she had pent up inside shine out of her eyes. He gave a small gasp and gathered her against his chest. "I'm sorry I was such an idiot," he murmured against her hair. "I was so sure you weren't interested in me except as a friend. I thought you'd gone out and gotten a new look to attract that Mike fellow. You don't have to be glamorous for me. I love you just for who you are. Can you forgive me for being such a fool?"

"I already did," she said softly.

His lips sought and found hers. She made a sound that was half sob, half sigh, and wrapped her arms around his neck. She felt a crackle in his shirt pocket. "What's that?" she asked.

"Oh, just a deed," he said. He pulled it out of his pocket. "I thought this might induce you to accept my proposal, but I'm glad I didn't have to resort to bribery."

Her forehead creased in puzzlement, but she took the paper he handed her. Scanning it quickly, she gasped when she realized it was the deed to Timeless Treasures made out in her name. She cupped her palms around his face. "You are full of surprises today. You're the new owner?"

"No, you're the new owner," he said with a grin. "But would you mind sharing with me until I can get our house built? Will you marry me so I can be Andi's daddy?"

She pulled back and looked up into his eyes. "Is that the only reason?" she asked teasingly.

He kissed her again. "I might want a few more children," he said. "Especially if they have your eyes."

She smoothed the hair back from his face."I think that can be arranged," she said.

Andi's footsteps came down the hall. "Mommy, why are you kissing the Lone Ranger? Is he going to be my daddy?"

"I think so, Andi, I really think so," Belinda said as Rick's lips found hers again.

Colleen Coble

Colleen and her husband, David, have plenty of time on their hands since their two children, Dave and Kara, have flown the nest. They spend their spare time knee-deep in paint and wallpaper chips as they restore a Victorian home in Wabash, Indiana. Her husband is her biggest fan and loves to help with the research end of her writing. Colleen became a Christian in 1980 after a bad car accident when all her grandmother's prayers finally took root. She is very active in her church, New Life Baptist, where she sings and helps her husband with a young adult Sunday school class. She writes inspirational romance because she believes that the only happily-ever-after is with God at the center. Colleen has three published novels in the **Heartsong Presents** series and another novella in the *Spring's Memory* anthology.

Collette

by Kristin Billerbeck

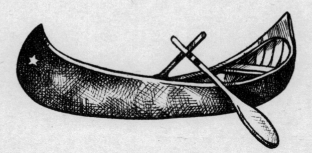

Chapter 1

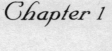

Collette Ambers exited customs and was swooped into a whirlwind of people, each of them going a different direction. The sounds of the noisy airport assaulted her senses. She instinctively retreated from the crowds and stood frozen at the customs door, unwilling or unable to advance into the overwhelming chaos.

She didn't belong here. San Francisco was a city with more folks than she'd seen in her lifetime. She looked at the myriad of faces, all so intent on their destinations. It was a painted sea of diversity, and Collette was reminded again how they were all strangers. Not a friend among them.

Collette had been to the States on several occasions: for Christian camp, for fund-raising efforts, but never without her parents or her camp friends. Never without someone waiting to greet her. Never alone.

At twenty-nine, Collette was embarking on independence for the first time in her life. And she didn't like it one bit. Twenty-two hours of flight had done nothing to prepare her for life outside Africa.

"Get out of the way, lady!" an angry-looking older woman snapped.

Collette's shoulder slammed into the side of the wall as another mob of passengers rushed past her. She defended herself by remaining against the wall while the irritated droves passed her.

"Wake up! You dreaming or something?" another questioned sarcastically.

Collette's fingers dug against the wall for support, and tears formed. How could things get any worse? She was in a foreign land called home by her father, but it wasn't her home. Africa was her home, at least it had been since she was seven. The wilds of San Francisco seemed far more dangerous than her life in the mission compound in Africa.

"Collette?" A gentle male voice broke into her thoughts. For a moment she thought she might have dreamed it. But then, through her blurred, tear-filled eyes, she viewed a man. He was tall, with dark, wavy hair, and his deep, chocolate-brown eyes held compassion. The first sign of that emotion she'd seen in America. Her heart sank when she realized she didn't know him, but he didn't leave. He remained before her as a welcome mirage, willing her to believe in him. She felt her lip quiver, and he took her hand in his own, guiding her toward a quiet corner. He grabbed her carry-on with his free hand and led her to a row of seats. The action spoke volumes. Collette had been too afraid to move. Were it not for this handsome stranger, she didn't know how long she might have stood against the wall.

"Collette Ambers?" he clarified.

She only nodded, wanting to rush into his embrace for protection. Simply the fact that he knew her name was enough. "Yes," she finally managed. "Should I know you?"

"No, we've never met," he whispered in a gravelly tone. "I'm from Bayside Community Church. I had business at the airport today, so I mentioned to Pastor Holmes I'd pick you up. Are you all right? You look a little shaken."

"Uh-huh, fine."

"I'm Kyle Brighton, from the singles' Sunday school class. Our class supported your father's ministry. We were so saddened to hear of his passing."

Her head nodded involuntarily. "Thank you. Did you know my father?" she asked hopefully. Anyone that could share in her loss would be so welcome.

"No, I didn't, but I've heard some wonderful things about him." He lowered his head and spoke softly. "I could tell by his monthly newsletters that he was a caring and loving man. You must miss him greatly."

She blinked away fresh tears. Not again. It was bad enough her father had gone to be with the Lord, but the loss of her home had been a double blow. It was more than she could bear, and it was all coming back to her again. She had to find a way to get back to Africa. And quickly.

After an uncomfortable silence, Kyle spoke again. "I hope you don't mind my coming to get you. If you're uncomfortable with this, I could call someone else—perhaps one of the secretaries at the church?"

"No, no. I'm sorry. It's not you. My mind just isn't up to speed yet. It's been a long flight, and I'm tired and a little overwhelmed. Hearing about my father. . .well, you know." She held her tightened forehead in one hand, trying to rub away the awful headache.

"Of course, that's completely understandable. Would

you like to sit for a while? Your bags can wait."

"To tell you the truth, I'm anxious to get out of here. All this bustle makes me nervous."

"Fine; let's get your luggage and get you to Mrs. Combie's house so you can rest. You must be exhausted."

"Mrs. Combie?"

"She's offered to have you stay with her until you can find a place of your own. The church is very excited to have you start as a new secretary. I know this all seems like so much, but it won't take long to get settled into city life. San Francisco is a wonderful city. We have a great singles' ministry. I'm anxious to tell you about it when you're ready. You are single, right?"

Terminally, she thought wistfully. "Mr. Brighton, I appreciate everything the church has done, but I'm not staying on long. I don't plan to be a charity case for the rest of my life for your church. Just because it supported my father is no reason for it to feel responsible for me now. I'm just here long enough to raise support to continue the work in Africa. I'm sure you understand."

Kyle's brow furrowed. "Miss Ambers, I don't mean to sound heartless at such a difficult time, but our church doesn't support women-run missions in foreign countries."

"I know that, Mr. Brighton, but I'm convinced God wants me to continue what my father started. And He'll find the money for me," she said with conviction. "I don't doubt it for a minute." *I can't doubt it,* she thought. *There's nothing else for me.*

"I'm sure if that's what He wants, He will, Miss Ambers," he answered evenly. "Let's go." He sounded annoyed.

As if his statement should have made her drop her life's work. *Men.*

"You don't believe me, do you?" She'd meant to sound confident, but her question came out as a pathetic whimper. She didn't need Kyle Brighton's approval, so why was she practically begging for it?

"Miss Ambers, if you believe this is what God wants you to do, who am I to question you? I just don't understand why you'd want to leave one of the most beautiful cities in the world—a mission field that's ripe for the taking, I might add—to go back to a desert in the middle of nowhere."

Because it's my home, Collette raged inwardly. Pasting a patient smile on her face, she explained, "Kassarani is close to Nairobi, Kenya, Mr. Brighton. I assure you we had many creature comforts. A nice townhouse with wood floors, a computer room available to us at the school in Nairobi, even an elegant church for Sunday worship." She didn't mention the stark, barren land or the eight-by-eight, block-built buildings that made up the Kassarani mission where she was stationed. It would only prove his point. "Besides, we're not trying to impress anyone financially. We're trying to win souls for the Lord."

Collette, usually so shy and withdrawn, had no patience with his inaccurate view of Kenya. Westerners never considered the hearts that deeply hungered for Jesus. They simply thought of the buildings and material items people in developing countries didn't have. Stuff that would all burn away someday. Stuff that didn't matter.

He raked his hand through his dark, short hair. "I did

not mean to offend you, Miss Ambers. I only meant that perhaps this is a new season for you. A chance to start fresh and see what God has for you. Perhaps He sent you here for a purpose." He stopped suddenly and changed his tack. "It was none of my business. I'm sorry I mentioned it. It's the accountant in me, always searching for the clear answer. Math, unlike life, only has one right answer, you know." He smiled.

Collette searched his warm brown eyes. Instinctively, she knew his apology was sincere. She looked at him with a downturned chin, studying him. He was good-looking in a city kind of way. Very confident in how he carried himself. She guessed he must be some kind of successful mogul by his shiny black loafers with tassels and the impeccably cut suit he wore. Even though he referred to himself simply as an accountant.

Although young, his face looked aged by experience, and she felt a spiritual maturity in him, even if it wasn't big enough to see Africa's need. She couldn't fault him for that—he was obviously comfortable with city life. Very few men would see the reasoning in wanting to return to Africa, but Collette had given up on trying to impress men. She would remain single, that much was certain. A striking man like Kyle Brighton would never look at her twice, so his opinion wasn't worth a second thought.

In Africa, her weight was never an issue. People there seemed to look within, not at the facade that fades away with time. But here in America, the image masquerade was clearly important. She could tell by the fine clothing on travelers at the airport that nothing had changed since her last visit. Society was still consumed with appearances. Collette felt frumpy. The way she always felt in the States. She wanted to turn and run as fast as her short, stocky legs would carry her. Back to Kenya, back where she belonged. In the little village of Kassarani.

"I guess my baggage is this way," she pointed.

"Are you hungry? Do you want something to eat?" Kyle asked.

Collette felt the pangs of hunger, but eating in front of Kyle would only remind him of her heavy frame and how different she was from the California ideal. She knew it shouldn't matter, but for some reason, it mattered a great deal. "No, thank you," she answered meekly.

"Well, I'm hungry. I haven't had dinner, and it's well past time. Come on, just a little bowl of crab chowder? The smell is driving my stomach crazy. I know you're tired, but you've got to eat and they actually have decent food at this little Crab Pot restaurant. Please?" He gave a half-smile that could have charmed the hardest of hearts.

She felt herself smile. "That would be very nice."

Kyle led her down the wide expanse of hallway. As he walked alongside her, she noticed nobody got anywhere within five feet of her. Something about Kyle Brighton commanded attention and made her feel safe. She felt his hand touch the small of her back and nearly jumped out of her skin. He hadn't even noticed he was touching her, until she started like a frightened jackrabbit. She felt so foolish when he looked at her questioningly. One thing was certain: Living in America was going to be an adventure.

Two French bread bowls of steaming, creamy soup were set before them. It took all of Collette's willpower not to devour it in one intense slurp. She was starving. She hadn't eaten a thing since the layover in Europe. Her mouth watered intensely as she waited through Kyle's prayer.

After praying, he leaned into the table and placed a hand on hers. "The singles' class is very active. We're going canoeing next weekend and to the ballet next month. It's a nonthreatening environment—just a big group of us together, not couples or anything like that. I think you'd enjoy yourself."

Collette knew enough about single society to know how these things worked. The men inevitably ended up hovering around the pretty girls. Whether or not it was a "couples" thing didn't matter in the mating rituals of men and beautiful women. A wallflower she would always be. There was no sense in believing anything would be different in San Francisco.

"I'm not very social, Mr. Brighton. I prefer a quiet night, curled up with a good book, to an evening out." The word singles was enough to throw her off. Not since her childhood camp days had she ever felt like part of the in crowd, and it was no fun to be reminded. A good book and secretarial work would keep her well-grounded until her return trip was secured.

The only good thing about America as far as Collette was concerned was her best friends. Amanda, Belinda, and Danielle had been there for her through everything. All her ups and downs in life, including her father's death.

They had sent the warmest notes Collette had received and, more importantly, had offered their constant prayers throughout his mission. She couldn't wait to join in their conference calls now that she was back in the States—to hear their sweet voices and outrageous laughter.

From the moment when those three girls had picked Collette's unathletic self to be on their volleyball team, the foursome had been bonded for life. With Belinda, Amanda, and Danielle, Collette knew she was loved for who she was inside and that the outside never mattered. She would never have another group of friends like that, so why bother? Besides, she had important reasons to get back to Africa. That had to be her priority.

"I just hope you'll give us a try at the singles' group. God wanted us to have fellowship with one another, and while you're here, you might as well join us." Kyle glanced at his watch. "Mrs. Combie's probably worried that I didn't pick you up. We'd better get going."

"Oh, yes." Collette took a last sip of ginger ale from her glass and set it back on the table. She rummaged through her purse before realizing she didn't have any American currency yet. "Kyle, here I've been bragging about not being a charity case, and I just realized, I don't have any U.S. money for dinner."

"Collette, do you really think I'd let you pay for your first meal on American soil in so many years?" He smiled warmly, and the light creases appeared in his cheeks. "Of course, it's my treat."

Collette found herself gawking at him. He did everything with a masculine artfulness. Something about him made her wish, just for one day, she could be the petite blond that men seemed to idealize instead of the round, mousy brown-haired woman in African clothes amid startling displays of American fashion.

After their light supper, Kyle drove them to a small tract house in a very nice section of town. It seemed familiar and, for some reason, reminded Collette of her mother. The front door opened widely and an older woman came out with arms outstretched. She took Collette's hand in both of her own. Mrs. Combie was a quiet-spirited older woman who seemed to hold a lifetime of wisdom in her knowing, clear blue eyes. What a stark and beautiful contrast they made against her white hair and faded skin tone.

"My dear, Collette, is it really you?" The older woman swept her up into a hug. Collette was, by nature, a hugger, so she didn't mind in the least. "Did you know I stood up at your parents' wedding? Oh, my dear, what a love they had for each other, and just look at you!" She held Collette's face between her hands. "You are the picture of both of them. You have your mother's flawless, porcelain skin and your father's bright smile. How on earth do you keep your skin so healthy in Africa? Kyle, look at Collette. Isn't she just beautiful?" Mrs. Combie had tears in her eyes, and Collette felt the awkward moment to her very soul.

Kyle set the bags beside the door and looked like the proverbial deer in the headlights. His expression said it all. No, she wasn't beautiful, and he was too polite to say it aloud. He smiled halfheartedly. "That's everything, Collette. I'll see you tomorrow at church. Bye, Mrs.

Combie." Kyle practically tripped over himself to get out the door.

Mrs. Combie laughed. "That Kyle, such a restless one. I wonder when he'll ever settle down. So shy." She nodded her head back and forth. "Let's get you situated in your room. Your friends from camp sent you some yellow roses—they're in your room in a vase. So nice of them to think of you. I can't believe you still keep in contact with women from Christian camp! They said they'd call on Thursday night. They can't wait for you to join them again. Oh, Collette, it is such a joy to have you here."

"Uh-huh," Collette answered, pitying herself. She felt like a lost puppy, nipping at Kyle Brighton's ankles as she stared longingly at the door he'd just shut. Why did he affect her that way? A man who didn't even believe in her abilities to run her father's mission. A man who she'd only known for an hour.

Why should it matter to her that Kyle Brighton didn't think she was beautiful? She wasn't, after all, and the poor man wasn't blind. Would she have rather he lied? Mrs. Combie had said he was restless. She'd even called him shy, but nothing about him struck her as being the quiet type. He was full of personality and life, something she distinctly lacked since her father had died. *Kyle is nothing special,* she told herself. *You're just lonely. Lonely and feeling sorry for yourself. Nothing a good Snickers wouldn't solve.*

Chapter 2

ollette had slept through Thursday as she combated jet lag. First thing Friday morning, she dressed in her finest dress to meet with Bayside Community Church's pastor, her new boss. There was nothing for her here in San Francisco. That fact was only reiterated by the intolerant reactions from strangers she'd received at the airport.

She reasoned if she met the pastor personally, he would see her deep desire to serve in Africa. Perhaps then he might reconsider the question of the church's support. After all, Collette had been taking on some of her father's duties at the mission since he had fallen ill eight months ago. Then there were those loose ends, the money issues, things she just couldn't put to rest until she got back to Africa and set them straight.

Pastor Holmes's answer was anything but promising. "Collette, you must understand as a church we feel responsible for the missionaries we send out. I realize Africa was once your home, but according to all reports, it is still a hostile environment in many cases. Your father trained new pastors, and not only does our church hold that women should not teach men, but you don't have the advanced theological degrees that are needed to teach new pastors in any event. I think your father would have wanted you here," he finished quietly.

"I don't think so, Pastor Holmes. I think my father would want me to continue his work the way I have been doing for the last eight months. There are things about that ministry that only I know, and I know my father would want me to be helping the African ministers he's trained. I would be working under them, so the question of a woman being in charge wouldn't even be an issue."

The pastor looked down at his desk silently. Then he answered her. "Collette, your father wanted you in the States. He left a detailed letter stating his wishes. He wanted you to have a husband and a family. We have a wonderfully active singles' group here at the church. I think once you get out and make some new friends, you'll love it here. Just take some time to get used to it."

She gave a short laugh. "Pastor Holmes, I don't fit in here. My father loved me, maybe a little too much. He saw me as the mirror image of my mother, but you knew her. She was a great beauty, and I'm afraid that legacy wasn't passed on to me. My father made decisions based on his heart if he told you that I belonged here. I'm not a sleek, San Francisco sophisticate, the kind of woman men here would be interested in for a wife. My father may have had many dreams for me, but that doesn't mean there's any hope of them coming true. I know the mission in Kassarani. I can make it work if given the chance. It needs me. And it needs a church back in America to help meet its financial needs."

"Collette, I'm sorry. There's nothing I can do. Kyle does the financial books for the church, and he has backed your father's wishes, saying the mission in Africa must stand alone now. Our singles' group is—"

"Your singles' group is full of eligible Christian bachelors, I know. I've heard that speech before, Pastor, but getting married is not the answer to my problems!" Collette closed her eyes when she realized her impertinence. "I'm sorry. . .I'm sorry; I didn't mean to sound ungrateful. I appreciate all you've done for me, Pastor Holmes, really I do. I know my father would be so thankful as well, but there are reasons I must get back, reasons I don't think even he understood at the time of his death."

She saw by his expression that she was getting nowhere.

"My hands are tied, Collette."

"Fine. I'm going to get back to answering phones. I'm sorry," she repeated.

As Collette exited the large conference room, she ran directly into Kyle Brighton's broad chest. "Kyle!" She looked back at the room, wondering how much he'd overheard, but it was apparent from his expression of pity that he'd heard more than enough.

"I have free tickets tonight for a play," he blurted out. "Would you like to go with me?"

"I don't think so." She wasn't that desperate. She might have to rely on the church for a job temporarily, but she didn't expect to be a complete charity case, relying on them for entertainment as well. A Snickers bar and a good book were her evening plans.

"That's too bad. I was hoping to get to know you better. Find out a little more about your ministry in Africa. I only know it by the numbers, not personally." He smiled. "I thought maybe we could exchange ideas and stories." He paused for a moment. "The tickets were donated to Inner Team Ministries." He took the tickets from his chest pocket and held them up. "I work for them, running after-school Bible studies in my spare time. But I suppose the tickets can just go to waste," he shrugged. "They won't know."

That stopped her from walking away. "Really? You work for an inner-city ministry?" Finally, she had something in common with him. The first person in San Francisco she'd found she had anything in common with.

He didn't answer her question. Instead he simply announced, "I'll pick you up at Mrs. Combie's at six. We'll grab a quick dinner. Okay?"

"Yeah, fine." Collette tempered her response. *Does Kyle have any interest in my ministry, or does he simply feel sorry for me?* He was obviously intelligent, handsome, and had a heart for the Lord. But this goodwill gesture only made her question his motives. As he turned to walk into the pastor's office, her eyes narrowed with apprehension. Remembering his inability to agree with Mrs. Combie's assertion that she was beautiful, Collette sighed. Clearly, to Kyle Brighton she was simply a charity case.

Mrs. Combie zipped up Collette's dress. "I'm as nervous as a mother of the bride. Do you know how long it's been since I helped one of my daughters dress for a big date?"

"I would hardly categorize this as a big date, Mrs. Combie. Kyle had free seats to a play. I happened to be in the right place at the right time." *Right in his chest, as a matter of fact,* she thought blushingly.

Collette's dress was a black polyester knit that camouflaged her hips and covered her abundant bosom discreetly. Wear had taken its toll on the dress, but it was still one of the nicest things she owned without an African pattern on it. She wanted to at least appear American for her evening, even though she felt as African as the veldt itself.

She studied herself in the full-length mirror. Her bare complexion looked pale next to the darkness of her outfit, her hair more mousy than normal, and her lips disappeared into her skin. She was sorely disappointed with the image staring back at her. Mrs. Combie seemed to sense her frustration, grabbing Collette by the shoulders.

"You look beautiful, just a little washed-out, that's all. Probably from the long trip. Would you like me to help you with some makeup?" Mrs. Combie asked.

Collette shrugged. "I don't own any makeup, Mrs. Combie. Just a lot of sunscreen," she crinkled her nose. "I don't think it would help anyway."

"Nonsense. Sit down. I'll be right back." Mrs. Combie pressed on Collette's shoulders and placed her in front of the vanity table that inhabited Collette's guest quarters. It was a lovely piece from days long gone. A time when furniture was made to be a lifelong investment. Three mirrors surrounded her, reminding her from all angles that she was dowdy and colorless. A big, blank canvas.

Mrs. Combie came back with a small metal box and

opened it to a variety of lipsticks, foundations, and blush samples all in little pink packages. She smiled a guilty grin. "I used to sell makeup from my home. I never did sell very much. My husband used to tease me about how my investments never quite paid off. I always tended to give it away to someone who couldn't afford it. Then one day everyone seemed taken care of, so I just put the case away."

"Looks like you're still giving it away to someone who can't afford it." Collette laughed.

Mrs. Combie shrugged. "So be it. I can't think of anything better to do with it. Putting makeup on someone makes me feel like I'm creating Esther to go before the king."

Collette laughed aloud. "I don't think I have much in common with the stunning Queen Esther of the Bible. My beauty certainly isn't going to save my people!"

"Now, Collette, Esther had to go through a year of beauty treatments before she was presented to the king. That's a lot of effort for one meeting. I can't see how one night of makeup would hurt. Let me play."

"Very well," Collette relented. "But it feels strange to be pampered this way."

"Sit back and close your eyes; I won't take long. It's like having my very own full-size Barbie doll. It's been a long time since I got to do this. My daughters never did care much for makeup."

Collette couldn't stop a giggle from escaping. If Mrs. Combie had attacked them with her collage of colors, Collette could imagine why they'd never cared for makeup. Still, she was more than appreciative. Anything had to be an improvement. Mrs. Combie wet a sponge and applied foundation to it before blotting it gently on Collette's skin.

"Oh, to have skin like this. Like a baby's bottom." The older woman sighed.

"Is that supposed to be a compliment?" Collette laughed.

"Absolutely. Your skin is as fresh and flawless as a baby's behind. Now hold still," Mrs. Combie chastised. "Look up. It's time for mascara."

"Am I going to look like myself? I've never worn makeup before. I don't want to look like a floozy."

"Trust me; do I wear too much?"

"You don't wear any," Collette answered.

"That, my dear, is the secret to wearing makeup properly. Now hush up, so I can finish." Collette felt her lips drawn on by a pencil tip and then finally the lipstick. "Ta-dah!" Mrs. Combie turned her around in the swivel chair to face the mirror.

A stranger looked back. Collette moved closer. "Oh my! My eyes look so much bigger. And greener."

"That's the eyeliner and mascara. See, just a light touch with that moss-green eyeliner and the green comes out. You have beautiful eyes, Collette, and look at your skin—it glows." Mrs. Combie stood back with crossed arms. "I'm better than I remember. It looks like you just stepped off the runway."

That was exaggerating things a bit, but Collette had to admit, she'd never looked better. Her mousy brown hair had been lifted and placed in an elegant bun. It actually looked vibrant against the gentle pink color on her lips.

For once, she looked like an American, not a downtrodden missionary's kid from Africa. "How can I ever thank you, Mrs. Combie?"

"You can go and have a fine time with Kyle. He's a wonderful young man, and he needs to find a woman who understands him and his ministries. Being chief controller for that big company keeps him from getting too intimate with anyone."

"That's a pretty tall order for a simple dinner with a friend."

"Not really. I've been praying for Kyle Brighton for some time now, and maybe God has you in mind to answer it." Mrs. Combie winked just as the doorbell rang. "I feel just like a fairy godmother."

Collette hated to break the spell, but she was no Cinderella. Poor Mrs. Combie had grand illusions, and perhaps her eyesight wasn't what it once was. A fairy tale indeed.

Collette gave her hair one last pat and looked in the mirror again to see that strange image gazing back. She looked like a woman with big, interesting-looking eyes and full, vivid lips. Her skin *did* look like her mother's. She was mesmerized by her own reflection for a full minute before realizing Kyle was at the front door waiting. For the first time, Collette saw something other than her weight in the mirror. She walked toward the door, feeling like she was hiding behind a mask. An attractive mask. She felt confident and pretty.

Until she saw Kyle. "Hi, Kyle," she whispered softly.

"Collette?" Kyle's deep-brown eyes lingered on her

face, studying her. Collette looked to the floor. "You look gorgeous." The way he'd said it, she almost believed him. She brought her eyes to rest on his clean-shaven jaw. She seemed drawn to the tiny laugh lines alongside his mouth. They told her how much he smiled.

Collette felt Mrs. Combie pinch her elbow from behind. "Thank you," Collette answered after the prodding. "Ready?"

Mrs. Combie pushed her toward Kyle. "You kids have fun tonight and keep your wallets out of sight. The theater district is famous for its pickpockets."

"We sure will, Mrs. Combie. I will have Collette back as soon as the play is over."

"Take your time; it's Friday night. I'll simply expect her by one."

"One?" Collette shrieked. "I don't think I've ever seen what 1:00 A.M. looks like!"

Mrs. Combie and Kyle both laughed. "I'll have her home at a decent hour; I promise."

Kyle took them to an elegant restaurant that catered to the theater crowd. It had everything on the menu from rich pasta dishes to peppercorn steaks to salads. It all made Collette's mouth water. The waiter handed Kyle a wine menu, and he handed it right back. Collette respected the way he did it, without calling attention to the fact that it wasn't necessary.

"What looks good to you?" Kyle asked.

"I was thinking maybe a salad."

"A salad? In this place? You've got to be kidding." He looked up, ready to laugh when her expression made it clear that she wasn't kidding. Collette watched his countenance change.

Who was she trying to fool? It had to be obvious she ate more than light salads, but still, she didn't want him to judge her for eating a big meal. She'd just fill up later on that grand-size Snickers she had waiting at home. Besides, she wanted to be sure she'd have enough to pay for her meal. She'd already been a charity case once.

Kyle broke her Snickers dreams. "Hey, I have an idea. The peppercorn steak is just huge here. Why don't you order your salad and get some soup and then split the steak with me? I'll do the same. Would that bother you?"

"To share your meal, you mean?"

"Yes; is that considered bad taste in Africa?"

Collette laughed aloud. "Um, no. We generally eat with our hands in a collective bowl when we eat in Kassarani, so I'd say sharing a plate would be fine."

He stared at her, the most serious cast crossing his jaw. "Collette, you have the most beautiful eyes and laugh when you smile. I wish you'd do it more often. Ever since you arrived, you've had this pained expression."

She felt the heat rise in her face. "It's the makeup. I'm not used to wearing it." Did she really say that? What an inane thing to say.

"No, I don't think so. It was there before the makeup. Your sweet spirit just lights up your eyes, and they sparkle. Reminds me of Rachel in the Bible."

Rachel? Collette had always thought of herself as Leah, especially when she heard it meant cow. Rachel was the pretty one. The one Jacob wanted. Leah was the leftovers.

"I do not understand your meaning," she finally answered.

He explained, "Leah was dull-eyed. That's how she's described in the Bible, but Rachel, her eyes sparkled. Just think how important that must have been in a time when women's faces were covered by veils with only their eyes showing."

"Rachel was also described as lovely in form and beautiful," she reminded him, while she sank lower behind her menu.

"As are you, Collette," he said with conviction, lowering her menu with his palm. "I feel I should apologize for our first meeting. I may have come off as judgmental, when I really just was worried about the welfare of a woman alone in Kenya. I think I made it seem like I had all the answers."

She exhaled, and her entire body seemed to relax. "Thank you."

"Let's order, okay? So, do you like steak?"

"Uh-huh," she nodded. He called the waiter over and ordered both their dinners for them. Collette had never been treated so gallantly, but deep in her heart, she knew it would end. Feared it. Which made it even harder to accept Kyle's graciousness. He was a loving, caring soul with a great deal of compassion, but at some point, he would wake up. He would realize Collette wasn't as pretty as the other women in San Francisco or as slender. Then he would move on to another maiden who needed to be rescued. And she would go back to Africa and save her father's ministry.

Chapter 3

The theater was something out of Collette's wildest, old-movie dreams. Something like she imagined must have been the height of fashion at the turn of the century. The walls were lined with private balconies and decorated with gilded cherubs and a color scheme that defied today's muted taupes. Antique lavenders, blues, and mauves blended in a collage of color that created excitement in itself.

It was the first live play Collette had ever seen, other than the skits she'd watched performed at Christian camp. The acting was so real, Collette felt like a fly on the wall in someone's kitchen. She relished the story, lapping up the dialogue hungrily, not imagining what could be next. When the lights went up for intermission, her shoulders slumped.

"They expect us to wait?"

"Only for fifteen minutes, Collette. Come on; we'll get some ginger ale or cola in the lobby."

"That's just not fair, to leave us hanging like that."

"No, I suppose it isn't. So what do you think so far?"

"I love it. I can't thank you enough for bringing me.

The acting is marvelous. I feel like they're living this family tragedy and I'm right in the middle of it. I almost found myself wanting to pray for them."

"Is that a good thing?"

She laughed and bit her lip. "I think so. The main character is such a fool. I just want to hit her on the head. She reminds me of Anna Karenina, how she just threw everything away for some guy, trying to find romance. Oh, it irritates me just to think of it. That's how this heroine is. I want to go up on stage and give her a good knock on the head."

He laughed. "Maybe we are sitting a little too close. Did you read many books in Kenya?"

"As many as I could get my hands on. The other missionaries' kids were all playing sports, and I have two left feet, but luckily my eyesight is good and I'm not likely to have any serious accidents reading."

It wasn't long before the lights dimmed a few times, and Collette once again felt transported into another era as they walked into the elaborately decorated theater and made their way to their seats. Until the second act started. Then she was confident she was in modern-day America. A bathtub had been moved out onto the stage, and as the act progressed, Collette soon realized the bathtub was more than a prop. The actors were about to remove their clothing.

Suddenly she felt Kyle's hand under her elbow, propelling her up from her seat. Although the theater rows were incredibly close together, Kyle walked with determination, apologizing to those patrons they passed. Collette felt uncomfortably aware of her size as she tried to squeeze through the too-small row. Kyle's whispered words were loud enough to be heard on stage, and the actors actually watched them leave. Since they had been a mere ten feet from the stage, their exit could not go unnoticed.

Kyle escorted Collette up the aisle resolutely. When approached by an usher and told to sit down, he only replied firmly, "We're leaving. Now." They made their way in the dark out into the marble-lined foyer where Collette breathed a sigh of relief.

"I guess I really am left hanging now, huh?" She grinned as they approached the glass exit doors. She heard some shuffling behind her and turned around to see other patrons also heading toward the exit.

"Uh, did we just start that?" Collette asked. "How did you do that?"

"Do what?"

"Get people to follow you out like that." She pointed behind them. "Are you the Moses of the theater, leading your people out of Egypt?" She lifted her eyebrows.

"I guess I wasn't the only one who didn't want to see that naked man from ten feet away! That's a little too 'fly on the wall' for me," Kyle exclaimed.

"I was looking forward to it." She looked at him with the utmost seriousness before breaking into a giggle. "I'm just kidding!"

"I am so incredibly sorry for taking you here, Collette," Kyle apologized. "I should have read the reviews. I feel like such an idiot. The tickets were free, and I just never thought to check. It is kind of ironic that the reason I didn't offer to take you to the movies was because I was worried that something in them might offend you." He looked at her, his brows furrowed in concern, and suddenly they both burst into a loud laugh.

Collette's laughter slowly died. Kyle was a man of his convictions. Partial nudity was a common part of life in many areas of Africa, but what she had just seen in the theater was not representative of everyday life in America. That scene had been created intentionally to shock the viewer and offend traditional values. She respected Kyle immensely for caring about what she saw, and his actions only caused her to admire him more. A feeling she was beginning to fear. Everything about Kyle made her feel like a princess who was looked after, in every detail.

"Kyle, thank you for doing that."

"You're welcome."

The couple walked up the well-lit street together, passing all-night restaurants and six-story parking garages. Kyle held her hand for safety reasons along the crowded, dirty sidewalk, and she found herself wishing the gesture meant as much to him as it did to her. His touch electrified her.

"Thank you for asking me to spend the evening with you, Kyle. Adjusting to San Francisco has been difficult, and I appreciate your trying to make it easier." *This sure beats a Snickers bar,* she admitted to herself.

He bowed dramatically. "It has been my pleasure, my lady."

"You have made my short stay so much fun, and I will be eternally grateful for your friendship." The comment was for him. To let him know she didn't hold him account-able for future get-togethers. She appreciated the night for what it was, an attempt to make her feel better, but she didn't expect any more from him.

"Maybe next time we'll get to see a whole play," he quipped.

"Maybe not! Walking out was much more adventur-ous. Any tourist can go see a play, but to annoy the entire theater in order to stand by Christian convictions—now that's what I call living." She smiled, but noticed he didn't. "What's the matter, Kyle?"

He squeezed her hand and stopped to face her. "You make it sound as though you're not staying, Collette."

Do you care? she wanted to ask, but afraid of the answer, she replied, "Kyle, I don't belong here. I want to go back to Africa. I'm working on my fund-raising letters at home, as we speak."

"Why do you want to go back? Do you mind my asking?"

"I'm useful in Africa. I'm comfortable there," she shrugged. "I guess Africa makes me feel like I have a pur-pose. Here I just feel. . .in the way. Like everyone has got somewhere to go, and I'm just standing in their path, blocking the road." She shivered.

The fog was rolling in over the hill, and San Fran-cisco's autumn night had quickly turned frigid. Kyle took off his suit coat and wrapped it around her shoulders. It was big on her, due to Kyle's muscular build and strong arms. Arms she couldn't help but desire to have around her. If only Kyle would give her a reason to stay. She was dreaming, of course, but for the moment, it was a nice place to be. Locked away in her own special world.

"You're useful here, Collette. You just haven't found God's calling yet." Their long, meaningful gaze made both of them uncomfortable, and Kyle began walking again. He took her hand more firmly as they walked past several homeless men, lined along the sidewalk and building stoops.

"So, do you still think there isn't a need here in San Francisco?" He nodded toward a few men sleeping right on the sidewalk, curled up in fetal positions with their cardboard signs over them for warmth. Each sign carrying a different reason, a different plea for money.

"I never said there wasn't a need here. I just don't know the first thing about filling it. In Africa, I know my purpose."

"It can't be that different here. Just ask Him what He wants." Kyle pointed to the night sky.

"I know He doesn't want me to see any more plays." She covered her mouth to stifle a giggle, but he pointed at her in mock anger.

"Collette Ambers!" He dropped her hand and put a fist to his hip. "I feel bad enough as it is." She couldn't contain her giggle. She broke out with an infectious laugh and grabbed his hand to show her repentance.

"You are incorrigible." Suddenly, his laughter stopped and his brown eyes looked into hers intensely. She felt herself warm under the gaze as his grasp tightened around her hand. Could he possibly be feeling anything of what she was experiencing? Could he possibly know what his brown eyes did to her?

He bent down, and Collette felt his lips come within an inch of her own. "Come with me next week on the canoe trip." His voice was low and held intent. "At least make plans to live life while you're here."

She shook her head no. She had to remain focused. Getting back to Africa was her priority. Her father's dream must live on in her. She pulled her hand away.

"Collette, there are so many people I want you to meet. We'll have fun, I promise. Just one day out of your life."

"Kyle, it's not the day, it's the activity. I'm not wiggling this body into a skinny little boat designed to tip over easily. I've been to camp, you know. I'm not totally naive."

"You've just never had a proper canoe master, that's all. Come with me. I'll take care of you."

"I think those exact words were used by my friend Belinda right before we tipped over in front of the entire Christian camp. Are you asking me to relive the most embarrassing moment of my life in front of my peers?"

"You see? Dwelling on the negative. You and Belinda made an unforgettable memory that day. I'm telling you, I'm a master rower. Say you'll come."

"Why are you and Pastor Holmes so intent on getting me in the singles' group?"

"Because we want Collette Ambers to spend time with her peers. To have fun and quit worrying about the life she left behind. We want her to move forward!" He nuzzled his nose against hers. "Get it?" She closed her eyes, and she felt his lips brush against hers ever so slightly. He pulled away quickly, leading Collette to wonder if he'd kissed her at all, or if he'd just come too close and accidentally touched her.

She ignored the possibility. "I get it; I get it."

"The Russian River is beautiful this time of year. You'll love it. I'm sure of it. I'll even pack us a lunch," he offered.

"I'll pack a lunch, not that I don't trust you or anything. But I don't! You know far too much about restaurants to be good at packing a homemade lunch."

"That means you'll go?"

"Against my better judgment, yes, it does." If only she were strong enough to say no and stay home, working on her support letters, but an invitation from Kyle Brighton was far more exhilarating.

Kyle took her hand again, and they walked to the dark garage where their car was parked. He opened her door, and she noticed his quick glance to her legs. He abruptly forced his eyes upward, and she smiled. Perhaps he did find her attractive. Was it possible? Or was her fairy-tale imagination working overtime?

Collette got home and dreamily plopped onto the couch. Mrs. Combie was waiting with a knowing grin. "I told you, you two would hit it off. I have a sixth sense."

"Yes, you did tell me."

"So?"

"So. . .he's gorgeous, he's a gentleman, and when I'm with him, I feel like I look like Sophia Loren!" Collette answered in a thick, faux Italian accent.

"That's amoré!" Mrs. Combie announced.

Chapter 4

When Collette realized the irony of her taking a canoe trip down the Russian River, the first thing she did was call Belinda. Only Belinda, who had gotten dumped into the water with Collette so many years ago, could fully appreciate the situation.

Belinda answered immediately, and Collette could hear the constant chatter of her daughter, Andi, in the background. The sound was both exhilarating and frightening. Thrilling because Belinda, a young widow, had a darling daughter to share her life with, and no one deserved happiness more. Frightening because Collette knew such happiness would probably never happen to her.

"Belinda, it's Collette. Did I catch you at a bad time?"

"Oh, Collette, you could never catch me at a bad time. I just finished reading to Andi. She's off to bed now. The camp gang has been thinking about you constantly since you got back to the States. I'm just running the store as usual, nothing too thrilling. Is everything going well?"

"As well as can be expected for living in San Francisco. What a nightmare this place is. People everywhere." They both laughed. "I just started fund-raising this week, and so hopefully, I'll get back to Africa right after our reunion in

February. That's my goal."

"Collette, are you sure you want to do that?"

"Belinda, my father's ministry was having some troubles before I left. Just some bookkeeping things I'd like to attend to. It's important that I get back there and insure that his legacy goes on—the way he would have wanted it to prosper."

"Andi and I are praying for you every day. So, enough of this serious talk; tell me about the men of San Francisco." Belinda giggled as if they were back at camp, toilet-papering the counselor's cabin. "Any cute ones? Anyone worth getting me in a black polka-dot bridesmaid's gown for?"

"Oh, you must mean the men that are beating at my door right now? Hold on a second; I need to tell them to cut it out. I can barely hear you." Collette paused a moment. "I'm telling you, Belinda, they just can't get enough of me. I have to keep a stick nearby. Always. Oh," she sighed, "the life of a beauty queen—it can get so tiring."

"Are you through?" Belinda asked through a chuckle.

"In all seriousness, that is why I called. You will never guess what I'm doing this weekend. Only you could appreciate this to the fullest, so I had to share."

"You've got a date with destiny," Belinda answered dramatically.

"Well, sort of. This is what I called to tell you. I'm going canoeing with a man from church."

Uproarious laughter filled Collette's ear. "You're going canoeing? You? Now, this man I have to meet. If he can get you into a canoe, he must be something special."

"Well, it's not really a date," Collette clarified. "Kyle is the leader of the singles' group at church. He asked me to accompany him, but the entire Sunday school class will be there, so I don't know if he's just being kind because I'm the new gal. The missionary's kid."

"Collette, don't sell yourself short. No one is doing you any favors by spending time with you. Quit feeling sorry for yourself and remember how lucky that man is to spend time with you!"

She smiled widely. "Oh, I knew I could count on you, Belinda. I feel better already. And you're right—who wouldn't love to spend the day with me?" She giggled. Collette and Belinda continued to talk until late into the night. It was as though they'd never been apart.

The bitter chill of the cold, moist wind rushed through Collette, and she questioned the sanity of cruising down a whitecapped river on this unseasonably cold, autumn morning. Kyle looked dashing in a black, formfitting wet suit that accentuated his muscular body and covered him from neck to toe. Collette sighed. In that outfit, he wouldn't have any motivation to keep the two of them out of the water. He'd be toasty regardless.

Kyle held up another wet suit as they stood on the bank of the rushing Russian River. "You may need this. I had an extra one, so I brought it along for you." He smiled.

Collette took one look at the tight-fitting apparel and thought, *There is no way I'm going to look like an overfilled Michelin, ready to blow, by snuggling into that thing.* "I thought you told me how excellent you were with a canoe.

There was no way we were going to tip over. Is any of this ringing a bell?" she asked with a grin. "I'm safe with you, remember?"

"Now, Collette, look at that water. I can't guarantee anything but fun." He smiled a lopsided grin and handed her the wet suit.

"I'm not putting that thing on." She let out a short laugh to let him know how ludicrous the idea was.

"Okay, but when you look like a drowned rat, don't blame me."

"I'll use it for my dry clothes." Collette took the suit and wrapped her extra set of clothing in it. She wore a navy sweatsuit, and Mrs. Combie had applied waterproof mascara for the day. She zipped up the provided life jacket and hoped for the best. She'd rather get wet than wear a rubber suit any day. Any sane woman would.

Collette went to the edge of the river and put her things into the long, silver, battered canoe that awaited on shore. The thrashed condition of the boat did nothing to build her confidence. All of the other adults were milling about, pairing off to get into the boats. It was then that Collette was approached by a tall, svelte brunette in a navy wet suit that left nothing to the imagination.

The woman spoke. "You must be new. Kyle mentioned you would be coming along today." Collette felt herself scrutinized by the taller lady. "I'm Trisha. I was Kyle's partner last year at this event. I was new then, too. I guess you're the lucky one this year."

Nothing the woman said was impolite or even unfriendly. It was the way she said it—in a tone that exuded superiority. Collette knew she was oversensitive, so she returned the greeting warmly, hoping she'd just misunderstood the woman's implication.

"I'm Collette Ambers, and I have to agree Kyle is wonderful with people. He definitely has a gift for making one feel welcome," she responded with a sweet smile.

Trisha gave a short grunt followed by a slight, haughty laugh. "Sure, he does. Kyle is always giving his time to some charity." The smile from Collette's face evaporated, and her confidence flew away on the morning breeze, leaving her feeling like the gawky seven-year-old waiting to be picked. The fat girl. The one the last team got stuck with.

She watched the athletic, slender woman sashay off to flirt with a canoe partner. Like a pack of ducks, all the men followed down the hill to catch Trisha's attention. Men. Waddling toward her without the slightest understanding about why.

Collette knew better than to be upset by such a calculated move. Still, logic flew out the window, leaving only a sharp, aching pain in her heart, reminding her that Kyle was only doing her a favor. She tried to recapture Belinda's words and even prayed for God's strength right then and there.

Kyle returned with a broad grin, holding up his fists like a victorious boxer. "You ready? Everyone's paired off and it's time to go!" He started to hum the *Rocky* theme and took her hand to help her into the canoe. She remained stoic along the riverbank. Noticing her reluctance, he stopped his winning tune.

"What's the matter, Collette? I'll do everything I can

to make sure we don't end up in the drink. Come on; this is going to be so fun. Did you get the lunch packed in the canoe?"

Collette's bottom lip quivered when she tried to speak. A tall man yelled from up the river. "Kyle! Lynn just got here, and she doesn't have a partner."

Kyle patted her arm. "Collette, I'll be right back. Duty calls—just a minute." He ran to fix the problem, and Collette wished more than anything that she had a car and could get back home. That would solve everyone's problem. Lynn would have a partner, and Kyle wouldn't have to feel responsible for Collette. She didn't feel like wearing a game face all day. She just wanted to disappear under a rock so Kyle could enjoy his day with friends.

"Collette?" A woman of about thirty-five approached her. She wore a warm smile.

"Yes." Collette wiped the uncooperative tear from her cheek.

The woman pointed behind her. "I saw you just talked to Trisha. I don't know what she said to you, but she's done that to all of us women. Made us want to cry. I saw it the minute she walked away from you, and I remembered that feeling. I think it's Trisha's version of the initiation ritual. Don't let her get to you. She's just a jealous, bitter woman. Try and see her for the lost soul she is. I'm Audrey, by the way." The woman held out a hand.

Collette swallowed the huge lump in her throat. She would never understand the type of person who intentionally hurt another. Her parents had always taught her to care for others as part of simple good manners.

"Is Trisha a Christian?" she asked tentatively, looking toward the slender brunette.

"Let's put it this way. She claims she is, but I have yet to see any fruit. Not that I'm one to judge anyone's Christianity. But Trisha's faith comes on pretty strong when Kyle is around. When he's not, it all but disappears." Audrey let out a guilty laugh. "I'm sorry; now I'm no better than her. Do you have a partner for the canoe?"

"I think Kyle is coming back. I just hope I'm not ruining his fun. This isn't exactly my sport. Trisha looks a little better prepared." The pangs of jealousy struck.

"Are you kidding? With Kyle's love of all things ministry? You two were made for each other. Trust me; Kyle sees right through the likes of Trisha Waring."

"Kyle and I are just friends. Nothing more," Collette corrected. "I didn't mean to imply anything," she added nervously.

"That may be, Collette. But I'll tell you something about Kyle. The woman that catches his eye will have to be more than beautiful on the outside. Like Trisha there. Kyle and I have been friends a long time, and he stays in the Word, Collette. He won't fall for the temptress of Proverbs." Audrey winked. "See ya at lunch!" With a wave she was gone, leaving only her wake of enthusiasm.

Kyle came back, and Collette felt a marked improvement in her emotions. They settled into the little canoe, which rocked unstably, and Collette's heart raced. She knew her ride was bound to end just like the one with Belinda had. In the water—the cold, swirling, racing water. She felt a rush of adrenaline as they pushed off into the whitecapped river. Her stomach felt as though it were still back on shore.

"Wooo-hoo!" Kyle yelled. "Is this fun or what? This is my favorite social of the whole year! Woo-hoo!"

Collette couldn't help but crack up. Kyle, whom she knew as the sophisticated controller of a high-tech company, the man who took her to an elegant dinner and play, was acting just like a teenager on a roller coaster. He maneuvered the canoe through the water with ease, barking out orders, which Collette instantly followed. The canoe raced easily through the rushing water, making the shore pass at a lightning speed.

Kyle and she were soon in a rhythm of rowing, and their speed increased. Collette's enthusiasm started to surface. She laughed relentlessly at the thrill their speed caused. It was so exhilarating to be streaming through the water with the knowledge that at any moment they might be thrown into it.

One by one they passed the other canoes, tipped and empty of their inhabitants. Kyle would raise his arm in victory, with every boat. "Teamwork," he'd yell, then laugh.

Collette felt a guilty pleasure as they passed Trisha with her flat, wet, stringy hair, screaming at her partner. Her copilot, on the other hand, laughed mightily, unswayed by her outrage.

Collette began to let her guard down and actually started to enjoy the swift, adventurous ride. Soon, her confidence had increased, and she knew just which way to lean when they'd approach a raging whitecap swirl. Suddenly, she noticed they were coming dangerously close to a gnarled, knotted collection of tree roots along a cliff. "Ahhhh!" she screamed.

The path of the water was leading them right to the cliff and a branch that hung ominously over the river. Collette closed her eyes to prepare for their destiny. Now she knew why the canoe was so mangled.

"Lean straight back!" Kyle yelled.

Collette went back without a moment's hesitation. She opened her eyes just in time to see the tree's leaves go right over her head as the canoe slid alongside the shore between the cliff edge and the overhanging branch. She heard the scrape of the branch alongside the canoe, but she and Kyle were unscathed. And dry.

"Woo-hoo!" Kyle held up his oar straight over his head. "Triumphant!" He began to sing the *Rocky* theme again and Collette was lost in her laughter.

"Pride goeth before destruction, you know." Collette raised her eyebrows and put a fist to her hip.

"I am invincible today."

Collette just rolled her eyes.

When the two-hour ride was over, Collette felt like it had lasted a mere two minutes. The constant action and the effort to stay focused had made the time fly. She was disappointed when the water smoothed and their canoe washed ashore, just in time for lunch.

Kyle hopped out onto shore and held out his hand for Collette. "My lady."

"We made it. I can't believe it. I'm dry!"

"I told you. We are incredible together, don't you think? When I told you to go straight back, you never even flinched. You just did it. What a pair!" Kyle's encouragement was unwavering.

"I agree," she replied.

"Why didn't you hesitate?"

"Hey, in Africa when somebody tells you to get down, you don't waste any time. I was trained for this."

Kyle looked around for signs of other singles' group members. "Well, no sense in waiting for the rest of them. Clearly, we are the only ones who didn't dunk, or others would be here by now. What did you bring for lunch?"

"Egg salad."

"My favorite!"

"I know. Pastor Holmes told me he can always tell when you're in the office because he can smell your sandwich."

"I think I'm offended."

She crinkled her nose. "He's right, you know."

"Now I'm definitely offended. All that free audit work I do, and what do I get? Criticized for my choice of sandwich."

"You're serving the Lord, remember?"

"Where in the Bible does it say a man serving the Lord with his mighty accounting skills should be subjected to grievous sandwich mockery?"

"Blessed are ye, when men shall revile you and persecute you."

"A woman who knows her Bible," he said nodding his head. "Impressive."

"Yes, but I do think it's stretching things a bit to complain of persecution just because people observe that your sandwich stinks."

"Never fully appreciated. The story of my life."

She unwrapped the sandwiches, which she'd folded up in the wet suit. "I put tomatoes and pickles on them. I hope you don't mind."

"Mind? That's the way I like them best. I'm just too lazy to get it all out in the morning. This is ideal. You are fabulous, Collette." He planted a short kiss on her cheek.

She grinned sheepishly and waited for his prayer.

They enjoyed a quiet lunch, discussing their plans for the future of their ministries and all the ways God had blessed them. Slowly the other canoe pairs trickled in, wet and cantankerous.

"Hey, Collette!" Her new friend Audrey approached them. "How on earth did you stay dry?"

"She had the best partner," Kyle quipped.

"Certainly not the most humble." Collette raised her eyebrows at him.

"A couple of us are getting together next Saturday and going to an amusement park. You want to come?"

Collette hesitated.

"You know—roller coasters, cheesy stage shows, cotton candy, basically acting like we're twelve."

Collette smiled. "I'd love to."

"Great. I'll get your number from Kyle, and we'll work out the details later. Enjoy your lunch, although I don't know how you can stand to eat next to him. Pee-ewww. He's either eating egg salad or liverwurst. Ack!"

Collette and Kyle broke into laughter.

Chapter 5

Collette arrived home that evening to several letters from possible supporters and a single letter from Africa. It was sent by her father's ministry partner, and she tore open the envelope, anxious to hear word of back home. She hoped it contained some choice morsel of souls saved that would help her raise more money, but its contents left her numb.

Dearest Collette,

As you know, your father's ministry continues even in the wake of your absence, with the Kassarani people taking most of the burden. We have lost funding due to your father's death, but I am certain you are taking care of that as this letter finds you.

I have come up with an idea that I think will meet both our needs, and I hope you will consider it seriously. Although it may come as a shock to you, I am talking of a marriage between the two of us. I, being unmarried, am not as trustworthy to the Africans as your father once was. You, being a woman alone in the world, can use your married status to build more funding for the mission.

Beyond that, I think it adds legitimacy to your ministry to be a married woman. We would no longer live in the run-down mission station at Kassarani. I have taken a nice flat in Nairobi, which would be more than ample to raise a family in. Please contact me as soon as possible so I can make arrangements for your passage. There is funding available to pay for your prompt return.

Sincerely,
Hank Guilding

Collette read the letter again and again, uncertain of its meaning. Hank had never given her the time of day before this letter arrived. She barely knew him, and now he was discussing children like they were stockholdings. Hank had taken over shortly after her father had taken ill. Collette wondered how they would run the Kassarani mission from Nairobi but felt Hank must know what he was doing. He had, after all, raised money that allowed the church school in Nairobi to gain computer access, which made training new pastors much easier—easily allowing them to translate Bible verses.

The letter seemed to offer her everything she said she wanted: passage back to Africa, a continuation of her father's ministry, and a future with children. So why did her mind drift to Kyle? What did Kyle Brighton have to do with any of this? She knew she had to pray. Pray and call her friends from camp. They would know what to do.

She dialed Amanda immediately. Amanda had been

engaged long enough to know if marriage would be a good decision. Yes, Amanda would know.

"Amanda? It's Collette."

"Collette? Oh, Collette, how are you? Are things going well in San Francisco? I can't wait to see you in Washington. Have you gained enough support to go back after February? You're not going to miss our reunion, are you?"

"Amanda!"

"What?"

"Let me answer a question," Collette jokingly chastised.

"Oh, sorry. I'm just so excited to hear your voice. Your letters have been so few and far between lately. Tell me; what's happening?"

"I–I'm thinking about getting married."

"Married? To whom? Did you meet somebody in San Francisco? Belinda told me you went canoeing. Is it him?"

Collette's eyes closed. No, it wasn't Kyle. With the mention of him came the painful realization that she wanted it to be. She coveted the idea of Kyle offering marriage, but that was ridiculous. Two mercy dates were hardly going to bring a proposal. She shook the thought from her head. "No, no; it's my father's ministry partner, Hank Guilding. He wants me to come down and help him get the mission back on its feet."

"Well, how long have you known him?" Amanda asked casually.

"I don't even know him really," she admitted.

"How can you even think of spending your life with a man you don't know?"

The question brought tears to her eyes. *Because I'm not*

sure there will ever be anybody else. Certainly, there will never be someone like Kyle Brighton.

This was a chance for marriage, for children, for her ministry. But how did she share that without sounding desperate? Even with her closest friends, the idea of letting go of her deepest fears proved too difficult.

"My father's ministry is having trouble. Hank wants to solve the problem, and so do I. That's reason enough, isn't it?"

"Why not let God solve it? I'm sure He can do a better job than either of you."

"Amanda, that's easy for you to say. You've always had men around. You don't know what it's like to be alone. Really alone."

"Maybe not, but being together with someone and still being alone can be worse," Amanda answered cryptically. "Collette, I don't want you to do anything until you've prayed deeply about this. Didn't Belinda just tell me you had a date this weekend? Was that Hank?"

"No, Hank is still in Africa. And it wasn't a date. It was a canoe trip with the singles' group, and the leader took pity on me and dragged me along. Kyle," she said wistfully. "His name is Kyle."

"Well, what does Kyle think of you getting married?"

"Trust me; he wouldn't care. He just feels sorry for me. It's part of his ministry to assimilate the new people. I'm his ministry," she answer pitifully.

"Okay, I'm confused. Do you care about Kyle?"

"Kyle is incredible. He's gorgeous, sweet, loves the Lord, and works tirelessly for the church. He does audits, runs the singles' group, works with inner-city kids. You name it, Kyle is there."

"And Hank?"

Collette shrugged her shoulders unconsciously. "I don't know. He runs my father's ministry now. That has to say something for him."

"Collette, it sounds to me like you're falling in love with Kyle. A marriage of convenience would never live up to that."

Collette let out a long, deep sigh. "Amanda, Kyle would never look twice at me. He thinks of me as a puppy that follows along enthusiastically. He's handsome and sought after by all the beautiful women. I very nearly got attacked by a jealous woman at the canoe trip. Kyle wouldn't think of me in that way. He just wouldn't."

"Have you asked him?"

"I've only known him for a short time." But it felt like so much longer. "How can I possibly ask him if he's interested? It's not exactly my style."

"You said yourself you're going back to Africa. So if Kyle rejects you, what do you have to lose? You'll never see him again. Don't leave without finding out. It will torment you."

"I can't. I can't do it."

"Just don't do anything until you've prayed. You can't leave for Africa until after February anyway, so just let this proposal ride. If it's meant to be, Hank will wait for you," Amanda, the voice of reason, said.

※ ※

A month passed. A long, arduous month of praying and

trying to avoid Kyle's friendly advances. Every week he picked her up for church and took her out to brunch afterward. It was a welcome diversion from her typically boring life. Kyle and she would reconvene every week to discuss their ups and downs and share their triumphs of the week. Kyle had such an easygoing air about him; he didn't realize how his simple phone calls and casual lunches led her on, elevating her hopes. She hoped he felt an inkling of the love that was growing inside her.

The hope was enough, and it brought her joy, more joy than she would ever receive marrying a man she didn't love. Collette couldn't bring herself to accept Hank's offer. Not yet. Not until she'd exhausted anything that might exist between her and Kyle. It wasn't like Hank loved her or was waiting anxiously for her answer, but at the same time, she couldn't close the door. Not when it might be God's will for her.

Finally Collette decided she had to send some kind of acknowledgment to Hank that she'd received his letter.

> *Dear Hank:*
> *Needless to say, your offer of marriage came as a complete shock, but I understand your love for the ministry and our partnership makes good sense. I am prayerfully considering your offer and promise to answer you by January.*
>
> > *Serving Him beside you,*
> > *Collette Ambers*

She looked at it. There was nothing romantic in the

letter, nothing that implied any attachment to her heart. That fact saddened her. Collette added up her pledges from missionary supporters and thought she finally had enough to work with. Perhaps she could go back to Africa without the aid of marriage or a sponsoring organization. Hank would be there, and they could get to know one another. She had to be sure about the finances.

Collette drew in a deep breath and dialed Kyle's number at work. She hated to bother him there, but she had important business to discuss. Important business he could help her finish and then get her out of his hair forever. He would probably be grateful.

"Kyle Brighton's office," a young woman answered.

"Um, yes. This is Collette Ambers. Is Mr. Brighton in?"

"Sure, Miss Ambers. Can you hold a moment please?"

Almost instantly, Kyle picked up the line. "Collette! I'm so excited to hear from you. This week has been so hectic. I haven't had time to call, but I've been thinking about you. How's life? Audrey said you did the ballet last week. Was it fun?"

Collette ignored the questions; she was too intent on her purpose, too nervous she'd give away the feelings she was trying to keep to herself. She steeled herself, trying to gain the nerve to ask for his help. "Kyle, I was wondering if—"

"We might have dinner tonight?" he interrupted. "That sounds wonderful. What time should I pick you up?"

"Kyle!" she scolded. "I'm trying to ask you something important."

"I'm answering you. I'm not busy, and I'd love to have

dinner tonight. I thought I made that clear."

"I didn't ask you to dinner tonight," she said through her grin.

"Then, I guess I'd better ask you, huh? Collette, would you like to have dinner with me tonight?"

"You are impossible."

"But lovable, don't you think? So what time?"

"I called to ask you something about my ministry. Something very important."

"So you can ask me tonight over dinner. What time?"

"I give up!" Collette relented. "Seven o'clock."

"Great. Oh, and Collette, thanks for the invitation."

"Good-bye, Kyle."

"Bye, hon. See ya tonight." Hon? If only that word carried the romantic meanings for him that it did for her. She knew Kyle saw himself simply as a big, overprotective brother for her.

Kyle selected a quiet little Italian restaurant in the heart of North Beach. The ambiance was less than stellar, so Collette had to assume the food was spectacular. There were only eight tables in the entire restaurant, and tacky, smudged still-lifes of fruit lined the walls.

"So what was so important that you had to see me tonight for dinner?" Kyle looked at her with his deep brown eyes, the epitome of sincerity. "You were a little pushy with the invitation, but I didn't want to say anything." He winked.

"I'm going to ignore that. I wanted to speak with you about my father's ministry. I have a chance to go back home and run it again."

Kyle's face went ashen. "How? How do you have a chance?"

"Well, I've raised quite a bit in support from my dad's friends. Apparently, they want to see the mission continue. Since they're not members of Bayside Community, they aren't concerned about a woman running the ministry. I was hoping you'd look at the numbers and tell me if you thought it might be enough, if I've figured in all the expenses properly, or if you think I should secure more funding. I want to spend the money wisely."

"Sure, I'd be happy to check it, but, Collette, I have to question your going into Kenya without a sponsoring church."

"I'll be fine, Kyle. The Lord will look after me."

"There's a reason organizations are so particular about who they send."

"Are you saying I'm not capable of running the ministry? Because I already did so for eight months while my father was sick."

"No, I know you're capable; I just don't know that you'll be safe from the harms that can befall a young woman alone in a strange country."

"It's not a strange country, Kyle. It's my home. This is a strange country."

"Still, being alone—"

"There's something else, a little detail that would help me secure more funding, perhaps even from Bayside Community Church itself, and I wouldn't be alone. My father's successor asked me to marry him to help further the cause of the ministry."

"Hank Guilding?"

"Yes. Do you know him?" Collette was incredulous.

"Collette, you're not going back to Africa." The line of his mouth was severe.

"Of course I am. What do you mean I'm not going back?"

"I mean only over my dead body are you going back to Africa to run that mission with Hank Guilding. Does that make it any clearer?"

"Kyle, I've never seen you like this. What on earth has come over you?"

"Collette, you can't be seriously thinking of marrying Hank Guilding to further the cause of this ministry."

"Why not? I think it's a noble thing to do." She squared her shoulders. "It's not like staying here gives me any better offers."

"There are reasons that ministry has come to an end. You need to accept that."

"It hasn't come to an end."

"Maybe not, but the African nationals are capable of running it now on their own."

"How would you know that, Kyle?"

"I do the books at the church, remember? Your father left that ministry in the hands of the Kenyans. He wanted you in America. Let it go. Your father's final ministry report—"

"Has been some kind of secret, hasn't it, Kyle? I've never seen that report, yet I'm just supposed to trust you that my father wanted to end his ministry."

"Yes. When have I given you any reason not to trust me?"

She ignored his beseeching brown eyes. "We were training three new pastors a year down there, Kyle. You would stop that work? Hank Guilding seems to think—"

"Hank Guilding is an idiot."

She gasped. "Kyle! I can't believe you said that."

"Collette, there are things you don't know. Reasons you need to stay here and out of Kenya."

"Kyle, if you have something to tell me, you should tell me."

"I've already said too much. Why can't you just trust me like you did that day in the canoe? Without asking questions—just knowing that I'll take care of you."

"Because you won't take care of me, Kyle. I'm a grown woman, and it's not your place to take care of me. If you have reasons why I shouldn't go back to Africa, you should tell me openly. Don't make me play a game of twenty questions. Following your orders in a canoe is a little different than deciding on my life's work."

"Do you love Hank Guilding?"

"I don't even know him. Well, barely. He was there at the end of my father's life, but I can't say I was interested in much else at the time. I was so busy attending to Dad's needs and making sure the ministry was operating effectively."

"Collette, there's your reason right there. You are going to sit here and tell me you're considering marrying someone else, a man you don't even love, when you're on a date with me?"

"I didn't know I was on a date. We go out all the time; when did this become a date? I thought we were friends. I called you to ask you for accounting advice. To find out if I had enough money to go back to Africa, and you bamboozled me into this dinner. Just tell me if I have enough money, and I'll leave you alone if that's what you want."

"I can't believe you're asking me this. No. You don't have enough money, and you are not going back to Africa."

"Kyle, my whole life has been run by others. I am finally independent, and now you want me to abandon my life's work with no other reason than that I'm supposed to trust you."

"Yes," he said simply.

"No, I won't do it. I'm going back to Africa, and I'll find another accountant to handle the funding."

"No, Collette, you won't."

"Check please," she said to the waiter, getting up from her seat.

"Collette, sit down." Kyle pulled her down, his patience clearly waning.

"Why are you doing this to me?" she said desperately, fighting back the tears that welled up in her eyes.

"I don't know how to make it any plainer to you. Your father didn't want you in Africa. He left explicit instructions that you were to remain in America."

"Not to me, he didn't. Kyle, everyone seems to know this but me. As far as I'm concerned, my father wanted me to continue his ministry just as I had been doing while he was ill. My father had a love for the Kenyans that surpassed words. It would have been his crowning glory to have me follow in his footsteps. He never said anything to me about coming back to the States, and he had plenty of opportunity."

Kyle looked down at the table. "I know."

"Then explain this to me. If you have all the answers, give them to me. That's all I'm asking from you. I thought we were friends."

His head shot up. "Of course, we're friends. Collette, I care deeply for you."

"Then tell me why you don't want me to go back to Africa." Collette hoped against hope it was because he cared for her, that he wanted her to stay in America, but somehow she knew that would only be true in her dreams. Kyle Brighton was beyond her. Way beyond.

"I can't. Isn't it enough that your father wanted you here in America?"

"No, because I don't believe he did. To see his daughter on the mission field would have brought him more joy than I can say."

"I don't know why he never told you that Kassarani was finished, able to stand on its own, but he told Pastor Holmes, and it was in his final mission report."

"Kyle, my father wanted me to marry and have a family. I can have all that in Africa, don't you see?"

"You can have that here," he said confidently, sitting back in his chair.

"Can I, Kyle? Can I really? You're the only man here that seems to avoid the fact that I'm fat. I'm fat, Kyle. In case you haven't noticed, I'm fat, and the Christian men of America are looking for Christie Brinkley with a godly heart. I don't fit your mold here, where women bounce around on television in nothing but swimsuits. In Africa, Hank Guilding will see me for who I am on the inside, a woman who loves the Lord and is willing to serve Him no matter what. A woman of character with a penchant for Snickers bars. That's who I am."

"Do you think I don't see inside, Collette? Do you think I'm so shallow that I would focus solely on your outside? Which, by the way, I find beautiful and curvaceous. What kind of man do you think I am? Do you think I would ask you out relentlessly to make you feel better?"

Yes, yes I do. Collette burst into tears. "No, I don't want you to say all the right things to make me feel better, Kyle. I want you to tell me the truth."

Kyle dropped a ten-dollar bill on the table. "Come on; let's go. Neither of us will be able to eat now." They scampered out of the restaurant, and Collette fell into Kyle's outstretched arms, needing his comfort, yet despising herself for falling victim to it. "Collette, I would never lie to you. Ever. I have no reason to lie to you. You're my friend, and I love you."

Like a brother loves his sister. "Then why can't you tell me why my father insisted I stay here?"

"Because the information was given to me as an officer of the church. I don't have the right to tell you. It would break my vow to keep financial records to myself. If I tell you, Collette, I ruin my reputation at the church and harm Pastor Holmes's leadership."

"But if you don't tell me, I'm going back to Africa. Because there's no reason for me to stay here."

"There are plenty of reasons to stay here. What about me?"

"What about you, Kyle? You're a really sweet man with heartfelt intentions, of that I have no doubt. But does it really go any further than that?" She searched his warm brown eyes. He couldn't answer the question, and she wanted to kick herself for asking it. She knew the answer to her question.

Amanda was right about one thing—she'd never wonder again. She could leave for Africa free and clear. Kyle's silence spoke volumes. There was no future for them, and Hank's proposal remained the only one she'd ever receive. Without love or emotion.

The stillness continued as they drove to Mrs. Combie's. Neither one was able to break it. Walking into the modest house, she took one look at Mrs. Combie, and her tears started again. She retreated to her room and sobbed some more, heart-wrenching tears that made her wish two things: one, that she'd never met Kyle Brighton, and two, that she was a size four, model-thin waif with sunken cheekbones that he might fall in love with.

❧

Collette went into work early the next morning, anxious to get her mind on anything else. Anything other than Kyle Brighton and his blatant refusal to love her. She had some typing to finish up, and it was best done before the constant ringing of the phone caused interruptions. Once at the church office, she was surprised that the door was already unlocked. She heard Pastor Holmes in the back, and she walked down the hall to let him know she was there. Kyle's voice stopped her.

"I'm telling you, Pastor Holmes, she has a right to know. I feel dishonest for keeping it to myself, and she keeps pressing me."

"Kyle, we had an agreement with her father. I can't break a dying man's vow because his daughter doesn't understand his last wishes. Just wait until we have word on Hank Guilding, then everything will be out in the open. Your work at the church must be confidential or it breaks the bond we have with members. The accountability issues, in my opinion, are more important than her knowing why right now."

"You're right. I just needed to be reminded."

Collette started to back away, feeling her presence was dishonest, but something willed her to stay and listen.

"Kyle, your work with Collette is done. Your ministry making sure she's settled into the singles' group is over. She's had plenty of time to assimilate and make friends. There are plenty of young women who can take over for you now. You're overstepping your boundaries, and it is time to find a new ministry."

A ministry? Collette *was* just a ministry to Kyle. She closed her eyes in agony. It was worse than she'd first expected. She scrambled to get out of the office, tears streaming freely once again as she rushed through the glass doors, throwing them open.

She ran across the parking lot and headed to a spot behind a nearby grandfather oak where she wouldn't be seen by anyone in the church. She threw herself down on the ground, crying with all the strength she had left within her.

She would make arrangements that very afternoon to get back to Africa. Even if it meant missing her reunion with her beloved camp friends. Even if it meant marrying a man she didn't love.

It was only early December. Three more months of life in the States seemed beyond her grasp. It seemed like all she did in America was cry. She wanted to know what it felt like to laugh again. To feel elevated and surrounded by God's love instead of being trampled on and alone.

She stopped crying. Reality hit her like a ton of homemade Kenyan bricks. She wasn't sad because she was lonely, or in America, or even because she was over-weight. She was despondent because she was wallowing in self-pity, focusing only on herself. In Africa, she never had time to feel sorry for herself because she was always caring for someone else.

Collette needed to get into a ministry and fast. Even if it only lasted for the next three months until she left for Africa. She needed to quit wallowing in her pathetic existence and start thinking of others.

Collette waited until Kyle's Saab pulled away from the church and then wandered back into the office. She wiped her eyes with the back of her hands and marched directly into Pastor Holmes's office. He looked up and sat back in his chair. He seemed to expect her visit.

"Collette," he said evenly.

"Pastor Holmes, I need something more to do here than just my job. I need a ministry. I want to work with the homeless. Can you suggest anything?"

"There's Inner-City Ministries downtown."

She held her palms up. "No, nothing where Kyle Brighton is involved. I want something else. What else is downtown?"

"Collette, you shouldn't blame Kyle. He's just doing his job."

"I know. I don't blame Kyle, but it's time he moved on," she said, repeating the pastor's own words.

He simply nodded.

"Pastor Holmes, I feel badly we've had so many rough encounters. I know what you did for my father. I know how you supported him, so I know that your intentions have to be good. I'm sorry we don't see eye-to-eye on the subject of getting me back to the mission."

"I am too, Collette. Very sorry, indeed." He handed her a business card. "Audrey Banks works for them part-time. It's a soup kitchen near Grace Memorial Church in the Tenderloin District."

"Thank you, Pastor Holmes."

"Do you know what the Tenderloin is?"

"No."

"It's where the drug addicts live, Collette. It's probably the worst section of the city, so keep that in mind when you go down there. Kassarani may have the poor, but the Tenderloin has the desperate and drug-induced."

"Thanks for the warning. I'll be careful."

Chapter 6

ollette spent Christmas Day serving up turkey and stuffing for the homeless of San Francisco in a sparsely furnished warehouse with makeshift counters. The people were so appreciative that Collette chastised herself for waiting so long to serve. She gave each person a smile and wished them a Merry Christmas, longing to do more than simply provide one meal. The faces she saw were drawn with pain and years of hard living. It was nearly impossible to tell how old each person was because they were prematurely aged from years of drug abuse and suffering.

After an eight-hour day on her feet, she was exhausted. The backbreaking work of carrying and serving turkeys all day was more than she'd bargained for. When the last helping was served, she retreated to a corner table and dropped into a chair with a deep heavy sigh.

"You's a good lady." She looked up to see an older man sitting in front of his turkey dinner. He was alone and hunched over the meal. He didn't look up when he spoke, but since there was no one else about, she had to assume he had spoken. His clothes were filthy, and his shoes had holes in them. "We don't see many young women down here alone. God bless you for coming."

"May God bless you too," she answered.

"He already has, missy. I got a nice meal set before me today by a right pretty gal that gave up her day to come down here. You's a nice girl. You'd do your daddy proud."

His comment gave her the will to get up. She patted his back. "Thank you. I needed to hear that today." She smiled and walked back into the kitchen to finish cleaning up.

God's message came to her that very second. He didn't want her in Africa. She had pushed so hard to make it work when God had kept sending her negative answers. The homeless man was right: Her father would have been happy no matter where she served, as long as she was serving. She looked to the man once again, certain God had sent him to give her the message, but he was gone. His plate and any sign of him had been removed. She blinked a few times, wondering if she'd imagined the whole thing.

She looked to the ceiling. "Thank You, Lord. Thank You for making it clear." She had wanted to save her father's ministry, which, according to the Kassarani people themselves, didn't need saving. She'd wanted to marry and have children, but Hank Guilding's offer made her cringe. How could she marry someone she didn't love when she loved another? She wanted to be useful, but she had learned today she could be useful wherever God placed her. For now, it looked like San Francisco was home. She would have to learn to be content here.

"Collette?"

She looked up to see Kyle's brown eyes gazing down on her.

"Kyle, what are you doing here?"

"I miss you, Collette. I came to tell you why your father didn't want you to go back to Africa. You need a reason, and I'm here to give you one. It's my present."

"No, I can't let you do that. You have a reputation to protect, and the fact is, it doesn't really matter. I can serve just as easily here in San Francisco. I just didn't want to. There's not a route back to Africa that makes sense. No route that comes from God, anyway. They're all created solely on human power to accomplish my will instead of His. It's just so hard to believe that His will doesn't have me out on the mission field somewhere. It seems so selfless, but I guess when you put yourself on the throne, nothing is selfless. Listen to me; I'm rambling."

He didn't say another word. He just bent down and hugged her, taking her up in his muscular arms. She grabbed him with all she was worth. *I love you, Kyle. I love you. And I'll never marry another for less than this feeling. Never.*

"You're going to need clothes," he stated emphatically.

"What?"

"Clothes. What's that they say? When in Rome, do as the Romans do? Well, you need to dress like the San Franciscans."

"I don't need any clothes. I can just get a naked role, acting in a play downtown." She giggled.

"Collette Ambers, you are never going to let me live that down, are you?"

"Probably not."

"I want to take you shopping. I want to buy you a San Francisco wardrobe, befitting of a queen. Well, at least a church secretary."

"Kyle, I can't allow you to do that. I'm perfectly capable of supplying my own clothes. I've learned some very valuable lessons today."

"The truth is, I'm actually very selfish. If I see you in that worn-out black dress one more time, I'm going to personally rip it from your closet and destroy it. Is that clear?"

Her mouth dropped open, mocking her fake astonishment. "Well, I never. At least my sandwiches don't stink." She gave a lopsided grin.

"Tomorrow all the clearance sales begin. We'll start early, say eight o'clock?"

"You're kidding me, right?"

"I've never been more serious. I make a controller's salary and live like a missionary. Nothing would give me more pleasure than to spend money on my best friend. Because she deserves it and because I love her."

Collette swallowed hard. His compliments were getting harder and harder to take with a simple smile. Just exactly what did he mean by his best friend? They'd gotten to the point that spending time together and talking on the phone were natural to them—perhaps that's what he had meant. But she couldn't stop herself from hoping, from wishing he meant more. That he was beginning to love her just a little like a man loves a woman.

Macy's, San Francisco. Eight floors of nothing but retail.

And it was all on sale. When Collette had arrived in the city, months earlier, she would have never ventured into such a crowded frenzy. Or allowed Kyle to know she shopped in the women's section for bigger sizes. But ever since that evening in that tiny little Italian restaurant, when she'd blurted out that she was fat, she'd been given a new freedom.

Now she had complete confidence in her appearance and the newfound knowledge that God truly looked at the heart. Yes, she was fat. So what? Neither one of them had ever mentioned her size since, but it was no longer the white elephant in the room. She'd said it; he'd heard it. It was over. Their friendship had survived.

They took the elevator up to the women's section, and Kyle found himself a chair. Collette picked up a dress with a similar pattern to her African clothes, and Kyle got up from his chair. "Uh-oh. I can see we're going to need a little guidance here."

"And, excuse me, but since when did you become the editor of *Vogue*?"

He laughed. "Humor me. I'm picturing you in something stylish. Something that shows off your beautiful figure. Something you can wear to my company dinner next week. I was thinking a new black dress, definitely a new black dress. We'll have a funeral for the other one."

"Your company dinner?"

"You know, schmoozing with the boss, avoiding all annoying coworkers, that kind of thing."

"You want me to go?" She laid a hand on her chest.

"Of course, Collette. Maybe I haven't made my

intentions clear. I'm a little shy in this area." He looked at the floor.

"You, shy? Now that's a good one." She laughed, but he didn't join her.

The line of his mouth straightened. "All men are shy when they think their hearts might be trampled on." He crossed his arms in front of him and didn't look at her.

She grabbed his shoulder to turn him toward her. "Do you think I would ever trample on your heart, Kyle?" She put the dress on a nearby rack and stared up at him. She forced his chin down, so he'd look at her.

His uninterrupted gaze held her eyes intently, and Collette waited with anticipation, the noise and chaos around her disappearing in his deep brown eyes. He bent down and kissed her, his lips firm and his intentions much more than friendly. He pulled away momentarily, but then kissed her again when he felt her response. It was her first kiss. And it was everything she'd dreamed about. Kyle's kiss warmed her to her toes.

"I love you, Collette," he whispered.

"Well, after that kiss, I don't think I'm your little sister anymore." He didn't smile. "I'm sorry. I'm nervous. I joke when I'm nervous. I love you too, Kyle. I think I have from that very first night when you replaced my Snickers bar with an elegant steak dinner and a play. Even if I didn't get to find out what happened in the second act."

"It doesn't matter what happened in the second act. It's more important what happened in the theater that night. When you followed me out and you didn't complain, I knew you could be content anywhere. None of the women I've ever dated have been comfortable with the fact that God could call me out of the high-tech controlling business at any time, leaving me with next to nothing for salary. You're the kind of woman who would follow a man to the mission field."

"I most certainly am that, but a woman who would follow you through the jungles of San Francisco? Hmmm, that's debatable."

"I love your sense of humor, I love your smile, I love your servant's heart, and mostly, I love how you make me feel. You make me feel like I'm the strongest, best-looking man in the world. When I thought you were going to Africa, I was sick."

"You are the strongest, best-looking man on earth. As far as I'm concerned, anyway. And I can't leave for Africa. You just promised me a new wardrobe."

"Yes, I did. Are we standing in Macy's?" His eyes thinned.

"Uh-huh."

"Did I just kiss you for the first time in a department store?"

"Uh-huh."

"Boy, I'm romantic. Well, we're here. Let's get you some nice outfits, but first. . ." He bent down and kissed her again. "I'll never get tired of that."

"Me, either."

"Did you two need some help?" A salesgirl approached. It probably wasn't every day two people kissed right in the women's department at Macy's, but there they were. Two people who were so overcome by the excitement of retail, they shared their first kiss in the middle of the racks.

"Yes, we do need some help," Kyle replied. "My beautiful girlfriend here." He threw an arm around her. "She has a disastrous wardrobe. Do you think you can help us with that?"

Collette laughed. "Do you see the ridicule I must endure?"

The salesgirl smiled. "Right this way. Do you have particular colors you like?" she asked Collette.

"I like green and black. Oh, and navy. Maybe a little bright pink," Collette said as she spied a nice pantsuit.

"Great; I'll grab a few things to get you started." The salesgirl must have guessed her size because she never asked, and all the things Collette tried on in the dressing room fit well. She twisted in the three-way mirror. She looked sophisticated, stylish, and beautiful. She felt beautiful. Kyle loved her. God had blessed her in every way. If only her mother and father were here to see the happiness on her face and meet the man who had stolen her heart.

"Collette, come out here," Kyle called from outside the dressing room. "I want to see what you look like in all this."

Collette walked out in an emerald-green pantsuit. It was cut so the jacket was long, and it created a waist. She felt glamorous and shapely. "Well, how do I look?"

"Stunning. I wish your father was here to see you."

"He'd never believe it. I think I was always the little girl with the scraped knees."

"Not anymore. You've become a gorgeous woman, both inside and out. You've done them proud."

Collette looked away shyly. "There are a few nice out-fits in there, but I don't need all this. Just the one for your company dinner is enough. Do you want to see the rest?"

"I want you to have the clothes, Collette. Please let me do this for you. You are simply a ray of light when you feel confident."

"There's so much more you could do with the money. And the fact is, I plan to be working a lot at the mission. I don't want to appear too full of myself with fancy clothes."

"Collette, just go get the things you like. You can argue with me later." He winked. "Trust me; you have the wardrobe for the mission already."

Chapter 7

January came upon her quickly, and Collette needed to let her supporters know she wouldn't be leaving for Africa after all. San Francisco was a bustling, exciting town with more needs than she could count. If only she'd opened her eyes earlier to the plight of the homeless, she wouldn't have wasted so much time trying to finagle some way back to Africa.

Although Collette felt comfortable with the idea of remaining in the States, one thing still bothered her. She still didn't know why her father wanted her back in America so badly. And the list of reasons set her mind in constant motion. Her father had been open and honest with her about everything. Why would he keep this important fact to himself?

At the end of his life, he'd gotten forgetful. He'd even lost some of the donations for the mission in the books somewhere. She'd tried to find the money and had spoken to the Kenyans about it, but it never showed up. She worried that in his old age, her father had simply used the money and not written it down. She wanted to make things right, and she wondered if his illness hadn't played some kind of part in his desire for her to stay in America.

The missing funds were the reason she'd been so adamant to get back to Kenya. Would the Kenyans understand when they noticed the missing funds? Would her father's reputation be ruined? The idea of it haunted her. She wanted her father's name to rest as peacefully as he did now.

A letter arrived from Kassarani. It was written in Swahili, and Collette knew by its contents that she couldn't remain in the dark any longer. The missing money had been noticed, and Collette felt compelled to find out where it went. Translated, the letter read:

> *Dear Miss Collette:*
>
> *I'm sure your church has told you of our troubles. We are still trying to build back up what was taken, but it will take time. Much time. I think it best for your safety for you to stay in America. Hank had announced you two were to be married before his disappearance. It would be best for you to stay.*
>
> > *God's blessings,*
> > *Kadju*

Collette's mind reeled. What was going on in Kassarani? Where had Hank gone? None of it made any sense. Did the Kassarani people think her father had taken the funds? Was Hank paying for that? She knew there was money missing, but nothing of consequence and probably only on paper. It was only about seventy-five dollars. Something she could easily replace.

She wondered what Kadju had meant would take time to build up—the church or the donation till? She rubbed her temples. All the letter did was raise more questions. She had to know. She couldn't move on until she knew things were right back home.

"Mrs. Combie." She exited her room. "Mrs. Combie?"

"What is it, Collette? You look as white as a ghost."

"Mrs. Combie, would you mind driving me to the church?"

"But, Collette, it's Saturday. No one will be there, honey."

"I need to look at my father's last mission statement. According to this letter, funds are missing from the mission. I need to find out what he wrote regarding the funds. If he knew where the missing funds might have gone."

"Well, Collette, your father would never take money from the mission if that's what set your heart to stir."

"I know that, Mrs. Combie, but something had to happen to the money, and if my father knew, he would have written it down. The Kassarani people need to know the truth. It sounds like it's tearing the church apart. I want to prove my father's innocence, even if it takes a trip down there. I can't have his memory tarnished. He worked too long for the Kenyans, too long for God, to have this happen to his memory."

"Collette, I'll drive you to the church, but you need to know it's in God's hands now. Your father's reputation doesn't need saving. His life spoke for itself, and he's in peace now. You need to move on. Besides, reading confidential files seems below you."

Her speech didn't satisfy Collette. They drove the short mile to the church, and Collette raced to the missionary files. She found the file she needed and took a deep breath. She put any guilty feelings aside and prepared for whatever she found.

Collette gasped, bringing her hand to her mouth.

"What is it, dear?" Mrs. Combie came alongside her and rubbed her back.

"My father did know the money was missing. Look here—he wrote it in his last statement before he became ill."

"See, I told you, dear."

"This mission file was audited by Kyle. He discontinued the mission because of improper use of funding! Kyle closed my father's ministry!" Collette sat slowly, sliding down the front of the file cabinet. "Look—he's signed it and everything." Scrawled across the file in Kyle's red pencil was a short note: "Mission funding cancelled. Over five thousand dollars in donations missing."

"Five thousand dollars! My father didn't lose that kind of money!" Collette shouted. "We didn't have that kind of money! In Kassarani that would be like a million dollars."

"Kyle knows that, honey."

"No, look. Funding was cancelled before my father's death. Look at the date." Collette thrust the manila folder toward the older woman. "Kyle thinks my father took that money or that he was at least responsible for its being missing." Collette felt her heart racing. The man she loved. How could he do this to the only other man that meant anything in Collette's life: her father?

Mrs. Combie looked at the folder and remained stoic. She pursed her lips but didn't make any reply and handed back the file.

Collette rifled through the rest of the pages in the file. "Kyle told me my father's reasons for having me stay in America were in his final report, but look, they aren't. Look, Mrs. Combie, it doesn't say anywhere in here that I was to stay in the States." She held the report up. "I've got to find Kyle. I need to ask him why he lied to me. I knew he was too good to be true. I should have known. Why did I let my feelings allow me to trust him? I should have never trusted him!"

"Collette, you're making assumptions." Mrs. Combie tried to keep her calm. "Kyle is an upstanding man. He would never do anything to knowingly hurt anyone."

"No, he lied to me. Kyle told me my father's reasons were in this report, but they're nowhere to be found. He and Pastor Holmes must think my father stole that money, and they didn't want me down there to steal more. I've got to find him. Kyle's going to tell me the truth!"

Collette dialed Kyle's cell phone from the front office, tears streaming freely down her face.

"Hello," he answered.

"Kyle, where are you? I've got to see you."

"I'm at the office, Collette. Is everything okay?"

"No, everything's not okay," she said through her sobs. "I need to see you. Right now. I'm at the church."

"I'll be right there." The phone clicked.

Collette paced the floor of the church office, her anger

accelerating at a rate she didn't know was possible. How could the man she loved betray her father? How could Kyle betray her?

Kyle yanked open the office door with vengeance. He rushed to Collette's side. "Collette, are you okay? You had me worried sick!"

Mrs. Combie went into a back office to give them privacy. "No, I'm not okay. This is my father's last report, Kyle! The one where you said he wrote that I was to stay in the States. But there's nothing in here, Kyle. Nothing. I want to know why you lied to me!"

Kyle fidgeted uncomfortably, clearly upset he'd been called upon for the answer she needed. She searched his brown eyes, but he couldn't look at her. "I didn't lie to you," he answered quietly.

"Then explain this to me, Kyle. You closed my father's mission. You put an end to his funding from this church. Before his death! He knew about it. My father knew his mission was ending. That's how he ended his life, Kyle! Knowing his life's work wouldn't go on! Tell me why."

"There were problems at the mission, Collette."

"Problems I could have worked out, if you'd only told me what they were. How could you let me stay here in the States when you knew my father's reputation was at risk?"

"Your father's gone, Collette. It doesn't matter."

"It matters to me. It matters a great deal. I love my father, Kyle. He worked his entire adult lifetime at that mission for the Lord. He doesn't deserve to have his reputation tarnished in the end. I need to go back."

"His reputation isn't tarnished. He handed the mission

over to the Kassarani people, not to Hank Guilding. He trained three pastors last year before he became ill, Collette. That mission station was more than capable of being run by Kenyans."

"How would you know? Did you eat with them? Sleep in an eight-by-eight cubicle of bricks? Wash your clothes alongside them? My father did. Hank did!" she screamed bitterly.

"I don't know an easy way to say this." He tried to wrap his arms around her, but she avoided any contact with him. "Hank Guilding was a con artist who took advantage of your father."

"No, Hank lived with the people in Kassarani. He loved them. You're just jealous because I almost married him."

"I would never have let you marry that. . .that ungodly wretch. Hank Guilding took advantage of the poorest of the poor. He stole from God. He came to Nairobi with computers for the mission to prove his value. But the computers were stolen, Collette. They were only a ruse to get your father to trust him."

"And the five thousand dollars that's missing on paper?"

"Stolen. It's not in the mission report because your father wanted to insure you were safely in the States while authorities tracked down Hank. He's wanted in America for tax evasion and now in Nairobi for diverting funds. He's disappeared."

"How do you know all this?"

"Your father was on to Hank almost from the first, but with his illness, there was little he could do. He passed the work onto Kadju, but made Kadju vow his silence to get you safely back here. None of the details of Hank's stealing were ever written down. Hank was too volatile. One thing Hank was good for is that computer equipment. We've been getting updates daily on the mission's state. I have the records locked in Pastor Holmes's office if you want to see them."

"So Hank only wanted to marry me because of the funding? He didn't want to do the Lord's will?" Collette fell against the file cabinet.

Kyle came toward her and wrapped her in an embrace. "I don't think so, honey. Hank Guilding is truly an idiot, and he only proves it time and time again. First, thinking he can get away with stealing from God, and secondly, to not recognize the value in Collette Ambers as a life partner. I can think of a hundred reasons to marry you."

Collette cut him off. "Where is Hank now?" she asked fearfully.

"I don't know, but I'm afraid he may have been the victim of vigilante justice. His condominium in Nairobi was untouched, but he's gone. None of the expensive computer equipment was missing, his stereo was intact, even his shoes were by the door."

Collette looked at her feet. "He would have been better off turning himself into the authorities."

"He thought he was smarter than he actually was. Hank took advantage of your father's sickness, and he might have taken advantage of you if God hadn't intervened. And your father. He spoke to us by phone during his illness. In our last phone report from him, he made us promise we wouldn't let you go back. Not until Hank was arrested. That's why I said your father's request for you to stay in the States was included in his last report."

"So my father knew about Hank? But he never let on."

"He handled things the best way he knew. He wanted you safe, and he thought that if Hank figured you didn't know anything about what was going on, you would be less likely to get hurt. He knew you had plans here in America."

"Yes, to see my friends next month in Seattle. He knew how much it meant to me."

"Little did he know you'd be getting married and starting a family too."

She looked up at him with wide, innocent eyes. He dropped to one knee and took her hand in his. "Collette Ambers, I would never lie to you or do anything to harm you. I love you with everything that is within me to love you. Your devotion to God is admirable and I want to spend the rest of my life serving Him beside you. Wherever that takes us."

She fell onto her knees before him and looked directly into the deep, chocolate-brown eyes she had come to know so well. "How could I have ever mistrusted you? I love you, Kyle."

He wiped away a single tear with his gentle thumb. "The Enemy plays wicked when it comes to keeping Christians apart, Collette. Marry me and stay beside me."

"Oh, Kyle! Yes, yes, I'll marry you."

He stood and pulled her up, taking her into his arms. "The sweetest words I'll ever hear." He kissed her, first along her jaw and then moved to her lips. Collette closed her eyes and savored the moment. There would never be another like it.

Mrs. Combie came out into the foyer and discovered the young couple in a passionate embrace. She shrugged. "So, I guess you two got everything worked out."

The couple separated and laughed. "I suppose we did, Mrs. Combie." Collette walked toward the older woman and hugged her. "I'm getting married!"

Mrs. Combie shrugged again. "I knew you would be. I told you. I've been praying for Kyle for a long time. You were just the missing part of the equation."

Kyle came and kissed Mrs. Combie's cheek. "Thank you for praying. You couldn't have been praying for a prettier, more wonderful bride for me. God certainly heard this one and answered with a resounding yes!"

❧

Collette tried on her wedding gown one last time before her trip. Her future was settled. A reunion with her best friends and then the wedding of her dreams. It was so exhilarating, she thought she might burst from sheer happiness. Getting engaged had brought two added pleasures for Collette. The first was sharing her news with her best friends Amanda, Belinda, and Dani. The second was the look of horror on Trisha's face when she learned Kyle Brighton had not fallen for the prettiest, the most successful, or even the slimmest member of the singles' group. Kyle had sought Collette out, focusing on the longings God had developed in both of them. A heart for missions and for one another. It was truly a match made in heaven.

Collette's gown was a simple shantung silk. It boasted a straight skirt, a high scoop neckline, and a delicate waistline. The elegant dress emphasized her shape without making her appear larger because of extra ruffles and gathers. She looked like a princess. Or at least she felt like one. She no longer saw the mousy brown-haired, overweight, gawky little girl she felt like when she stepped off the plane in San Francisco. The image gazing back at her was of a confident woman who'd won the love of an intelligent, handsome man of God. A woman who was ready to serve her Lord wherever the path might lead.

Kristin Billerbeck

Kristin lives in the Silicon Valley with her husband, Bryed and their three sons, Trey, Jonah, and Seth. When not writing, Kristin also enjoys reading, painting, and conversing with her on-line writing groups. She has three published novels with the **Heartsong Presents** line and one novella out with Barbour Publishing. Visit Kristin at www.getset.com/kristinbillerbeck

Danielle

by Carol Cox

Acknowledgment

Heartfelt thanks to Paul Kinnison,
pastor of Grand Canyon Baptist Church,
who graciously answered my many questions.

Chapter 1

Is this the one you'd like to see?" Danielle Gallagher reached inside the glass-enclosed display case and indicated a delicate silver and turquoise necklace. The man across the counter nodded vigorously, beaming when Dani laid the necklace on a piece of black velvet for his inspection.

"How much?" he asked in a strongly accented voice. Dani named the price, which the man looked up in a currency converter. He nodded again, satisfied, and slowly counted out the amount.

"*Danke schön,*" he said when Dani handed the necklace to him, carefully wrapped and tucked into a bag marked Bailey's Curios.

"*Bitte,*" she responded. "And enjoy your stay at the Grand Canyon." The man blinked in surprise, smiled, and left.

Genial Mr. Bailey peered at her over his half glasses. "How many languages can you say 'thank you' and 'you're welcome' in now, Dani?"

"Seven," she replied. "Eight, if you count English. I love watching people's faces light up when they hear their own language."

"You mean you love people," Mr. Bailey corrected. "And it shows, Dani. They love you back." He glanced at his watch. "Go ahead and take your lunch break now. You've put in quite a morning."

Dani grabbed her purse, slung it over her shoulder, and waved a cheery good-bye. She walked out back to the employee parking area, fishing in her purse for her keys.

"Hey, Dani, have you finally gotten a real car, or are you still driving that tank?" She turned to see the friendly face of Brad Taylor, who worked in park maintenance.

"Are you running down my Scout again?" Dani grinned and paused to stroke the bright yellow fender with a loving hand before unlocking her door.

"Come on. They don't even make these anymore. Doesn't the fact that an International Scout hasn't come off the assembly line since 1980 bother you?"

"That's all part of the Scout mystique," Dani said, giving him a mock glare from her perch in the driver's seat. "You drive a Jeep. You just wouldn't understand."

With a mischievous smile, she pulled away, cautiously threading the blocky four-wheel-drive vehicle through the line of cars circling the parking lot in the hope of being on hand when a new space opened up. August was one of the Grand Canyon's busiest months, and today Dani was convinced a hefty percentage of the park's visitors had found their way into Bailey's.

She shook her head in amusement, remembering one of last year's summer workers who had flung up her hands and quit after her second day on the job, declaring, "I can't take it! You can't see the scenery for the tourists!"

Those same tourists were one of the blessings of living at the canyon for Dani. How many places were there where you could live and work in one of the most beautiful spots on earth, meeting tons of people from all over the world? *It just doesn't get any better than this*, she reflected. It was the perfect environment for someone who loved both people and outdoor life with equal fervor.

Her longtime friends from camp had kidded her for years about her obsession with the great outdoors. The two weeks they spent each year near Deception Pass in Washington State only whetted Dani's appetite for more time away from city life. When a temporary job at the canyon had opened up one summer after camp, Dani leaped at the opportunity.

What started out as a summer job led to Mr. Bailey's offer of full-time employment. After two years, Dani felt more like she was on a long-term vacation than holding down a regular job.

How in the world had all this happened to Danielle Gallagher? *I don't understand why You've blessed me like this, Father, but thank You for making this part of Your plan for my life.*

Dani parked in the lot in front of the post office and crossed the broad concrete walkway to the slump block building, humming a praise chorus. Twisting her key to open her mailbox, she found a single envelope inside. The foreign stamp told her it was from Collette, even before she glanced at the return address.

Ripping the envelope open with her thumb, Dani

scanned the letter, hoping for good news and a positive answer to their prayers for Collette's father. Dani's face clouded. The news wasn't encouraging, Collette wrote. Her father's health was failing, and she was concerned about the future.

Dani went back to the beginning of the letter and read it again, slowly this time, while she walked back through the lobby. Poor Collette! She must be worried sick, not only about her father, but about what would happen to her if he didn't survive. Deep in thought, she pushed through the lobby doors and started back toward the parking lot, stuffing the letter into its envelope.

Her left shoulder collided with something solid, sending the envelope fluttering through the air. Dani looked up, startled, into a pair of dark gray eyes. *They could be the color of a placid lake,* Dani thought, but just now their irritated expression reminded her more of towering thunderheads before a storm.

"I'm sorry," she said with an apologetic smile. "I guess I wasn't looking where I was going."

"That's fairly obvious." Scowling, the man she had run into knelt to retrieve the handful of envelopes that had scattered on impact, scooping them up with both hands. When he stood again, Dani realized how tall he was. Even without the cowboy boots, his chin would just skim the top of her head. The gray Stetson he wore added even more height. He gave her an exasperated look and turned to leave.

"Wait a minute; I think that one is mine." Giving the startled man a friendly grin, Dani reached into the middle of the stack he held and tugged until she pulled Collette's letter free. "See?" She held it up for his inspection, pointing to the stamp. "It's from my friend. In Africa," she clarified, her grin fading when he simply stared at her blankly.

He raised one eyebrow without speaking, then turned and walked away. *What a grouch!* At least she didn't have to deal with him, whoever he was, on a regular basis. Dani watched him disappear through the glass doors, then pocketed her letter and walked across the lot to the Canyon Cafe.

Dani lifted her tray at the end of the serving line and looked around for a place to sit. A flurry of movement caught her attention, and she turned her head to see her friend Lorna Fredericks waving at her frantically.

"Over here!" Lorna called, pointing to the empty chair at her table. Dani wove her way through the lunchtime crush to join her in the atrium, settling into the padded vinyl seat with a sigh of relief.

"What a morning," Dani sighed, unloading a chef salad from her tray and sipping her iced tea. "I'm beat."

Lorna gasped dramatically, placing one hand over her heart and making a broad, sweeping gesture with the other. "I don't believe it! Did Dani Gallagher, Human Dynamo, just admit to being tired?" She held a soup spoon in front of Dani's mouth the way an interviewer would hold a microphone. "Our listeners are desperate to know. To what do you attribute this unprecedented lack of energy?"

Dani assumed a deadpan expression and spoke earnestly into the spoon. "This unusual sapping of my strength is the result of three factors. One, we've had a million jillion customers already today.

"Two," she said, holding her fingers in a V shape and wiggling them in front of Lorna's nose, "I have just fought my way through traffic that would do Manhattan proud.

"And three. . ." Dani heaved a deep, theatrical sigh. "I just walked right into some guy at the post office." She wrinkled her nose. "And that one's no exaggeration." She described the encounter to Lorna. "You'd think I had done something really awful, the way he glared at me and then stalked off."

Lorna stared, forgetting her mock reporter's role. "Someone got mad at you? I don't believe it. Everybody loves you! Who is this guy?"

Dani shrugged. "I never saw him before. He's mid-thirtyish, I think. Tall, with gray eyes. Kind of a rugged, outdoorsy face, athletic build. It looked like he had wavy light brown hair, but it was hard to tell because of the Stetson. I have no idea who he was, but I'd just as soon not run into him again."

"Hmm. . ." A faint smile curved Lorna's lips.

"And what does that 'hmm' mean?" Dani asked suspiciously. "I don't trust that gleam in your eye."

Lorna propped her elbows on the table and rested her chin on her cupped hands. "Let me see if I have this straight. You nearly bowl this guy over and knock his mail all over the place. He is less than pleased and spends most of the time glaring at you. So far, so good?"

Dani nodded slowly. "So?"

"How long did this little episode last?"

"A minute, maybe. No longer than two. I still don't see—"

Lorna pursed her lips and nodded judiciously. "And in that brief amount of time, you collide, he scrambles to pick up his mail, you try to get your letter back and make amends. But you still have time to notice his height and build, the color of his eyes, and possibly the color of his hair. I repeat: Hmm."

Dani held up her hands defensively. "Hold everything. There is nothing significant in that. If you're thinking what I think you're thinking, forget it. I refuse to be the target of another one of your matchmaking schemes."

"Nothing significant, huh?" Lorna's eyes held a speculative glint. "Describe Brad Taylor."

"Brad?" Dani's tone was incredulous. "Um, he's four or five inches taller than I am. Probably a couple of years younger. Why?" she demanded.

"Hair color? Eye color? Does he have dimples? Are his teeth straight? Come on, you've known him for the two years you've been here. This should be easy," Lorna said, smirking.

"Blond hair, blue eyes," Dani shot back. "I don't know about dimples, and who cares about his teeth besides his mother and his dentist?"

Lorna leaned back in her chair as if satisfied. "I rest my case."

Dani rolled her eyes and tried to keep a straight face. Lorna's attempts at matchmaking were legendary, but it was impossible to be upset with her good-natured friend for long.

"Save it for someone who appreciates your efforts," she said, trying to sound stern. "Remember me? I'm the one who got tired of the dating game and all the phoniness and pressure that goes along with it. After a couple of dates, guys were pushing either for intimacy or marriage. Who needs that?"

"Dani, don't let a few bad apples sour you on the whole idea of marriage," Lorna pleaded. "My husband and I have the greatest relationship in the world, and I'd love for you to find that with the right guy."

"That's just it: It needs to be the right guy. What you and Eric have is wonderful, but marriage to the wrong person would be a disaster. Every time I've gotten a proposal I've prayed, and you know what? God said no every time. It finally got through to me that He knows the right man for me, and He'll bring him into my life when the time is right. Until then, I'm not going to worry about it. And neither should you," she added, smiling to take the sting out of her words.

Lorna raised her hands in surrender. "Okay, okay; I know when I'm licked. Besides," she said, trying to suppress a laugh, "I just remembered what you did to the last guy I set you up with."

Dani sputtered with laughter. "I tried to tell you that one wouldn't work out, didn't I?"

"Yeah, but do you really think he deserved to find a frog in his sleeping bag on the singles' camping trip?"

Dani pressed both hands over her mouth, trying to stifle her giggles. "He asked for it!" she insisted, her voice muffled by her fingers. "He kept telling me what a nature lover he was. All I did was let him enjoy a bit of nature, up close and personal." The two women slumped in their chairs, laughing helplessly.

"I still think—" Lorna broke off and stared open-mouthed at a point beyond Dani's left shoulder. "As I live and breathe, look who's back. It's Chase Sheppard! Yoo-hoo, Chase! Over here." She flailed her hands wildly to attract his attention.

Dani, wiping tears of mirth from her cheeks, was aware of someone approaching and stopping just outside her range of vision. Breathing deeply to control the laughter that still threatened to erupt, she turned her head and found herself staring at a long denim-clad leg. The yoke-fronted shirt above the jeans looked oddly familiar. With a sinking feeling, Dani forced her gaze up beyond the shirt collar to confirm her suspicions.

Dark gray eyes shadowed by a darker gray Stetson glanced at her quickly, then looked back at Lorna, who was still bubbling with excitement.

"Chase Sheppard, I can't believe it! What brings you back here after all this time? How long has it been now—two years?"

"Three." The deep voice showed little emotion. "I didn't like Yellowstone as well as I thought I would. When I heard my old job was opening up again, I applied for it, and here I am."

"That's wonderful!" Lorna gushed. "Chase, have you met Dani? Danielle Gallagher, this is Chase Sheppard. He's a contract specialist."

Chase glanced at Dani again with a cool stare that

made her feel like he was looking right through her. "We bumped into each other earlier at the post office," he said dryly.

The tingling heat in her cheeks told Dani her face was still red after her bout of convulsive laughter. *Probably just as well,* she thought. It would help hide the flush of embarrassment she knew stained her cheeks now.

"At the. . ." Lorna blinked, then looked from Chase to Dani and back again. "Ohhh. I see," she purred.

"Look, Lorna, I need to get going," Chase said. "Thanks for the welcome back." He gave the barest sketch of a nod in Dani's direction and headed toward the door with long, sure strides. Lorna watched him leave, then turned back to the table and looked around with a puzzled expression, as if searching for something.

"What are you looking for?" Dani asked.

Lorna looked up, her face a picture of confusion. "Sparks," she said. "They're supposed to be flying around like mad, and I don't see a single one."

Dani chuckled and patted Lorna's hand. "Don't feel bad, kiddo. You can't win 'em all." She glanced at her watch, then scooted her chair away from the table. "I've got to get back to work. Talk to you later." She left Lorna sitting at the table, shaking her head.

※

Chase drove through the heavy traffic, his mouth drawn in a thin line of disgust. *Wouldn't you know Lorna Fredericks would still be at the canyon!* And it figured he'd run into her his first week back. Chase pursed his lips and blew out a long, slow breath. When he'd worked there before, Lorna seemed to feel duty-bound to match him up with every single woman she could find.

If that hadn't been bad enough, the women she'd picked out for him invariably made Chase want to turn and run. He felt the same way now. If that long, drawn-out "Ohhh" of Lorna's wasn't enough to put a man on guard, there had also been that unmistakable "Have I got a girl for you" look in her eyes.

Chase snorted. No doubt that Gallagher woman was the one she had in mind. Chase had to admit she was good-looking, with those sparkling hazel eyes and the glossy dark brown hair that curved under where the ends skimmed her shoulder. The jeans and the black polo shirt emblazoned with Bailey's logo didn't disguise her trim figure, and her glowing tan attested to the fact that she was an outdoor girl.

Just the kind of girl he would have been attracted to once. Her generous mouth with its contagious smile would have stopped him in his tracks only a few years ago. Before Elise. . .

Chase shrugged his shoulders, as if he could shake off the bitter memories. Escaping those memories was the biggest reason he had for transferring back to the Grand Canyon. Even two years after their breakup, Yellowstone was full of reminders. Chase needed a place to come home to, someplace familiar and comforting, where his wounded soul could heal, and this was the perfect spot.

Except for Lorna and her ditzy friend. Chase shook his head, remembering the impact that had sent his mail sailing in all directions. What had she been thinking of, waltzing along like that without paying the least bit of attention to her surroundings? He knew right away she was a flighty female, one to avoid.

He might have granted her the benefit of the doubt, chalking their collision up to her being distracted, if it hadn't been for seeing her with Lorna. He had spotted the two before Lorna ever saw him. What in the world had they been doing, Lorna shoving a spoon practically up her friend's nose, then the other woman waggling her fingers in Lorna's face, and both of them laughing like maniacs?

It was just as well I saw them, he reflected. It confirmed his first impression of Danielle Gallagher, and it put him firmly on guard against Lorna's machinations. Forewarned was forearmed. Never again would he allow himself to be taken in by a frivolous airhead who was more interested in her own pleasure than the things of God.

Chapter 2

Dani grimaced and burrowed deeper into her pillow, pulling the comforter up over her head to muffle the insistent ringing of her phone. She gritted her teeth and counted—eight rings. Ten. Twelve.

With an exasperated moan, she flung back the covers and reached over to the bedside table, yanking the receiver off its cradle. "Hello?" Her voice was husky with sleep.

"Did I wake you?" The bright voice on the other end of the line made Dani cringe.

"Lorna, Sunday's a day off. I don't have to get up at six today. Give me a break."

"I will in a minute, but first you have to hear what I discovered. It explains everything."

Dani kept her eyes closed and concentrated on relaxing her tense muscles. As soon as Lorna hung up, she would go right back to sleep. "Explains everything about what?" she asked drowsily.

"About Chase Sheppard and why he acted like that the other day."

Dani moaned. "It doesn't matter. I do not care how

he acted. What I do care about is getting a little extra sleep, so—"

"It didn't make sense," Lorna continued as if Dani hadn't spoken. "I mean, everybody likes you. And Chase has always been such a warm, caring person. . . ."

"Uh-huh. Anybody can see that," Dani muttered.

"Exactly," Lorna enthused, missing the sarcasm completely. "That's what made it such a mystery! But," she added, her voice full of pride, "I am happy to report the mystery has been solved."

Dani squeezed her eyes tight, beginning to despair of this conversation ever ending. "Lorna, what are you talking about?"

"I made a few phone calls and did some investigating, and guess what I found out?" Lorna's voice dropped to a dramatic whisper. "Chase is suffering from a broken heart."

The only response was a muffled groan from Dani.

"Don't you see?" Lorna persisted. "He's been hurt. Wounded. No wonder he was standoffish. He's being protective of his heart," she finished in a solemn tone.

Dani gave a resigned sigh. "Okay, Lorna, he's one of the walking wounded. I'll try to remember that so I don't step on his tender feelings. Now may I go back to sleep?"

"How can you think of sleep at a time like this?" Lorna yelped. "We have to think, to plan. This could be your Mr. Right, and we can't—"

"Whoa," Dani commanded. "You make this sound like a safari, with him as the big game. Listen carefully, Lorna. I am not looking for Mr. Right. I do not have a problem being thirty-one and single. I am through with all those false starts along the way. I've been through it too many times, and that kind of life is not for me.

"No more looking at every single man who comes in view, wondering if he's the one. If God has a Mr. Right for me, He'll let me know. Until then, I am enjoying each day as it comes." Dani's tone carried such a note of finality that Lorna gave up after only a couple of feeble attempts at protest.

After she hung up, Dani lay still, but her body and mind refused to relax. Disgusted, she threw back the covers and swung her legs over the edge of her bed. So much for sleeping in.

Two hours later, fortified by three mugs of strong black coffee, Dani slipped through the crowd in front of the Shrine of the Ages. Entering the foyer, she made her way along the crowded corridor, smiling and greeting other worshipers along the way.

"Dani! How's it going?" Pastor Ben Stevens gave her a genial smile and held out his hand in welcome.

Dani shook his hand and laughed. "Even after two years, I'm still amazed at how the congregation fluctuates."

Ben chuckled in return. "You mean, two hundred during the summer and eighty the rest of the year?" He nodded, still smiling. "With the summer workers and the tourists, it brings the mission field to our doorstep."

Dani nodded in agreement, her eyes sparkling. "How many other places can you do what amounts to foreign missions right at home? I love it!"

She slipped away while the pastor greeted other arrivals and slid into her favorite seat at the far side of the sanctuary, near the four huge windows that made up most of the north wall. Dani loved to look through them during the sermons. Watching the changing panorama of the seasons in one of God's most spectacular settings never failed to bring peace to her soul and focus her mind on Ben's godly teaching.

The remaining seats filled up quickly. Many people waved across the room to Dani, who smiled and waved back. A tall man with wavy light brown hair entered and looked around for a vacant seat. Dani recognized Chase Sheppard, and some of the joy of the morning dimmed.

Oh, boy, it's Mr. Charm himself. A twinge of guilt pricked at her conscience. It wasn't like her to be so uncharitable. *Maybe Lorna's right,* she mused. *He's been hurt and wants to keep his defenses up. Maybe the poor guy just needs to lighten up a little.* The piano and organ began to play, and Dani turned her attention to the worship service.

After the final amen, she gathered up her Bible, notebook, and tote bag and headed for the door, her thoughts intent on the sermon on building your relationship with God. Ben had made some important points. *I'll go over my notes this afternoon,* she thought, opening her tote bag and sliding the notebook inside. *Right after lunch would be a good—*

Whump! Dani felt the jarring thud all the way to her toes. When did they put a post in the middle of the sanctuary? She looked up to see a shaken Chase Sheppard.

"I hope this isn't going to become a habit," he said, eyeing her warily.

For the third time that week, Dani watched him walk

away. Three contacts with the man, and she hadn't failed yet to come across as an absolute idiot. *That must be some kind of record*, she thought gloomily, pulling the strap of the tote bag onto her shoulder.

On the other hand, he's not doing a thing to help matters any, she reflected, walking out into the late summer sunshine. *He'd be a lot happier if he dropped that sour attitude and relaxed a little.*

"Hey, Dani, over here!" Dani turned in the direction of the voice and spotted Cindy Kepler, one of the college-age students who came to do summer missions work at the canyon. "Some of us are leaving tomorrow, so we're taking a group picture now. Come on!"

Dani's mood brightened instantly. She had gotten closest to Cindy, but she'd enjoyed the contact she'd had with the whole group of committed young Christians, some of whom had come every summer of their college years.

They stood in front of the laminated beam archways, lined up in two decorous rows facing Pastor Stevens, who stood with his camera at the ready. Dani took her place next to Cindy and smiled at the camera for two shots. Behind her, Fred Collins called out, "Okay, enough of the formality. Now show us as we really are!" He pulled out a pair of eyeglasses with fake nose and mustache attached, positioned them on his face, and struck a comic pose. Immediately, the rest of the group started clowning for the camera.

Ben Stevens picked up on the mood and snapped one picture after another. "Hold it a minute!" Cindy yelled. "Isn't that Chase over there?" She darted through the pole fence and jogged along the parking area, grabbing Chase by the arm and leading him back to the group.

Dani's mind whirled. This was Cindy's fourth consecutive summer at the canyon. Apparently, she remembered Chase from before and in a positive way. But there was no way Dani would have paired the stolid Mr. Sheppard with the fun-loving Cindy.

Chase allowed himself to be towed back and introduced to the boisterous group. He even submitted, with reasonably good grace, to being positioned near Dani for another photo.

Dani looked at him with new eyes. This was a side of Chase Sheppard she hadn't seen before, hadn't even suspected. This relaxed, smiling man was much more appealing than the one she kept bumping into. Her diagnosis had been correct. All he needed was a little loosening up.

Dani motioned to Fred to hand her the glasses while Ben moved closer and refocused his camera. With one quick motion, she stood on tiptoe and slipped them over Chase's head just before the shutter clicked. "Good one!" Ben laughed.

Chase swept one hand over his face, snatching the glasses away. He turned and fixed his eyes on Dani, his features frozen into a stiff mask. Thrusting the glasses into her hand, he pivoted and stalked off down the parking area where he was lost from sight in the crowd of tourists.

After four strikes, I think I'm definitely out. Dani looked into Ben's startled face and shrugged, forcing a grin and hoping her rapid blinking would hide the tears she knew glistened in her eyes. It was official, no doubt about it; she would never be able to do anything right as far as that man was concerned.

And why, she wondered, *should his disapproval bother me so much?*

⁂

Chase stormed through the door of his tiny duplex and slammed it behind him, raking his fingers through his hair. He returned to the canyon for peace, for healing, and what did he find instead? A scatterbrained woman apparently intent on creating havoc at every turn.

Flipping his Stetson on top of the stereo, Chase flopped onto the couch and tried to think. His first impulse was to grab his belongings and pull out, but after leaping at the chance to come back here, he couldn't very well pack up and leave right away. He'd have to be watchful and figure out how to avoid Danielle Gallagher. He would never regain his peace of mind with her around.

Chase kicked off his boots and propped his feet on the worn coffee table. He folded his arms behind his head and settled deeper into the cushions. If he acted like he was relaxed, maybe he could ease the stress that tightened his body like a wound spring.

He rolled his head from side to side, trying to loosen his stiff neck muscles. It was crazy to let her get to him this way. After all, he barely knew the woman. *And let's keep it that way, okay, Lord?*

Chase shook his head, remembering the way Danielle sat during the sermon, alternately staring out the window and scribbling in her notebook. *Probably making out her grocery list,* he thought sourly. It was obvious she hadn't been paying the least bit of attention to the sermon.

And what was that stunt with the glasses? He hadn't minded posing for a picture with the missions group, had been flattered to be remembered and asked to join them, in fact. How Miss Gallagher had wormed her way into the photo, he couldn't imagine, but he'd assumed she would be able to maintain some semblance of dignity long enough to have a picture taken.

Wrong. The moment he felt the glasses sliding over his face, he knew who was responsible. But what could he expect from someone who made a practice of walking along, trusting some obviously faulty internal radar to warn her when she was about to plow into somebody?

It's a shame, he thought, his eyes drifting shut. *She sure is easy to look at.* Cut it out! Chase shook himself awake. Thoughts like that were not going to be helpful in keeping his guard up where Lorna and her bubbleheaded protégée were concerned.

Dani reached into the refrigerator in the back room of Bailey's and retrieved two apples and a pack of string cheese, dropping them into her fanny pack.

"Going out to your quiet spot?" Mr. Bailey smiled and reached past her for a fresh roll of the shop's distinctive gift wrap.

Dani flashed him a smile in return and checked to make sure her pocket Bible and small notebook were in the pack as well. "Uh-huh. Fall's on the way, and before you know it, it'll be too cold to sit around outside. I want to take advantage of it while I have the time."

Mr. Bailey nodded in approval and hefted the heavy roll of paper a notch higher in his arms. "Smart girl. You never know when the snow will start to fly. Thanks for filling in for Marian today."

"No problem," Dani answered. She slipped out the back door and walked the few yards to the paved path that made up the Rim Trail. No matter how many times she made that short walk, she marveled at the sheer blessing of spending her days at the edge of one of the Seven Wonders of the World.

Turning right, she hurried east along the trail to the spot she had found within weeks of coming to live here. Her initial awe over the canyon's overwhelming size had gradually subsided into a deep-seated desire to know as many of its varied views and moods as possible. She had spent her days off trekking sections of the Rim Trail until she knew it from end to end.

To Dani's delight, she found a favorite spot within walking distance of the store. In several places, the trail curved away from the edge of the canyon. In one of them, a crest of rocks rose in the space between the trail and the precipice, and atop the crest was the place Dani liked to call her own. She climbed up a short, steep path between limestone outcroppings.

The scene before her never failed to take Dani's breath away. She settled on the ground, setting the fanny pack to one side, and nestled against the massive trunk of a Ponderosa pine. The twisted trunks of two stunted piñons framed the magnificent vista—striated cliffs set against the backdrop of the sapphire sky.

Dani rested her head against the pine and drank in the sight, watching a pair of ravens rise and dip as they rode the thermal updrafts. *It's never the same,* she thought, even after spending as many hours there as possible over the past two years. Every change of light, every shift of the towering cloud formations altered the colors and the sharpness of the shadows. Dani opened her Bible and began to read, munching on one of the apples.

She had finished her snack and was busy recording how God had spoken to her when a twig snapped only a few feet away. Dani started and gasped, a hand to her throat.

She looked up into the equally startled gray eyes of Chase Sheppard. She groaned inwardly. In all the time she had been coming here, she had never, not once, been interrupted in her hideaway. Tourists seemed content to stay on the trail or the more level approaches to the canyon edge where the wide-open view beckoned.

And when someone finally intruded into her special place, it had to be this man! She had studiously avoided him for the past two weeks following the photography fiasco. She wondered what he'd find to fault her for this time. At least she wasn't walking, so she couldn't crash into him again.

Chase seemed just as astonished to see Dani. "What are you doing here?" he asked in a voice so bewildered it would have been funny if Dani hadn't been on edge.

"I was having my quiet time," she answered. "I come here nearly every day when the weather's good."

Chase seemed to have a hard time finding words to say. "You do?" he finally managed.

Dani nodded slowly, trying to figure out what was bothering him. Feeling an unexpected twinge of sympathy for his awkwardness, she reached into her fanny pack. "Have an apple," she invited, tossing it to him with a friendly grin. "Maybe you'll feel better."

Chase snagged the apple in midair. He looked at it, then at Dani, seeming to come out of his daze. "I'm sorry," he said. "I was just surprised to see you here."

"You surprised me, too," Dani admitted, beginning to relax. "Nobody comes up here besides me. I've always thought of it as my special spot, and I don't go around telling people about the gorgeous view they're missing."

Chase looked out at the magnificent panorama. "I never did, either," he said, almost to himself.

Dani drew back her head and studied him. "Never did what?"

"Told anyone what a beautiful place this is," Chase responded. "When I lived here before, I came here to pray as often as I could." He stared out across the great chasm. "It's spectacular just before sunset, isn't it?"

Dani could see the sadness in his eyes, as though he were wishing he could recapture some joy from that earlier time. She rose to her feet, dusting off her knees and the seat of her jeans. "Then I'll let you get reacquainted with the place," she said. "I was nearly finished, anyway."

Chase held up his hand. "No, you stay. I'll come back another time. Really, it's okay," he said when she started to protest. He smiled and added, "I'm glad someone else has been praying here."

Once again, Dani watched him walk away, but this

time they had parted on friendly terms. Given the obvious meaning this place held for him, it took a generous spirit to leave it to her. Maybe she'd have to revise her opinion of him. *Or maybe,* she thought with a giggle, *he was just afraid to let me walk past him again.*

Chase followed the Rim Trail back to his parking spot near the Visitor Center, walking slowly and savoring the cool afternoon air. After three years in Yellowstone, he'd almost forgotten the effect the vastness of the canyon had on him.

He hadn't forgotten his favorite viewpoint in Grand Canyon Village, though. It had always been his place to think, to pray, to wrestle with his problems.

And now Danielle Gallagher, of all people, had invaded his special haven.

Somehow, the idea didn't bother Chase nearly as much as it would have a couple of weeks before. While he'd admittedly gone out of his way to keep his distance from Danielle, he had seen her around the village more than once and watched her being her bubbly self with the people she met. Everyone lit up as soon as they saw her, seeming to think of her as their best friend.

He'd watched her in church, too, seating himself surreptitiously several rows behind her, unnoticed among the summer crowd. He saw the joyful way she sang the hymns and praise choruses and how intently she followed Pastor Stevens's Bible reading.

Seeing her today, utterly absorbed in her time alone with God, until he came blundering along, made Chase wonder whether he truly had an accurate perception of this woman. He had to admit he might have to reassess his first impression. And his second, and his third, he realized, remembering the collision at church and the scene with the glasses. *Will the real Danielle Gallagher please stand up?* he thought wryly.

Chapter 3

A light drizzle was falling when Chase maneuvered into the parking area, pleased to find a vacant spot in front of the Shrine of the Ages. *You can always tell when summer is officially over,* he reflected with a grin. The amount of available parking increased in inverse proportion to the size of the crowds.

He scooped up the tapes he'd offered to loan Ben Stevens, stuffed them in a plastic bag, and trotted soundlessly across a carpet of wet pine needles toward the archways framing the entrance. Already, there was a distinct nip in the air. It would be long-sleeve weather before long.

Chase could hear muffled voices coming from the sanctuary, but the entry corridor was still. He turned to the right, heading toward the pastor's office. Behind him, the glass doors into the sanctuary burst open and a gaggle of wildly dressed young people emerged, laughing and talking. Chase's jaw dropped at the sight of their garish garb.

One figure, in a bright orange wig and the gaudiest clothing Chase had ever seen outside a circus, stood with its back to the corridor, trying to get the attention of the noisy group.

Chase stood staring at the apparition. The six-inch flowers plastered all over the jeans would have looked more at home painted on a van from the sixties. The brightly hued shirt was enough to make him want to reach for a pair of sunglasses, even on this overcast day.

Who were these misfits, and what in the world were they doing in the church?

"Our next practice will be Saturday morning at ten. Can everybody make that?" The murmurs of assent covered up Chase's "Oh, no." That voice sounded all too familiar. The orange-headed figure turned, smiled, and waved at him.

Danielle Gallagher. It figured. Chase turned to knock on Ben's door. Didn't the woman have a serious bone in her body?

Fifteen minutes later, Chase emerged from the pastor's office. In answer to his baffled question, Ben told him Dani was teaching clowning to members of the youth group. "It's a viable outreach ministry," Ben assured him. "And Dani's the ideal person to lead it. She works very well with the young people," he added with a flicker of amusement, seeing Chase's doubtful expression.

The knowledge that this tomfoolery was a sanctioned activity of the church and not just an aberration on Danielle's part eased Chase's mind somewhat. But why couldn't she be content to do something normal, like teach children's Sunday school? Chase strode back to his parking spot, shaking his head. The sight of someone on all fours, peering under his front bumper, stopped him in his tracks.

"Did you drop something?" he asked in a loud voice.

Dani sprang up and sat back on her heels, narrowly avoiding hitting her head on the bumper. "You scared me!" she said in an accusing voice.

"What were you doing?" Chase asked, refusing to be put on the defensive.

He was relieved to see she had removed the wig and the clown clothes. Her own glossy brown hair was much more attractive than that orange monstrosity. Dani brushed a wisp out of her face, leaving a streak of dirt across her nose, then got to her feet and brushed herself off, looking slightly guilty.

"I was just checking to see if they'd used a lift kit to get that extra clearance."

One corner of Chase's mouth curved upward. "That's good. For a moment there I thought you might be gluing a big red clown nose on my Scout."

"Your Scout?" Dani's eyes widened. Surprise made her hazel eyes seem more green than brown, Chase noted, the color of the river he'd rafted the summer before. "I didn't know you drove a Scout."

Chase's smile broadened. "You never asked," he said. "Is it important?"

Dani picked up a large bag with telltale orange strands sticking out of the top and hoisted the strap onto her shoulder. She gave Chase a brilliant smile. "Only in that it defines you as a person of incredibly good taste."

Chase watched her stroll away, pleased but puzzled by the compliment until he saw her swing her bag into the rear seat of a bright yellow Scout and drive away. He stroked his chin, bemused. From Bozo the Clown to a knowledge of lift kits? The woman truly had a multi-faceted personality.

There was a time, he reflected on his drive home, when he'd thought Elise was a woman of wide-ranging interests, too. Beautiful Elise, with her artist's studio in Jackson Hole, who fascinated him with her passion for nature. . .and for him. But that was before he'd seen her true character and learned her only serious concern was herself. Before she found someone more to her liking and dumped Chase without a backward glance.

Memories danced in Chase's mind, and his lips thinned into a grim line. The way Elise had looked at him with that adoring blue-eyed gaze. Her faithful church attendance, which he'd taken as a sign of spiritual commitment, until he realized she looked on church as a place to find a better class of men.

Why, *why* hadn't he seen the truth before his heart was ripped in two? Chase slammed his fist against the steering wheel. It was over now, had been over for nearly two years, and still it hurt. He needed to get past the pain and get on with his life. And he couldn't do it by softening toward Danielle.

Never mind that she had a smile that went straight to his heart or that she spent much of her spare time involved in church. For all he knew, she was shopping, just as Elise had been. He'd thought Elise had a great sense of humor, too, until he realized her laughter was always directed at someone else.

The similarities were there, and he'd do well to heed

them. He knew from experience that a pretty face and a bubbling laugh could conceal an emptiness of soul.

He needed to be strong. It had cost him a lot to erect the barricade around his heart, and he wasn't about to let someone like Danielle Gallagher get past it.

❧

"You want me to what?" Chase stared dumbfounded at his pastor, not believing what he'd just heard. Sunday morning worshipers moved past them on their way to the exit. Chase would have slipped into the swirling crowd and joined them, but Ben still held his hand in a firm grip. *And I thought he only wanted to shake hands,* Chase thought, feeling betrayed. He gave another tentative tug, but the pastor's hold remained steady, strengthened, no doubt, by innumerable after-church handshakes over the years.

Chase heaved a sigh, admitting defeat. "Okay, I give up. You can let go now."

Ben grinned and released his hand. "I only said I thought your voice would blend well with Dani's. Why don't you go with her Friday night when she does her campfire program?"

Chase glanced across the sanctuary, where Dani was engaged in animated conversation with her clowning group. His eyes narrowed. "Did she ask you to do this?"

"I haven't even spoken to her about it yet, but I think this might be from the Lord. Let's go see what she thinks." He grasped Chase firmly by the elbow and propelled him across the room, giving him no opportunity to change his mind.

Dani saw them approach and gave a tentative smile.

Chase had seemed warmer, almost friendly at their last encounter, then inexplicably his attitude had cooled once more.

Ben beamed. "Chase is interested in the campground ministry. Can you fill him in on it?"

Interested, huh? Dani eyed the two men, Ben clutching Chase's elbow and Chase looking like he wished he were anywhere but here. What was going on?

"It's at Thunder Ridge Campground, just outside the park," she said slowly. "It changed hands a year and a half ago, and the new owners are Christians. They talked to Ben about starting some kind of ministry for their campers. A couple of the men from church lead Bible studies during the week, and on Friday nights I lead singing around the campfire." She shrugged. "That's about it."

Ben punched Chase's shoulder excitedly. "How many more weeks will it run?" he asked.

If Chase is the one who's interested, how come you're asking all the questions? Aloud she said, "Probably six. Maybe more. They'll shut down sometime in late October or early November."

"Perfect!" Ben looked like he'd just been awarded a prize. "Chase has a wonderful voice, and I think you two would sound great together. What do you think about him doing the program with you next Friday?"

Dani's lower jaw dropped so far she was surprised it didn't clatter on the floor. He couldn't be serious! She and Chase had done nothing but clash since the day they met.

"Come on," Ben urged. "It's a terrific idea. Don't you think so, Chase?"

Chase drew a deep breath, trying not to let his irritation show. The last thing he wanted was to be pressured into this, but he didn't want to appear surly, either. "I think it's entirely up to Danielle," he said shortly.

Oh, great, Dani thought. *Make me the bad guy.* It was obvious Chase would rather do almost anything than spend time with her, but she didn't see any way to decline without being rude.

"We can give it a try if you'd like," she said quietly.

"Great!" Ben clapped Chase on the shoulder and moved off to greet the rest of his congregation, the picture of satisfaction.

Chase shuffled his feet uncomfortably. What had he gotten himself into? "Do you want me to give you a ride to the campground?" Even he could hear the stiffness in his tone.

Dani shook her head. "You don't need to do that." *You don't even need to show up, if you hate the idea so much.*

"How about practice?" Chase asked. "Do we need to get together during the week?"

Spend more time with someone who obviously couldn't stand to be around her? No, thanks. "Let's just wing it," she answered, starting toward the exit. "Be there by six-thirty." She stopped and turned back to Chase. "One thing. If we're going to work together, do you think you could start calling me Dani?"

Dani paid for her chili dog and slid into the seat opposite Lorna. The General Store deli wasn't crowded at this time of day in late September, and they had the corner area to themselves.

"Finish the story," Lorna demanded. "You're doing the campfire program together tomorrow night. . .and?"

"There is no 'and,'" Dani replied around a mouthful of hot dog. "Pastor Stevens corralled us both and put us in a position where it was impossible to say no. Chase will sing with me tomorrow, and that's that. End of story."

Lorna's eyes grew round. "That's it? Come on, you must have had time to talk and get to know each other better this week. What about rehearsals?"

"We haven't had any." *Which might not be the great idea I thought it was Sunday,* Dani reflected. She didn't know how familiar Chase was with the songs she usually sang, or what his playing style was, or if he could even follow along in her key. *Bright, Dani. Really bright.* "It'll be fine," she assured Lorna, hoping she was right.

"This is not like you." Lorna frowned. "I know how much that campground ministry means to you. You practice like mad all week, and now you're telling me you haven't gotten together with Chase even once?"

Dani propped her elbows on the Formica tabletop and cradled her forehead in her hands. "Look, Lorna, he was obviously not happy about doing this. Why should I put either one of us in a position where we'll be miserable? We'll get through tomorrow night to satisfy Pastor Stevens, and then we'll never have to do it again. He'll be happy, I'll be happy. Okay?"

"I don't get it." Lorna finished her coffee and pushed her cup to one side. "You two could be so good together. You have so much in common!"

Dani rolled her eyes. "Somehow, the similarities do not leap out at me."

"Well, for one thing, you're both single." Lorna grinned impishly. "That's always a good place to start."

"Lorna—" Dani cautioned.

"For another, you both love the outdoors and you like living at the canyon. You're both interested in music, and you're committed Christians. How's that for starters?"

Dani shook her head. "You could say that about a lot of people here. But you're missing the point. Even if we were clones, it wouldn't matter. I'm waiting for God to show me the man He's already picked out for me. I don't need any helpful nudges from you."

Or from Ben Stevens, she thought dispiritedly. After pondering his motives for the past four days, she still couldn't understand why he had set this up. Dani shook her head and began clearing her place. Lorna was enough to deal with; she didn't need to worry about her pastor playing matchmaker, too.

"You know what I think?" Lorna asked in a stage whisper loud enough to be heard at the other end of the store. "I think the two of you are more alike than either one of you wants to admit." She gave Dani a quick good-bye hug and was gone.

Dani squeezed her eyes shut, comforting herself with the thought that by tomorrow night, it would all be over. How Lorna could see similarities between her and Chase was anybody's guess, but that was typical Lorna—rose-colored glasses all the way. When God brought someone into Dani's life, she was sure he and she would be obvious soul mates. People who intended to spend their lives together needed to be enough alike to be the best of friends.

Of course, she thought, *no one would ever mistake me for Belinda. Or Amanda or Collette, for that matter.* The four of them were as dissimilar as could be, but that didn't keep them from sharing a lifelong bond. Dani glanced at her watch. Only a couple of hours now until their monthly conference call. She could hardly wait.

"Come on, ring," Dani ordered the silent telephone. If she didn't talk to Amanda and Belinda soon, she'd burst. She had plenty of friends at the Grand Canyon; she made friends easily, no matter where she was. But there was a special connection between her and her camp friends, one even Lorna didn't share.

Maybe the fact that she made friends easily was part of her current problem, she mused. Usually people liked her, responding to her outgoing warmth and genuine interest. She wasn't used to having someone want to avoid her, and she didn't know how to deal with it. It would help to talk it over with her special friends. They had always been there for her in the past.

Amanda, Belinda, and Collette had agonized with her over early romances, prayed with her to find God's will, and cried over relationships that hadn't worked out. Every one of them understood and supported her decision to let God do the looking for her and enjoy life in the meantime.

They would completely understand her frustration with Lorna's and Ben's well-meaning interference. Dani curled up on the couch and wiggled her foot impatiently, anxious to unload her pent-up feelings.

The telephone jangled, and Dani snatched the receiver from its cradle. "It's about time!" she exclaimed.

"How did you know it was me?" Amanda asked, laughing. "It might have been a salesman."

"Not a chance." Dani felt herself relax deep down inside. Soon there would be two willing listeners who could help her put her problems in perspective. "Go ahead and call Belinda."

Dani listened while Belinda filled them in on Andi's excitement over her new puppy.

"Rick and Andi have really hit it off," Belinda said happily.

And maybe more than just him and Andi, Dani thought. That lilt hadn't been in Belinda's gentle voice the last time they'd talked. "You're sure Andi's the only one who's interested in him?" she teased. *Oh, brother. I sound just like Lorna.* But Belinda was so wracked by guilt over Andrew's death, she'd never give herself a chance at happiness unless she was nudged a little. She had so much going for her, with those gorgeous blue-green eyes and her sweet personality. All she needed was to start believing in herself again.

Dani's wandering attention was recaptured by Amanda's voice calling her name. "Dani? Are you still there?"

"Sorry, guess I was woolgathering. What did I miss?"

"Belinda asked if we wanted to chip in on some flowers for a welcome-home gift for Collette. What do you think?"

"That's a great idea. Count me in." The conversation shifted to other ways they could help Collette deal with the loss of her father and readjust to life in America.

When Dani finally hung up, she glanced at the clock. They'd talked less than an hour this time. Not bad, compared to some of their marathon calls.

Dani got ready for bed, thinking of all they'd discussed. Plans for the camp reunion in February were shaping up nicely. It had been way too long since the four of them had been together in person. Belinda, whether or not she realized it herself, had a definite interest in her new customer. It would be interesting to see how that developed. Collette would be back in the States well before the next conference call. With all four of them on the line, that one should set an all-time record.

She was almost asleep when she realized she hadn't said a word to her friends about her dilemma with Chase.

Chapter 4

Dusk was already settling over Thunder Ridge Campground when Dani parked her Scout near the owners' cabin. She grabbed her guitar case and joined Rod Weaver where he was arranging bundles of firewood.

"Nice evening, isn't it?" the sixtyish man asked. "Looks like we have quite a group of folks planning to come tonight."

"That's good." Dani forced a smile, trying to look more enthusiastic than she felt. Wouldn't you know there would be a crowd when she and her unwanted partner made their debut?

Dani settled onto one of the split log benches and lifted her guitar from its case, checking to be sure it was in tune. Looking around, she saw no sign of Chase. Good. Maybe he'd forgotten or decided not to come. It would be just as well.

Dani assessed the campers who were starting to look for seats around the campfire. Most were in their fifties or older, she judged. Probably a night for the old standard hymns, although she'd been fooled by people's musical preferences before. She smiled at a couple seating themselves near her.

"We want to be close to the orchestra," the man said, grinning. Dani laughed and introduced herself.

"We're Ed and Thelma Howard," he told her. "From Cleburne, Texas." Dani listened to his account of their travels, all the while looking around furtively for any sign of Chase. It was 6:35 by her watch. She'd allowed him plenty of time; he wasn't coming.

Buoyed by the knowledge, Dani smiled brightly and welcomed the campers to the program, then launched into an old gospel favorite. The campers smiled, recognizing the tune. Some followed Ed's lead in clapping to the lively rhythm.

"I'd like you to pick the songs this evening," Dani told her audience. "What would you like to sing?"

Thelma held up her hand. " 'The Old Rugged Cross?' " she suggested. Dani began strumming the opening chords, nodding to the group to join in. It was obvious they were all familiar with the song; no one fumbled for the words, even though Dani led them through all four verses. When the last note ended, she was rewarded by the peace reflected on each face.

Of all Dani's activities, these programs were her favorite. The opportunity to lead worship in the pine-scented forest never failed to leave her with a sense of awe, and tonight was no exception. After the second song, even the more reticent campers shed their reluctance to sing out loud and joined in with gusto. Tonight was turning out much better than she'd feared.

"Hey, Dani! Looks like you have backup." Rod Weaver's voice rang through the stillness. Dani turned to see Chase walking toward them, guitar case in hand. Her peace fled. Why did he have to spoil things by showing up now?

Chase didn't look any happier than Dani felt. Dani grimaced inwardly. *This will really liven things up,* she thought grimly.

"I got a phone call when I was heading out the door," was his only explanation. "Sorry."

Dani nodded, trying to recapture her earlier mood. Okay, he was here. Why let that ruin the entire evening? She leaned toward Chase and whispered, "We're getting ready to do 'Rock of Ages.' In G. Can you handle that?"

"You go ahead," Chase said. "I think I can keep up."

Talk about conceit! Dani began to play, hearing Chase join in immediately. The addition of another guitarist seemed to push the campers' enthusiasm even higher, and they sang the song with gusto.

"Who's your partner, Dani?" Ed Howard threw the question at her unexpectedly, and Dani froze. How could she say they'd been pressured into this so-called partnership? She settled for announcing Chase's name.

"What's next?" she asked with forced cheer.

"Let Chase pick one," called Thelma.

Thanks a lot, Dani thought. She glanced at Chase, who seemed to pick up on her discomfort.

"How about 'Power in the Blood?'" he whispered. "You pick the key."

The campers were obviously enjoying themselves

thoroughly, oblivious to the undercurrent of disquiet running between Dani and Chase. Testimonies and prayer requests followed, and Dani was ready to call it a night. It wasn't the worst campground program she'd ever done, but it wasn't the best, either. It wouldn't be over any too soon to suit her.

"One more, and then we'll have the closing prayer," she announced.

"How about a duet?" suggested a camper in the back row. "You and Chase."

Dani sighed and managed to keep from rolling her eyes. Everyone seemed intent on pairing her and Chase, and a more unlikely duo she could not imagine. So far, they hadn't done too badly, considering their lack of practice, but a duet? That was pushing it.

She looked at Chase, expecting him to protest. Instead, he was already picking out a melody. "Do you know 'Take My Life, and Let It Be'?" he asked in a quiet voice. Dani nodded resignedly.

I'll sing it for You, Lord, she prayed silently. *I know my attitude about this whole thing hasn't been good. Please forgive me and let this be for Your glory.* Closing her eyes, she began to sing.

The lyrics rang out sweet and clear. The song was one of Dani's favorites, expressing the desire to be totally consecrated to God's will. Chase had followed Dani up to this point, simply playing chords and matching his style to hers.

Now he added his rich baritone to Dani's clear alto on the second verse, his voice rising and swelling with hers, making her heart quicken. By the time they reached the last verse, with Chase singing harmony, Dani felt chills run up her arms and tears pooled behind her closed eyelids. She relaxed completely, knowing instinctively that Chase's tempo and phrasing would match her own.

Rarely did two people come together in such a way that each complemented the other absolutely, making the whole far more than the sum of the individual parts. This was one of those times.

Dani poured her whole being into the final words that promised total dedication of herself to her Lord, feeling that not only their voices, but their souls as well, blended and soared, reaching across the circle of listeners and into the night beyond. The last note hung in the air, and a stilled hush settled over the group.

Dani opened her eyes at last, too overwhelmed to speak. The faces around the campfire reflected her awe. Rod cleared his throat to say a brief closing prayer, and the campers quietly moved away from the fire, returning to their sites in reverent silence.

Dani felt a hand on her shoulder and looked up to see Ed and Thelma Howard standing next to her. Thelma was dabbing at her cheeks with a handkerchief, and even Ed's eyes were suspiciously damp.

"We've done a lot of camping since my retirement," Ed said, "and we always go to these programs when they are available." He paused to retrieve the handkerchief from Thelma and blow his nose. "But we want you to know this was something special. I haven't felt God's presence so clearly in a long time."

Ed motioned for Chase to join them. "I don't know

how long you two have been working together," he said, his voice cracking, "but you make a very effective team. Thank you." He patted Dani's arm, clapped Chase on the shoulder, and moved off into the darkness with his arm around Thelma.

Shaken, Dani watched them walk away, then turned to Chase. He met her gaze, and Dani stared into his eyes, feeling as though she could lose herself in their solemn gray depths. Without a word, Chase turned, picked up his guitar case, and went off toward the parking area.

Alone in the circle of light from the dying fire, Dani put her guitar in its case with trembling hands. What had happened here? One moment, she was looking forward to being done with an uncomfortable situation. The next, she felt bereft at the loss of Chase's company.

What about Chase? she wondered. Had their duet affected him as powerfully as it had her? The dark gray eyes loomed in her memory, and she had no doubt. He had felt it, too. Dani loaded her guitar into her Scout and started home, half her mind on the highway before her, and the other half reliving the last song and the connection she had sensed between them. How was it possible to harmonize so well musically, yet experience nothing but discord on a personal level?

Chase strode down the hall of the Shrine of the Ages, wondering what had prompted the urgent summons that brought him here. He tapped on Ben's office door and entered at his hearty, "Come in!"

Chase blinked when he saw Dani, lacing her fingers in

her lap and looking as confused as Chase felt. What was going on? He sat in the remaining chair, trying to appear unconcerned.

Ben beamed at them both. "Thank you for coming on such short notice," he said. "I just got a call from Rod Weaver, and I wanted to discuss it with you immediately." Chase shot a quick glance at Dani. Had there been some problem he hadn't been aware of? Her expression gave him no clue.

"He couldn't say enough about the program you did last night," Ben went on. "According to him, it's the most powerful one he's ever seen. Campers have been coming up to him all day, telling him how blessed they were."

Chase felt himself relax at the words of praise, but it didn't ease his confusion. Surely Ben hadn't called them both down there in such a rush merely to hand out compliments.

"He's hoping you'll agree to keep playing together, at least for the rest of this season." Ben looked from Dani to Chase expectantly. "What do you say? Will you at least pray about it?"

If anyone had told Chase twenty-four hours earlier he'd give a moment's consideration to spending extra time with Dani Gallagher, he would have told them they were crazy. After last night, though, everything had changed. Dani's joy in the campground ministry had been evident and genuine. Her smooth voice was one he could listen to for hours, and her love for the Lord shone through her music. And the song they had sung together. . .

Chase had never felt such a bond with anyone, such a

sense of being on exactly the same spiritual wavelength. The experience stunned him. Then the searching look Dani had given him afterward rocked him to the core. He had seen her soul when he gazed into her eyes.

This was no Elise, self-centered and shallow. Here was a woman whose love of God was as great as his own, one with whom he felt a special connection. One he had decided he would like to know better. He smiled, ready to say yes to Ben's request.

This time it was Dani who hedged. "It's nice of Rod to ask," she began, "and last night did go well. But that doesn't mean things would always work out that way. I'm not sure it's a good idea."

She looked at Chase, as if for confirmation, but he wasn't about to help her out of this. He'd been presented with a heaven-sent opportunity. There was no way he was going to turn it down.

Ben frowned. Clearly, this wasn't the response he'd expected. "What do you think, Chase?"

Chase swallowed and cleared his throat. Leaning forward in his chair, he said, "I agree with what you told me last Sunday. I think this is from God. We ought to at least give it a shot."

Ben sat back, relieved. "Dani?"

Her eyes were darker today, Chase noted, more brown than green. He wondered if their color made a good gauge of her emotions. He'd have to observe them more closely, which wouldn't be hard on him at all.

"All right," she said in a small voice. "We'll give it a try."

Chase wanted to shout with joy, but settled for a calm,

"Okay; when do you want to practice?"

Dani waved good-bye to the departing members of her clown troupe and headed into the ladies' room to remove her makeup and change clothes.

A glance at her watch showed her she had only a few minutes until Chase was due to arrive. She shoved her costume into her tote bag, brushed her hair, and applied a dash of tinted lip gloss. *You can catch your breath when you get home,* she promised herself. *Right now, it's time to get to work.*

Dani hurried into the sanctuary where she had left her guitar and checked to see that it was in tune. It wasn't going to be easy to do two very different types of rehearsals back-to-back, but she hadn't seen any way to get around it.

After Chase surprised her with his enthusiastic response to Rod Weaver's request, she hadn't had much time to think of a suitable place for them to practice. Her apartment was an obvious choice, and under different circumstances she would have offered it without hesitation. After what had happened at the camp program, though, neutral territory seemed safer.

She had insisted on them working right after her clowning practice, knowing Ben Stevens would be in his office then. It was a small point, but it made her feel better, and right now she needed all the comfort she could get.

After last Friday's duet and the response it brought from the campers, Dani had to admit God had used her and Chase to minister in a special way. If this was God's idea, she was willing to go along with it, but she drew the line on anything beyond the limits of ministry. She refused to allow the relationship to take on a personal note.

Chase strolled through the door, guitar case in hand. Dani breathed a sigh of relief when he got right to work in a businesslike manner, checking the tune of his guitar with hers. If he looked at her again the way he'd looked after last Friday's program, Dani knew she'd be in trouble. His gaze had evoked feelings in her she had no business feeling for anyone but the man God wanted her to marry.

Dani flipped open her music notebook to the first page. "I thought we'd go through as many songs as we have time for today," she told Chase. "That way we'll be comfortable with enough to get us through this week, and we can keep adding to that."

Chase nodded and gave her a smile that made her heart race. *Maybe I was better off when he ignored me,* she thought in a near-panic. *Lord, what's going on here? You and I both know I'm committed to waiting for Your leadership, so why is it so hard to remember that around Chase? Please help me keep my feelings from getting out of hand.*

❧

"Come on, gang," called Hank Watson, the singles' group leader. "It's time to plan another activity. Let's hear some ideas!"

Chase sat in the back row of the singles' class, arms folded and his ankle propped on his knee. He still didn't quite feel like he fit in with this group. Some of the old crowd were still there, but many of the faces had changed.

The new ones look a lot younger, he thought with a wry grin. *Most of the guys my age are old married men by now.* At thirty-four, Chase was well aware of the passing of time and his single status. Up until Elise, though, there had never been anyone in whom he was interested enough to consider spending the rest of his life with. After her betrayal, he'd closed himself off from romantic entanglements, not sure he would ever again meet a woman he could trust.

Until now. He glanced toward the front of the room, where Dani stood at a marker board, writing down suggestions as they were called out. Her dark brown hair gleamed in the sunlight coming through the windows, and her eyes sparkled as she bantered with various members of the group. *That smile could melt your heart,* he thought. It had finally melted the ice encasing his.

Chase shook his head slowly, wondering how he could have been so wrong about her for so long. He had allowed the pain of Elise's deception to blind him to the truth, seeing similarities where there were none and missing out on the godly woman before him.

And Chase was afraid it might turn out to be the biggest blunder of his life.

He had hoped her initial lack of enthusiasm for their joint campground project would diminish once they started working together, but it hadn't turned out that way. After three weeks of rehearsals and three more programs at the campground, he still felt like there was an invisible wall between them.

Chase couldn't complain about the way their music was progressing. The affinity he felt at the first campfire program was still there. Based on the responses they received from each new group of campers, he knew God was using their ministry.

Danielle showed up promptly for every rehearsal and program and consistently gave her best. No complaint there. But when it came to interacting on a personal level, things came to a screeching halt.

"Any more ideas?" Hank asked, scanning the room. "Then it's time to make a decision."

"Schultz Pass!" called a young woman in front of Chase. "It'll be gorgeous up there this time of year, with the aspens changing colors." A murmur of assent confirmed it as a popular choice.

"That'll work," Hank said, "as long as we have enough four-wheel-drive vehicles to take everybody. With the snow they had up there last week, those roads might be a challenge for anything else."

"I'll bring my Suburban," Len Thomas volunteered. "That'll hold eight."

"How many of us are going?" Hank asked. "We need a head count so we know how many vehicles we'll need." Fifteen hands went up. "Okay, we need one more Suburban, or a couple of smaller vehicles."

Chase kept his arms folded. He wasn't going to offer his Scout unless it was absolutely necessary. If he and Dani could ride in the same vehicle, he would manage to sit next to her. The drive to and from the mountain pass near Flagstaff should give them ample time to talk—and maybe make some dents in that wall she had erected.

"Come on," Hank urged. "I know more of you have four-wheel drives."

Dani's hand went up. "I can bring my Scout, if no one has anything bigger."

"That's one Scout and one Suburban," Hank called. "Who else?"

No one volunteered. Chase uncrossed his legs and waved a finger at Hank. "I'll drive," he said, hoping he didn't sound as sour as he felt. So much for spending the time on the road together.

※〜〜

The drive through Schultz Pass was every bit as beautiful as promised. Stands of white-trunked aspens blazed with glorious shades of orange and gold, making a rich contrast to the background of dark green pines.

It's a good thing Hank insisted on four-wheel-drive vehicles, Chase reflected. Already, they had crossed a couple of areas where they would have been in trouble with anything less. Dani's Scout rocked along the road behind Len's Suburban, while Chase brought up the rear. All the vehicles swayed over the ruts one after the other, reminding Chase of a line of waddling baby ducks.

The Suburban pulled off the road at a broad meadow. Dani and Chase followed. "This looks like a great place to have our picnic," Hank announced.

Fifteen hungry people made short work of spreading blankets on the ground over waterproof tarps and setting up the food. Minutes later, they were all sitting on the blankets, eating from plates piled high with ham, chicken, potato salad, and dessert.

Chase's plan to sit next to Dani was thwarted when she seated herself between two younger women. He shared a blanket with Hank and Len instead.

"I haven't seen much of you since you've been back, Chase," Hank told him. "It's good to have you with us again."

"This is where I plan to stay for quite a while," Chase told him. "I'm glad I made the move." He bit into a chicken thigh, hoping the conversation would stay on general topics. He didn't want to discuss his reasons for returning or his hopes for the future.

"When are you and Dani going to sing in church?" Len asked, dashing Chase's hopes of keeping the discussion on neutral ground. "I hear you're doing some great things together. You must make quite a team."

Not exactly the kind of team I'm interested in, Chase thought. Aloud, he said, "We'll just have to see when we both feel ready."

Small groups of people wandered across the meadow in twos and threes, exclaiming over the fall colors. Seeing Dani walking alone, Chase tossed his paper plate in the trash bag and hurried to join her. His hiking boots made little noise on the grass, and he had nearly reached her before she was aware of his presence.

Chase saw the way her eyes dilated with surprise when he approached and the way she looked past him, as if hoping someone else would come along. He stopped several feet away, not wanting to make her uncomfortable enough to leave.

"Len was wondering when we're going to sing in church." This was not the conversation he'd hoped to have, but seeing Dani's relief, he was glad he'd chosen that topic.

What made her look so spooked when he was around?

Dani smiled and shrugged. "It doesn't matter to me. Whenever you're ready, I guess." She circled around Chase, heading back toward the picnic site.

Chase sidestepped and put himself directly in her path. "You're rubbing your arms. Are you cold?"

"A little. I left my jacket in the Scout." Before she could take another step, Chase threw his jacket across her shoulders. He let his hands linger, wishing he could wrap his arms around her. How could she not feel the electric current that ran between them? It nearly knocked Chase to his knees.

Dani only looked up at the sky, saying casually, "The clouds are building up; we'd better go. We don't want to get caught here if it starts to rain." She started across the grass to call the group together, and Chase had no choice but to follow.

Chapter 5

The following Sunday, Dani felt the sense of anticipation that swept the congregation when Ben announced their duet. She made her way up the three steps to the platform, wondering for the thousandth time why she had let herself be talked into making Chase Sheppard a significant part of her life.

If she had put her foot down and said no when Ben first broached the subject of Chase accompanying her at the campground, none of this would have happened. They never would have sung together, never would have experienced that powerful connection. Rod Weaver would not have put the idea of making this a semipermanent arrangement in Ben's head, and she wouldn't have gone through the emotional turmoil she'd experienced the past few weeks.

Having Chase disapprove of her and ignore her had been difficult to deal with, but it was nothing compared to the difficulties of being near him on a regular basis. After that first night at the campfire, Dani knew she was in trouble. It would be entirely too easy to allow herself to be drawn into a deeper relationship, one that had no place in the life of someone who was waiting for the Lord's leadership.

She hadn't shared with anyone the struggle she faced every time he came near. Her only option was to hide behind a barrier of reserve, but keeping that distance between herself and Chase was easier said than done. Especially when it was contrary to everything she wanted to do.

When Chase placed his jacket around her shoulders at the singles' picnic, it had taken every shred of willpower Dani possessed not to lean back against him and melt into his arms. He would never know what it cost her to turn and walk away.

Now she picked up her guitar and tried to smile at the congregation. They had decided to repeat "Take My Life and Let It Be." After their first experience with it at the campground, they had repeated it at the end of every program since. Dani was beginning to think of it as their song.

Chase strummed the opening notes and Dani began the first verse. Once again, she felt like she was singing it with Chase for the first time. *Why, Lord? Why do I feel this affinity with him every time I sing about pledging my life to You? It doesn't make sense.*

When they were finished, Dani could tell by the looks on the faces of the congregation that many of them had been affected as deeply as she had. *Thank You for letting me be able to touch people for You with my music. I just wish I didn't have to do it with Chase Sheppard!*

Following the service, Ben approached Chase and Dani while they were packing up their instruments. "I knew from the first you two could do something special together," he said warmly, resting his hands on their shoulders, "but I had no idea just how special it was going to be. Thank you for giving this a chance."

Dani smiled and murmured a thank you, then left quickly. Ben turned to Chase, looking more solemn now. He lowered his voice so only Chase could hear. "I also wanted to check with you and see how things are going. To tell the truth, I'd expected Dani to jump at the opportunity to keep singing with you. After the way she hesitated that day in my office, I've been worried that I created a problem. Is everything okay?"

Is it? Chase wondered. With a practice session and a performance each week, their music had only improved. They seemed to be making a real impact at the campground. Musically, everything was a plus.

Personally, he was still trying to figure out how to make some headway with Dani. She was her outgoing, bubbly self with everyone. . .except him. With him, she remained cordial but distant, and he didn't have the faintest idea how to breach that barrier.

But Chase knew that wasn't what Ben had in mind. "Everything's fine," he answered.

"That's a relief!" A huge smile spread over Ben's face and he gripped Chase's hand. "Thanks for setting my mind at rest."

Chase's smile didn't quite reach his eyes. *I wish my mind was at rest, too.*

Chase peered through the glass door opening into the

lodge's lobby. One woman stood at the counter, filling out a registration form. She passed it across the counter to Lorna, who smiled and handed her a key in return. The woman picked up a bulging duffel bag and headed for the stairs.

Lorna was alone behind the counter. Chase ducked back so she couldn't see him, asking himself if he really wanted to do this. Probably not, but he didn't know any other way to get the information he needed. He pushed open the door and entered the lobby.

Lorna looked up and smiled. "Chase! What are you doing here?"

Good question. What was he doing here? He hadn't even had the foresight to concoct a plausible cover story. "Just out wandering around," he answered, wincing at the lame reply. If he couldn't convince himself, how was he supposed to persuade Lorna his visit was casual?

Lorna planted an elbow on the counter and rested her chin in her cupped palm. "Seen much of Dani lately?" Her knowing smile reminded Chase of a cat watching a bird. He pulled a tour brochure from a rack and stared at it as if he found the contents fascinating.

"Not too much. I see her when we practice and sing, and at church. That's about it."

"Are you interested in an outing to Lee's Ferry?" she asked sweetly, pointing to the brochure.

"I like to stay informed on what's going on," he said. "In case anybody asks me."

Lorna reached across the counter and reversed the paper he held in his hand. "You'll get more out of it if it isn't upside down," she said gently.

Chase tossed the paper down in disgust. So much for looking nonchalant. He scrubbed one hand across his face, then ran his fingers through his hair. What was he doing? He had known Lorna Fredericks since he first came to the canyon. Even then, he had considered her a meddler. So why was he here now?

Because she's the only one who can give you inside information on Dani.

"Okay, you win," he said, raising his hands in defeat. "I did come in here on purpose."

Lorna drummed her fists on the counter and did a victory shuffle. "I knew it. I knew it! I told Dani from the beginning you were meant for each other." She looked up at him appraisingly. "There is something between you two, isn't there?"

Oh boy, he'd done it now. "Actually, that's what I was hoping you could tell me," he said, throwing caution to the wind and telling himself he didn't care if news of his feelings for Dani was broadcast to the entire canyon community by morning. At the puzzled look on Lorna's face, he went on, "I thought there was, but she's been avoiding me. You talk to her a lot. Has she said anything to you?"

Lorna's brows knit together. "Every time I bring your name up, she changes the subject." Chase's heart sank. "I thought she was just being coy," Lorna continued, "and didn't want me to know. But if she won't talk to you, either. . ." She shrugged, looking dejected. "I don't know what's going on."

So much for his fount of information. Lorna glanced

up at him, the picture of gloom. "Want me to try some more girl talk and see what I can find out for you?"

"I'd rather you didn't say anything more to her. . .or anyone else, for that matter. I think this is something the two of us need to figure out on our own."

Lorna nodded slowly. "I guess you're right." Chase moved away and started toward the door.

"Chase?" Lorna called after him. He raised an inquisitive eyebrow. "I'm sorry it hasn't worked out. I was so sure. . ."

❧

"I guess that's it for today, then?" Chase settled his guitar in its case and fastened the latches.

Dani nodded, making an effort to smile. "Probably our last practice, too," she said carefully. "They're predicting the first major snowfall this weekend, so that will end our campground season."

Chase stiffened, then moved to pick up his case and walk to the door. "Then let's make our last performance our best, all right?" He flashed a warm smile at Dani and pushed open the glass door.

The door hissed shut with a sigh. Dani echoed it with a sigh of her own. She bit her lip and stared after Chase, watching him go out the main door and disappear around the corner of the building. She had tried to sound nonchalant, not wanting to give him the slightest inkling of the turmoil that churned within her.

Part of her wanted to shout with relief at not having to endure the torment she felt whenever they were together. Another deeper, more tender part didn't know how she would manage without Chase's deep laugh, the warmth of his presence, or the soaring joy she felt when their voices joined together in perfect harmony.

Lord, I'm so confused! I believed You opened the door to this ministry, and I'm grateful for that. But the feelings I have for Chase aren't feelings I should have for anyone but the man I'm going to marry. I didn't mean for this to happen, but You and I both know I'm in really deep, and I need Your help.

Please show me what You want me to do. You know how I love the music and how much I'd love the opportunity to do more, but if You want me to sing anymore with Chase, You've got to change the way I feel.

Dani felt the sting of tears behind her eyes. Chase's casual remark and the easy way he strolled away showed her how little it meant to him that the next Friday night would mark their last time of working together for this season. Maybe forever. She swiped the dampness from her eyes just before Ben pushed through the sanctuary doors.

"Chase is gone?" he asked, barely waiting for her nod before he continued. "I was hoping I'd catch you both, but you can pass the word along to him. I just got a call from Curt Wyman, who pastors a church in Cameron. The church is celebrating its fortieth anniversary a week from Sunday, and they'd like you and Chase to be part of the program. It's going to start at the usual morning worship service time and go on all afternoon. If you could do several sets during the day, he'd be really pleased."

He watched Dani, waiting for her answer. Her head whirled, and she didn't know whether to cry or cheer. Hadn't she just admitted to the Lord she'd love to do more in the way of her music ministry? But could she control her emotions around Chase?

"I'll talk to Chase," she said slowly. "But I think you can go ahead and tell them yes." Ben gave a cheery wave and left. *Our biggest fan,* Dani thought with a rueful smile. She walked slowly toward the exit, more mystified than ever. It appeared she had just gotten an answer to her prayer, and in record time, at that. But her feelings for Chase hadn't had time to change.

Cameron was nearly sixty miles away. Chase had grudgingly gone along with her insistence on meeting him at the campground every week, but Dani knew there was no way he would agree to that on this trip. How could she maintain her composure seated next to him in his Scout, listening to his mellow voice and smelling the woodsy scent of his cologne?

Gloomily, Dani pushed open the main door, welcoming the crisp air that stung her cheeks. If God wanted her to keep working with Chase, she'd do it. She would just have to find some way to deal with her feelings until God saw fit to take them away.

Dani rounded the corner and stopped in her tracks. Not twenty yards ahead of her, Chase stood in earnest conversation with an attractive young woman. A little boy about three years old stared up at Chase, smiling when he chuckled at one of the woman's remarks.

Chase noticed his young admirer and knelt down to his eye level. The little boy immediately threw his arms around Chase's neck. With a glance first to make sure the mother approved, Chase stood, holding the child in the crook of his arm. He and the mother resumed their conversation, unaware of Dani's presence.

Dani stood, unable to walk away if she had wanted to. And she didn't want to. She stared at the trio with a kind of morbid fascination. *They could be a family group.*

Chase patted the little boy's back while his mother talked, looking as though he'd done it all his life. The woman was taller than Dani's five feet five inches and had pale blond hair that swirled gracefully about her shoulders when she moved her head. The little boy's hair was a couple of shades darker than his mother's. *Just the color he'd have if Chase were his father,* Dani thought. A twinge she reluctantly recognized as jealousy knotted her stomach and tore at her heart.

Stop it! she told herself sternly. Chase had every right to talk to whomever he wanted. Even if she was blond and beautiful. Dani made a determined effort to walk past them to her parking spot without so much as a glance in their direction.

"Dani!" Chase's voice brought her to a stop. Dani tried to compose her expression before she turned, wanting to mask the turbulence within her spirit. She walked toward him with what she hoped was a friendly, interested look.

"Dani, this is Lainie Springer and her son, Jimmy."

Lainie held out her hand. "From Houston, Texas," she said, as if her accent wouldn't have given away her origin. Dani shook the proffered hand and patted Jimmy on the head. So far, so good.

"Lainie, here, has a little problem—"

"The worst sense of direction in the world," the animated blond cut in with a laugh. "I can find my way anywhere, as long as it's in Houston. Take me out of there, and I'm in trouble!"

"She and Jimmy have a room at Yavapai Lodge," Chase explained. "But she's having trouble finding her way back there."

Maybe she should have left a trail of bread crumbs, Dani thought, immediately regretting her uncharitable attitude. "It's just on the other side of the road, through those trees," she said, pointing helpfully.

Lainie laughed again, a tinkling, rippling sound. "I know where it is in general, but I can't find the turnoff to it to save my life. This is the third time I've stopped for directions. Chase," she said, taking his arm in a familiar gesture that made Dani grit her teeth, "said you might be able to help."

"You are going home, aren't you?" he asked. Dani nodded her head and raised a questioning eyebrow. "Could you let Lainie follow you and swing by the lodge on your way? I'd do it myself, but I have to meet with a contractor in fifteen minutes."

"Sure," Dani said. "No problem."

"Oh, thank you," Lainie cooed. "I knew as soon as I saw Chase that here was a man who could get things done." She batted her eyes at him and gave his arm a squeeze.

"Jimmy's father and I are separated," she explained to Dani. "He's a truck driver, so he's traveled all across the country, but I've never been anywhere. So I thought, why shouldn't I have some fun, too? And here I am!" She

322

reached out for Jimmy. "Come on, honey; let's get you in your car seat. We're going to follow the nice lady back to our motel."

Dani smiled at Jimmy, who stuck out his lower lip and began to whimper. She drew back, surprised. Kids usually loved her. She tried another smile, which brought forth a plaintive wail from Jimmy, then retreated and headed for her Scout.

"Hey, Dani," Chase called when she was halfway there. "Maybe he'd like you better in the orange wig."

Dani didn't bother turning around. After making sure Lainie and her son reached Yavapai Lodge, she drove home, wondering about their role reversal. Chase had made a joke, and she hadn't seen any humor in it. What was wrong with this picture?

An image of Chase laughing with Lainie flashed into her mind. He had looked relaxed and happy, his teeth gleaming white, and his eyes crinkling at the corners. Dani felt a lump in her throat, and she tightened her grip on the steering wheel. If she didn't watch out, she'd find herself sucked in even deeper than she already was.

Chapter 6

I thought it went well today, didn't you?" Chase squinted against the glare of the sun as he drove west along Highway 64 from Cameron.

"Uh-huh."

Chase winced. While they were singing, Dani's voice rang freely, like liquid silver, but whenever he'd tried to make conversation with her on the drive, the most he got was a wordless grunt. He risked a glance out of the corner of his eye. Dani sat staring out the window, arms crossed, her body language screaming, "I want to be left alone!"

Chase didn't get it. Was this the same woman who bounced around in the wildest clown costume he'd ever seen? The one who had been determined to put that crazy pair of glasses on him the day of the mission group's photograph? It looked like her, sounded like her, but something had changed drastically. The woman who sat beside him now bore only a superficial resemblance to the bouncy Dani he had first met.

Had he done something to offend her? Chase flinched, remembering his sullen behavior at first. It hadn't seemed to put her off, though. In fact, he recalled with a slight grin, it only seemed to make him a challenge to her. Lately, though, he had treasured being in her company, enjoying their times together more than he dared let on, given her cool behavior.

Last Friday at the campground and today at Cameron, she'd seemed even more distant than usual. Had anything happened recently that might have triggered this silent treatment? A picture of Lainie Springer swam unbidden into Chase's mind, and he frowned.

Lainie was a good-looking woman. He had to admit he'd enjoyed the story of her travels, at least until Dani showed up. At that point Lainie had started acting like a predatory female, grabbing his arm and holding on for dear life. It seemed far safer to ask Dani to help Lainie find her way back to the lodge, rather than stay in a situation that made warning signals go off in his brain.

But was that how the scene had looked from Dani's point of view? The thought took Chase's breath away. Could she have thought he was actually enjoyed Lainie's overtures? No, Dani knew him too well for that. Didn't she?

A new thought tingled in Chase's brain. If the episode with Lainie was the root of Dani's current attitude, it almost sounded like a case of jealousy. And if it was jealousy, that meant. . . Chase stole another quick glance at Dani. Was it possible she felt some of the same things he did? He'd love to ask her straight out, if only he could break through that wall of silence.

The sun had moved lower in the sky, beyond the point where Chase's sun visor was of any help. In only a few more minutes, it would move behind that layer of gathering clouds, giving him some relief. Chase's practiced eye told him those clouds should make for a spectacular sunset.

Chase stiffened, like a hound on the scent. They were nearing the turnoff to Grandview Point, one of the most beautiful vistas in the park. Sunsets at Grandview Point could be incredible, one of the most romantic settings Chase could imagine.

Oh, yeah. He swung the wheel to the right when they reached the turnoff. Dani turned to him, lips parted in confusion, and Chase's stomach muscles tensed. Stopping here was a great idea. He knew it was. Now all he had to do was convince Dani.

He cleared his throat. "The sun's been in my eyes all the way home," he said. "I thought we'd wait a few minutes until it goes down. Do you mind?" She shook her head, and Chase sighed. Still the silent treatment. *Lord, would You please make this sunset extra-special? I need all the help I can get.* If this didn't soften her up, he didn't know what would.

He pulled his Scout to a smooth stop along the edge of the road. Several other cars were already parked there, he noted with annoyance. He had hoped he and Dani would have the point to themselves, but he should have known better. *It might not be a bad thing,* he reflected. Having other people around should keep Dani from feeling threatened. It would help her relax, and the sunset would be just as gorgeous, no matter how many people were there.

To his relief, only ten or so were scattered around the

lookout area, most of them taking up their posts along the guardrail at the edge. Voices were kept low, as if in homage to the awe-inspiring sight before them. Chase noted the thickening clouds with approval. In about ten minutes, the colors should be glorious.

Dani stood quietly by herself, leaning on the rail several yards away from the rest of the onlookers. Chase moved to join her, careful not to crowd her personal space, and waited.

Behind them, car doors slammed, and quick steps hurried toward the viewpoint, breaking the reverent hush. Chase's brows drew together. *Settle down, folks. Don't ruin this for the rest of us.*

Two men and a woman hastened toward them, one of the men helping the woman stay upright on her high heels. Heels? Chase took a second look. The woman leaned on her companion's supporting arm, looking up at him with a glowing face. She was dressed in a calf-length white dress and jacket, and both of the men wore suits. The one walking alone held a Bible under his arm.

He and the couple took their places on a flat rock in the center of the viewing area. The couple joined hands and looked at their companion expectantly. Chase grinned. A sunset wedding! What better way to drive home his point? Breathing a quick "Thanks, Lord," he nudged Dani and pointed.

At that moment, the bride said something to the minister. He reached in his pocket and looked around, spotting Dani. "Miss," he called, beckoning to her, "would you mind helping us out?" He pulled a small camera from his pocket. "They'd like pictures of the ceremony, getting the sunset in the background, if you can."

Dani, looking like her old self again, grinned broadly and took the camera. She stationed herself behind the minister's right shoulder.

Chase restrained himself from shouting a jubilant "Yes!" This was perfect. Dani had to focus on the couple saying their vows and the wonders of the sunset, all at the same time. The minister opened his Bible and began, "We are gathered here. . ."

The sun sank to the horizon, shooting brilliant bands of purple, pink, and gold across the sky. Every one of the observers turned their backs on the breathtaking sight to watch the joining of a man and woman before God.

When the brief ceremony ended, the couple kissed and the crowd burst into applause. Dani snapped several more shots before returning the camera. The minister held out a paper and a pen and Dani eagerly bent to sign her name. "We need one more witness," the minister called out. "Who'd like to sign the marriage license?"

Chase leaped forward and wrote his name on the line indicated. *Are you watching this, Dani? Our names together on a marriage license—not a bad idea, is it?*

Dani was no more talkative than before on the rest of the drive home, but Chase was content to continue in silence, wanting to give Dani ample time to ponder what they had just seen. After giving up hope of ever finding love, Chase knew he was ready to risk his heart again.

Dani stared out the side window into the waning light,

keeping her face averted so she couldn't see Chase's rugged profile. The joy on the newlyweds' faces reminded her that someday God would bring that same happiness into her life, and for the first time, she hoped it would be soon.

Why now, God? After all the years I've been content to remain single, why is the desire for a husband so overwhelming? She refused to look at Chase, suspecting the answer to that question sat beside her.

Lord, I'm trying everything I know to keep my promise to You, but I need help. When I'm around Chase, all I can think about is how wonderful it would be to belong to him forever. Help me remember You have chosen someone just for me and that Your timing is perfect. You know who that person is, even though I don't. I've tried to find that person on my own, and it's caused nothing but problems. Help me to wait patiently until You show me the way.

A chill wind blew across the shopping center parking lot. Dani studied the heavy gray clouds massing overhead. It would snow by morning, maybe sooner. Time to leave Flagstaff and get back to the canyon before the storm hit. It was not an evening to chance being stranded in a snowstorm.

Stowing her purchases on top of the others in the back of her Scout, Dani felt the satisfaction of a successful shopping trip. She fished in her purse for her keys and shivered. The temperature was dropping, no doubt about it. In just a few minutes, though, the heater would be on. She slid her key in the ignition and twisted it.

Nothing.

Dani stared in disbelief and tried again, with the same result. She hopped out and jiggled the battery cables, but the engine still didn't respond.

Thirty minutes later, she was standing at a pay phone. "Lorna, I have a huge favor to ask. I'm broken down in Flagstaff. The good news is, I was parked right next to an auto shop. The bad news is, the guy doesn't think he can get to it before tomorrow, at the earliest. Could you possibly come pick me up?"

She winced at the squawk emanating from the receiver. "I know December's a super busy month, and I hate to put this on you, but I'm stranded." Her shoulders sagged in relief. "Thanks; I owe you one. I'm calling from the library. Could you pick me up here? That way I can stay inside and stay warm. See you in about an hour and a half."

Thank goodness for public libraries, she thought, hanging up. She could curl up in a cozy armchair in a heated room instead of freezing outside. She headed to the mystery section.

An hour and a quarter later, Dani stood in the vestibule watching for Lorna. Car after car pulled into the narrow parking lot, none of them resembling Lorna's Nissan. A blue Scout drew up at the end of the walkway. If she didn't know better, Dani would think it was Chase's. Her eyes widened in amazement when Chase himself opened his door and waved to her.

Of all the people she didn't want to run into. . . Dani hurried down the walk, anxious for him to move along and leave her to watch for Lorna.

"I didn't expect to see you here," she called with what

she hoped was a friendly smile. Friendly, she reminded herself, nothing more.

"Well, I expected to see you," Chase returned with a grin. "I was out in front of the General Store when Lorna walked by, all in a dither because she had to come pick you up and still get back in time for a party she's going to tonight. I didn't have anything else to do, so I volunteered to come in her place. Now, what's the matter with your Scout?"

"I'm not sure," Dani replied through lips that felt permanently frozen in that friendly smile. Lorna had let Chase come get her? Asked him to was probably closer to the truth. Some friend! Dani clenched her teeth, stifling a moan. She couldn't handle another long drive alone with him.

"Let me take a look before I drive you home," Chase offered, and Dani had no choice but to climb in with him. At the parking lot, he popped the hood open and stuck his head underneath. Five minutes later, he emerged with a smile.

"The solenoid on the starter's shot," he told her, wiping his hands on a rag. "If you had a standard transmission, I could pull it and get you started. With your automatic, I'll have to tow you home." Before Dani could protest, he started pulling a tow bar from the back.

"I came prepared," Chase said with a grin. "If I'd known it was your starter, I would have brought an extra one. They go out so often, all knowledgeable Scout owners keep a spare handy." He delivered the dig with a mischievous smile that melted Dani's insides.

This ride is going to be longer than I thought. Just wait 'til I get hold of Lorna!

The sun was low in the sky by the time Chase was ready to leave. Dani cast a worried glance at the overcast sky. "We'll make it back before the storm hits," Chase assured her.

He pulled out onto the road and turned up Highway 180. Dani checked her Scout in the side mirror from time to time. It would be nice to have it running again tomorrow, instead of being without a vehicle for days and having to beg a ride back to Flagstaff to pick it up. It was nice of Chase to come prepared to tow her home and to offer her his replacement starter.

It was nice of Chase to come, period. But then, Chase was nice. It was typical of him to come to her rescue without complaint, whether he had truly volunteered or been coerced.

"Do you ever drive down this way to see the fall foliage?" Chase's voice interrupted her reverie, making her jump.

Dani nodded. "There's nothing like driving through that mass of aspens, all waving those bright golden leaves." It was too late for fall color now. She watched the stark white trunks flash by. Against the overcast, colorless sky, they made little contrast. *It's a bleak picture,* she thought, watching the light pale as the sun dipped down behind the horizon. It matched the bleak mood that enveloped her.

Chase eased both vehicles off the road onto a wide turnaround area and let his engine idle. Dani reached for the door handle to check on her Scout, but Chase laid a detaining hand on her arm. "Nothing's wrong," he said. "I just needed to talk to you." With no place to go, Dani laced her fingers tightly together and waited.

"I've enjoyed spending time with you over the last few months," he began. "I'll admit I wasn't sure about doing music together at first, but something special happens when we sing together.

"But lately," he continued, "I feel like there's a barrier between us, and I don't understand why. There's something I've wanted to tell you, Dani, but I didn't know how to break through the wall. I still don't, so I'm just going to say it straight out and hope it won't make things worse.

"It's not just the music that's special, Dani. It's you. Neither one of us set out to make this happen, but—" He drew a deep breath. "I'm falling in love with you."

Dani shrank back in her seat, grateful for the blanket of darkness. Chase loved her? It was even worse than she'd thought. This was the very reason she had avoided any kind of dating relationship for years. All that came of it was stress and heartache. She'd led a happy life the past few years, able to be her own easygoing self, to have friendships without fear of them turning into anything more serious. All this had fit in perfectly with her commitment to wait for God's direction.

And then Chase Sheppard popped into her comfortable life. What was she going to do?

Dani could see Chase's outline in the dim glow of the dash lights. Even though she'd tried not to notice him, she was familiar with every contour of his profile. He stared straight ahead, his hands gripping the wheel, the lines of his body rigid, and Dani felt some of what it had cost him to make that admission. He had bared his soul to her, made himself completely vulnerable. She owed him the truth. The whole truth. The silence between them thickened while she tried to find her voice.

"You're right," she began. "I have kept a distance between us. I've never explained why, and that hasn't been fair to you." Dani twisted her hands in her lap and prayed for the courage to continue.

"The truth is, Chase, I'm in serious danger—danger of falling head over heels in love with you." In the dim light, she could see him tense, then turn toward her, hope radiating in every line of his body.

"Then why, Dani?" he asked hoarsely. "Why keep me at arm's length?"

Dani shook her head helplessly, tears pooling in her eyes. "There's no point in letting this happen. It won't work out."

Chase stared at her and shook his head. "How can you say that? Every time we're together, I feel like I'm being drawn toward you by a magnet. Don't tell me you don't feel it too?"

"That's just it. I do feel it, and that's why I've tried so hard to back off."

Chase raised his hands, then let them drop helplessly at his sides. "Am I missing something? This does not make any sense to me."

Dani reached out, then withdrew her hand before she touched his shoulder. More than anything, she wanted to throw her arms around Chase's neck and hug away the pain she heard in his voice. But if she did that, instinct told her Chase would fold her in his arms. And if that happened, she knew she would be lost.

Instead, she clenched her hands so tightly they hurt, wanting to explain, wanting to keep from hurting Chase, and knowing there was no way she could do both. She took a shaky breath and falteringly began to tell him how she had pledged to wait for God's guidance in finding true love.

"It made life so much simpler," she concluded, sniffling now. "I didn't have to get caught up in all the phoniness of the dating game. It was all so much fun and so easy. . .until you came along.

"I've never been so tempted to go with my feelings instead of waiting for a green light from God," Dani sobbed. "But I can't go back on my promise, Chase. I can't! I'm sorry."

She looked up at him, silently begging him to understand, and her mournful expression twisted Chase's heart. The faint light reflected on the tears shimmering in Dani's eyes, brimming over to stream down her cheeks. Chase stretched out his arm, tenderly wiping them away with his thumb. An aching sadness settled over him. Everything in him cried out that this was right; Dani was the woman for him. But how could he argue with God?

He leaned across the seat and brushed a gentle kiss on Dani's cheek, tasting the salty dampness. With a sigh that emanated from the depths of his being, he shifted into gear and pulled back onto the highway.

Chapter 7

Everything all right, Dani?" Mr. Bailey's kindly face peered into the back room where Dani was unpacking a shipment.

Dani blinked the moisture from her eyes and forced a smile. "Just give me a few more minutes. I'm nearly finished."

"I'm not trying to rush you. It's just that there's a gentleman here to see you. A very impatient gentleman," he added with an impish grin. Mr. Bailey ducked back around the corner and Dani could hear him talking to someone in the front of the shop. A familiar voice answered him, and Dani froze.

Chase. Chase wanted to see her? Her heart raced even as she told herself to act normally. As normally as she could after a week of sleepless, tearful nights.

Dani set the last pair of soft buckskin baby moccasins on the shelf and tossed the empty packing box on the stack with the others. Should she talk to him? After their last discussion, she'd had no contact with Chase. She'd even bought a new starter and had Lorna's husband, Eric, install it, hoping that distance would help to begin the healing process.

It had, however, exactly the opposite effect; Chase was in her thoughts more than ever. Dani squared her shoulders and pushed her hair back from her face with both hands, fighting the desire to duck out the back door and avoid him.

Chase was pacing the area in front of the jewelry case like a caged tiger when Dani came through the doorway. Seeing her, he stopped in midstride. "What time do you get off?" he demanded.

"Now," Mr. Bailey put in. "Unpacking that order was all that was left today. She can leave this minute."

Dani stared openmouthed at her employer. "But I was supposed to close—"

"Not anymore." Mr. Bailey beamed and gave her a roguish wink. "Something tells me this is an important occasion. Go, Dani." When she didn't move, he made shooing motions with his hands. "Go, go."

Outside, the brisk December air nipped at Dani's cheeks and nose. Chase guided her away from the cluster of shops and down the deserted Rim Trail before coming to a stop.

He turned Dani to face him, placing his hands on her shoulders and staring intently into her eyes. "I've done little but think and pray about what you said ever since we talked, and I need to know one thing. You said you were waiting for God's direction, but have you ever prayed about you and me?"

An electric current shot through Dani when Chase touched her. It was all she could do to nod slowly.

His grip tightened. "And how, exactly, did you pray?"

"I asked God to take away the feelings I have for you," she whispered through trembling lips.

"And did He?" This time she shook her head from side to side, and Chase relaxed his hold and smiled. "That's what I hoped." His eyes burned with intensity once more. "Hasn't it occurred to you there's a reason He didn't take those feelings away?"

When she merely stared at him, he continued, "You've gotten so used to waiting for God's answer, I think you missed it when it came along." He caught Dani's hands in his and pressed them urgently. "Think about it. Neither one of us tried to make this happen—just the opposite. But I can't get away from the feelings I have for you, and I think you feel the same way. Am I right?"

Dani nodded, her gaze never leaving Chase's face. Was it possible? Could this be the man God intended for her? Her heart pounded as hope surged through her.

"I have prayed my heart out over this," Chase said. "I have nothing but peace about it, but I don't want to pressure you into something you're uncomfortable with." He swallowed, and Dani felt his hands tighten on hers. "Would you pray about this one more time. . .only this time, would you ask Him to show you whether it's His will that you marry me?"

"Right now?" Dani felt a momentary sense of panic. If she prayed, got an answer now, and the answer was no. . . she didn't think she could bear it.

"Right now." Chase tugged gently at her hands, drawing her toward him. He held her loosely within the circle of his arms. "I can't stand not knowing for one more day," he said, resting his cheek on Dani's hair. He drew a shuddering breath. "If the answer's no, I promise to abide by that, but I have to know. We both do."

Dani nodded wordlessly. She pulled away slightly, resting one palm on Chase's cheek, her gaze locked on his. Chase lowered his face toward hers, then drew back. "No," he said. "Not until we know for sure."

Releasing Dani from his embrace, he asked, "Where will you be?"

Without hesitation, Dani turned and pointed. "Up there, at our special spot." She gave him a tremulous smile. "It seems appropriate."

"Take my coat," Chase told her, tucking it firmly around her shoulders. "Ben loaned me his key to the church building. I'll wait inside, but I don't want you to freeze." His hands lingered a moment on her shoulders, then he stepped back and turned away.

Dani watched him, wondering if she was seeing him walk away from her for the last time. With faltering steps, she walked farther down the trail and climbed to the crest of rocks.

Long shadows and the purple hues of the cliff walls told Dani the canyon would soon fade into darkness, but she would be aware of the yawning chasm before her even when she couldn't see it. Just as she was aware of God's unseen presence. She stared at the darkening sky, watching the stars appear one by one, wondering if she should have agreed to Chase's wild idea.

"Father," she began, "I'm not sure what has been

happening the past few months. You know I've tried my best to keep the promise I made to You. You also know that in spite of that, I feel drawn to Chase more than anyone I've ever known.

"Lord, I'm confused. It was easy—almost a relief—to say good-bye to the others. This time, I'm almost afraid to find out what You'll say."

Dani raised her eyes skyward, as if seeking her answer in the clear night sky. "Is it possible?" she whispered. "Is Chase the man You've had for me all along?"

She stood still, waiting, bracing herself for a negative response. Instead, a sense of approval enveloped her, warming her despite the winter chill. Dani's lips parted in wonder and her eyes glistened with unshed tears, buoyed by a peace, a rightness she'd never known before.

"Is this a yes, Lord?" she asked, scarcely daring to believe it was true. Joy and jubilation welled up inside her. Tears pooled in her eyes, turning the stars into a display of bursting fireworks, streaming white against the black sky. With an exultant whoop, Dani scrambled down from the rocks and ran down the trail to find Chase.

In the quietness of the sanctuary, Chase was on his knees once more. He had purposely left the light switched off, wanting only the starlight filtering in through the large windows. Those were the same stars Dani would be looking at right now. It gave him a sense of connection.

Once again, he poured out his heart to the Father. "Lord, I've put it all on the line tonight, and I hope it was the right thing to do. You know how I feel about Dani. I can't imagine loving anyone more. If it's Your will, show her this is right. And if I've been wrong about this whole thing. . ." He let out a long sigh. "Then help me to bear it, that's all I ask."

Chase stood and resumed his vigil at the window, wondering how soon he would have the answer to the most important question of his life, wondering if he would be ready for it when it came.

The sound of footsteps pounding along the pavement outside rang out clearly in the silence, followed by the rattle of the main door. Chase's mouth went dry. Ready or not, his answer was here.

A momentary doubt assailed him. Would Dani, dear, exuberant Dani, fly just as quickly to tell him bad news as good? His throat tightened convulsively. The idea of not having her around to liven up the rest of his life was unbearable.

Dani ran across the foyer, skidding to a stop in the doorway. She stood motionless, staring at Chase with luminous, wondering eyes. From where he stood, Chase could see her lower lip quivering. *Lord, You promised You wouldn't give us more than we can stand.*

The moment seemed to stretch on forever, with Chase willing her to speak, yet afraid of what he might hear. Dani's lips parted, and Chase thought his heart would stop beating.

"He said yes." The words were little more than a whisper. Then Dani's whole face lit up. "He said yes!" she cried, launching herself across the space separating them and into Chase's waiting arms.

He held her close, his heart pounding, scarcely able to believe what he had just heard. Tiny crystal droplets dotted Dani's eyelashes, and Chase felt his own eyes grow moist. "Thank You, God. Thank You!" he whispered in a choking voice.

Dani pressed her cheek against the soft warmth of Chase's flannel shirt. His fingers lifted her chin, tilting it upward until their gazes met and locked. Chase lowered his head and Dani closed her eyes, waiting to receive his kiss.

The fireworks were still going strong.

Carol Cox

Carol is a native of Arizona whose time is devoted to being a pastor's wife, home-school mom to her teen, active mom to her toddler, church pianist, and youth worker. She loves anything that she can do with her family: reading, traveling, historical studies, and outdoor excursions. She is also open to new pursuits on her own, including genealogy research, crafts, and the local historical society. She has had two historical novels published in Barbour Publishing's **Heartsong Presents** line, *Journey Toward Home* and *The Measure of a Man*, and novellas in *Spring's Memory* and *Resolutions*.

Forever Friends

by "The Friends"—Kristin Billerbeck,
Colleen Coble, Carol Cox, and Gail Sattler

epilogue

The camp near Deception Pass was just as they remembered it, full of memories that warmed the four friends' hearts. Amanda, Belinda, Collette, and Dani smiled knowingly when they spied the small stone church at the center of Wildwood Christian Camp. Fir trees towered over the modest building, their deep green contrasting with the red bark of the madroña trees. A more perfect setting for a wedding was hard to imagine.

Dani fluffed Collette's long veil. "Collette, you look radiant! I can't believe how beautiful you look with make-up, and that gown really flatters your figure."

"You always were an encourager, Dani. But what about you? Your dress is gorgeous, with all that satin and lace. And would you look at Belinda? Now that's a makeover! Her blue eyes just sparkle." Collette grinned.

Amanda looked up from stepping into her white satin slippers. "That's not makeup; that's true love!" she corrected.

Belinda's cheeks turned a becoming pink, then she gave a dazzling smile. "In that case, no wonder we all look so good. We've all found true love." She smoothed her elegant aqua dress, then knelt to give Andi a hug. "Haven't we, sweetheart?"

The little girl beamed at her mother and nodded. "Is this mine?" she asked, pointing to a basket of tiny pink silk rose petals. When Belinda nodded, she clapped her hands. "They match my dress!" she cried, with a dimpled grin.

Dani tucked a curl behind Belinda's ear. "Isn't it amazing how well all the guys get along?"

"Not really." Amanda shook her head. "If they fell in love with us, it only makes sense they'd become instant friends, just like we did."

Collette laughed. "Good point." She looked around the cabin, freshly cleaned for this special day. "What a flood of memories this place holds. We've spent so much time here together, but I never thought we'd be getting married here, and certainly not all on the same day!"

A ripple of laughter greeted her statement. "It was a great idea Amanda had to do this here," Belinda said.

Amanda flushed with pleasure. "It seemed so right. We were coming here for the reunion anyway, and this way we don't each have to make three cross-country trips to be at each others' weddings."

The Reverend John Milton, who had run the camp forever, tapped on the door and stuck his head inside the room. "Are you ready?" he asked with a paternal smile. "It's time."

The four brides picked up their bouquets and started for the door. Dani halted abruptly in front of the fireplace. "Wait a minute," she called, peering under the mantel. "Do you think it's still here?"

Her three best friends exchanged puzzled glances. Collette stepped toward the door. "We're getting married in just a few minutes. What's so important under there?"

Dani removed a knot from the log wall and slipped her fingers inside the opening, grinning triumphantly. "Yep, it's here. Can you believe it, after all this time?" She pulled a folded piece of paper from the hole and spread it open carefully. "Remember this? We hid it in there the first summer we met."

The other women gathered around Dani, staring at the yellowed note. "Amanda, Belinda, Collette, and Danielle," Belinda read softly. "Friends forever." The four of them looked at each other, their eyes misting over at the host of memories the scrap of paper recalled.

Once more Collette stepped toward the door. "We'd better get going," she said. "We have four wonderful guys waiting for us."

"Wait." Amanda gently removed the note from Belinda's fingers. She took a pen from the nearby desk and added two words in the middle of the note, then held it up to reread it: "Amanda, Belinda, Collette, and Danielle. Married together. Friends forever." She carefully tucked the note back into its secret slot.

"Now we can go," she said, smiling.

Exchanging a final loving glance, they stepped through the door to meet their future. . .forever friends.

A Letter to Our Readers

Dear Readers:

In order that we might better contribute to your reading enjoyment, we would appreciate you taking a few minutes to respond to the following questions. When completed, please return to the following: Fiction Editor, Barbour Publishing, Inc., P.O. Box 719, Uhrichsville, OH 44683.

1. Did you enjoy reading *Forever Friends?*
   □ Very much, I would like to see more books like this.
   □ Moderately—I would have enjoyed it more if _____
   _____
   _____

2. What influenced your decision to purchase this book?
   (Check those that apply.)
   □ Cover   □ Back cover copy   □ Title   □ Price
   □ Friends   □ Publicity   □ Other _____

3. Which story was your favorite?
   □ *Amanda*   □ *Belinda*
   □ *Collette*   □ *Danielle*

4. Please check your age range:
   □ Under 18   □ 18–24   □ 25–34
   □ 35–45   □ 46–55   □ Over 55

5. How many hours per week do you read? _____

Name _____

Occupation _____

Address _____

City _____ State _____ Zip _____

If you enjoyed
FOREVER FRIENDS
then read:

The Painting

Four Inspiring Novellas Show a Loving Way
to Make a Fresh Start

Where The Heart Is

New Beginnings

Turbulent Times

Going Home Again

If you enjoyed
FOREVER FRIENDS
then read:

Frontiers

Four Inspirational Love Stories
from America's Frontier by Colleen L. Reece

Flower of Seattle
Flower of the West
Flower of the North
Flower of Alaska
